THE ESTABLISHED AND
THE OUTSIDERS

Theory, Culture & Society

Theory, Culture & Society caters for the resurgence of interest in culture within contemporary social science and the humanities. Building on the heritage of classical social theory, the book series examines ways in which this tradition has been reshaped by a new generation of theorists. It will also publish theoretically informed analyses of everyday life, popular culture, and new intellectual movements.

EDITOR: Mike Featherstone, *University of Teesside*

SERIES EDITORIAL BOARD
Roy Boyne, *University of Northumbria at Newcastle*
Mike Hepworth, *University of Aberdeen*
Scott Lash, *University of Lancaster*
Roland Robertson, *University of Pittsburgh*
Bryan S. Turner, *Deakin University*

Recent volumes include:

The Body and Social Theory
Chris Shilling

Symbolic Exchange and Death
Jean Baudrillard

Sociology in Question
Pierre Bourdieu

Economies of Signs and Space
Scott Lash and John Urry

Religion and Globalization
Peter Beyer

Baroque Reason
The Aesthetics of Modernity
Christine Buci-Glucksmann

The Consuming Body
Pasi Falk

Cultural Identity and Global Process
Jonathan Friedman

THE ESTABLISHED AND THE OUTSIDERS

A Sociological Enquiry into Community Problems

Second edition

NORBERT ELIAS
JOHN L. SCOTSON

SAGE Publications
London • Thousand Oaks • New Delhi

Published in association with *Theory, Culture & Society*,
School of Human Studies, University of Teesside

 SAGE Publications Ltd
6 Bonhill Street
London EC2A 4PU

SAGE Publications Inc
2455 Teller Road
Thousand Oaks, California 91320

SAGE Publications India Pvt Ltd
32, M-Block Market
Greater Kailash – I
New Delhi 110 048

British Library Cataloguing in Publication Data

A catalogue record for this book is available from the British
Library

ISBN 0 8039 8470 7
ISBN 0 8039 7949 5 (pbk)

Library of Congress catalog card number 94-61329

TO

OUR FRIENDS

IN THE

DEPARTMENT OF SOCIOLOGY

UNIVERSITY OF LEICESTER

WHO HAVE GIVEN US MUCH HELP AND ENCOURAGEMENT

Contents

Foreword

The Established and the Outsiders was first published in 1965. It grew out of a study of a community near Leicester in the late 1950s and early 1960s by John Scotson, a local schoolteacher interested in juvenile delinquency. But in the hands of Norbert Elias this local study was reworked to illuminate social processes of general significance in human society—including how a group of people can monopolise power chances and use them to exclude and stigmatise members of another very similar group (for example, through the powerful medium of gossip), and how that is experienced in the collective "we-images" of both groups.

Ten years later Elias dictated, in English, a long new introduction for the Dutch translation of the book. This "Theoretical Essay on Established and Outsider Relations" spelled out how the theory could be applied to a whole range of changing patterns of human inequality: to relations between classes, ethnic groups, colonised and colonisers, men and women, parents and children, gays and straights. For many years it was thought that parts of the English text of this important essay had been lost, but they came to light in 1994, and the final version was assembled by myself and Saskia Visser. The essay is published in English for the first time in this volume, exactly as Elias dictated it, with only minor editorial changes. Shortly before his death in 1990, Elias added a brief appendix on Harper Lee's *To Kill a Mocking Bird* for the German edition of the book which is not included here.

May 1994   Stephen Mennell
                                          University College, Dublin

Preface

The Established and the Outsiders is a study of a small community with
a relatively old settlement as its core and two more recent
settlements which have formed around it. The enquiry started like
so many others because local people drew our attention to the fact
that one of the neighbourhoods had a consistently higher delinquency rate than the others. Locally that particular neighbourhood
was regarded as a delinquency area of low standing. As we began to
probe into the actual evidence and to look for explanations, our
interest shifted from the delinquency differentials to the differences
in the character of the neighbourhoods and to their relationships
with each other. In the course of a fairly intensive exploration of
the microcosm of Winston Parva with its three distinct neighbourhoods, one got to know the place and some of its individual
members sufficiently well. The fascination which its problems had
for us steadily increased—all the more so as we became gradually
aware that some of them had a paradigmatic character: they threw
light on problems which one often encountered on a much larger
scale in society at large.

As it turned out, the shift of the research interest from the
delinquency problem to the wider problem of the relationship
between different neighbourhoods within a community prevented
what might have been a waste of effort. In the third year of the
research the delinquency differentials between the two larger
neighbourhoods (which had supported the local idea that one of
them was a delinquency area) practically disappeared. What did
not disappear was the image which the older neighbourhoods had of
the newer neighbourhood with the formerly higher delinquency
rate. The older neighbourhoods persisted in stigmatising the latter
as a neighbourhood where delinquency was rampant. The question
why opinions about these facts persisted, even though the facts
themselves changed, was one of the questions which impressed
itself upon us in the course of the enquiry although we had not set
out to explore it. Another question was why the facts themselves

changed—why the delinquency differential between the two neighbourhoods more or less disappeared.

Thus the study as presented here was not planned as such from the outset. We often followed clues and took up new problems which appeared as we went along and, in one or two cases, what we discovered on the way changed the main direction of the enquiry.

An investigation conducted by not more than two people who were responsible only to themselves, and who were unhampered by set stipulations often entailed by the receipt of a research grant, could be conducted in a relatively elastic manner without the need to stick to a prescribed problem or to a set schedule. The opportunity to follow clues as they offered themselves and to change the main course of the enquiry if they appeared promising proved on the whole advantageous. It helped to counteract the rigidities of any set idea we had as to what was and was not significant in the study of a community. It enabled us to scan the horizon for inconspicuous phenomena that might have unexpected significance. And this seemingly diffuse experimentation led in the end to a fairly compact and comprehensive picture of aspects of a community which one can regard as central—above all of the power and status relationships and of the tensions bound up with them. We tried to discover the reasons why some groups in Winston Parva had greater power than others, and what we found went some way towards explaining these differences. On a wider plane the enquiry shed light on the merits and limitations of intensive micro-sociological studies. While proceeding with it, we ourselves were surprised to see how often configurations and regularities we dug up in the microcosm of Winston Parva suggested hypotheses which might be of use as a guide even for macro-sociological enquiries. Altogether the enquiry indicated that the small-scale problems of the development of a community and the large-scale problems of the development of a country are inseparable. There is not much point in studying community developments as if they take place in a sociological vacuum.

By and large the intention was to keep a balance between simple factual presentation and theoretical considerations. We are by no means certain whether we succeeded. But we tried not to allow our theoretical interests to overwhelm our interests in the social life of the people of Winston Parva itself.

An enquiry such as this would have been impossible without the friendly help and co-operation of others. We are indebted to the people of Winston Parva who helped to make interviewing a pleasant as well as an enlightening task. Intrusion into their homes brought no resentment. Many of them took a cheerful and encouraging interest in the research. We were greatly helped by the officials and members of voluntary organisations in Winston Parva. We owe a special debt of gratitude to the County Probation Service and to the Senior Probation Officer. Above all we are indebted to Dr. Bryan Wilson, Reader in Sociology at Oxford. In the final stages he has looked through the whole manuscript. It owes a great deal to his wise help and counsel, and to his power of persuasion which was often needed in convincing us of improvements he suggested.

February 1964   Norbert Elias
                                                    John L. Scotson

Introduction
A Theoretical Essay on Established and Outsider Relations

THE ACCOUNT of a suburban community presented in this book shows a sharp division within it between an old-established group and a newer group of residents, whose members were treated as outsiders by the established group. The latter closed ranks against them and stigmatised them generally as people of lesser human worth. They were thought to lack the superior human virtue—the distinguishing group charisma—which the dominant group attributed to itself.

Thus one encountered here, in the small community of Winston Parva, as it were in miniature, a universal human theme. One can observe again and again that members of groups which are, in terms of *power*, stronger than other interdependent groups, think of themselves in human terms as *better* than the others. The literal meaning of the term "aristocracy" can serve as an example. It was a name which an Athenian upper class of slave-owning warriors applied to that type of power relation in Athens which enabled their own group to take up the ruling position. But it meant literally "rule of the best". To this day the term "noble" retains the *double* meaning of high social rank and of a highly valued human attitude, as in "a noble gesture"; just as "villein", derived from a term that applied to a social group of low standing and, therefore, of low human value, still retains its meaning in the latter sense—an expression for a person of low morals. It is easy to find other examples.

This is the normal self-image of groups who in terms of their power ratio are securely superior to other interdependent groups. Whether they are social cadres, such as feudal lords in relation to

I am greatly indebted to Cas Wouters and Bram van Stolk. Discussing problems of translation into Dutch with them helped me to improve the text, and they stimulated me to write this essay.

villeins, "whites" in relation to "blacks", Gentiles in relation to
Jews, Protestants in relation to Catholics and vice versa, men in
relation to women (in former days), large and powerful nation-
states in relation to others which are small and relatively powerless,
or, as in the case of Winston Parva, an old-established working-class
group in relation to members of a new working-class settlement in
their neighbourhood—in all these cases the more powerful groups
look upon themselves as the "better" people, as endowed with a
kind of group charisma, with a specific virtue shared by all its
members and lacked by the others. What is more, in all these cases
the "superior" people may make the less powerful people themselves
feel that they lack virtue—that they are inferior in human terms.

How is it done? How do members of a group maintain among
themselves the belief that they are not merely more powerful but
also better human beings than those of another? What means do
they use to impose the belief in their own human superiority upon
those who are less powerful?

The study of Winston Parva deals with some of these and related
problems. They are discussed here with reference to different groupings within a small neighbourhood community. As soon as one talked
to people there one came up against the fact that the residents of one
area where the "old families" lived regarded themselves as "better",
as superior in human terms to those who lived in the neighbouring
newer part of the community. They refused to have any social
contact with them apart from that demanded by their occupations;
they lumped them all together as people less well bred. In short, they
treated all newcomers as people who did not belong, as "outsiders".
These newcomers themselves, after a while, seemed to accept with a
kind of puzzled resignation that they belonged to a group of lesser
virtue and respectability, which in terms of their actual conduct was
found to be justified only in the case of a small minority. Thus one
encountered in this small community what appeared to be a
universal regularity of any established–outsider figuration: the
established group attributed to its members superior human characteristics; it excluded all members of the other group from non-
occupational social contact with its own members; the taboo on such
contacts was kept alive by means of social control such as praise-
gossip about those who observed it and the threat of blame-gossip
against suspected offenders.

To study aspects of a universal figuration within the compass of a small community imposes upon the enquiry certain obvious limitations. But it also has its advantages. The use of a small social unit as a focus of enquiry into problems which one can also encounter in a great variety of larger and more differentiated social units makes it possible to explore these problems in considerable detail—as it were, microscopically. One can build up a small-scale explanatory model of the figuration one believes to be universal—a model ready to be tested, enlarged and if necessary revised by enquiries into related figurations on a larger scale. In that sense the model of an established–outsider figuration which results from an enquiry into a little community like Winston Parva can serve as a kind of "empirical paradigm". By applying it as a gauge to other more complex figurations of this type, one can understand better the structural characteristics they have in common and the reasons why, under different conditions, they function and develop upon different lines.

Walking through the streets of the two parts of Winston Parva, a casual visitor might have been surprised to learn that the inhabitants of one part thought of themselves as vastly superior to those of the other. So far as the standards of housing were concerned, the differences between the two parts were not particularly evident. Even if one looked more closely into the matter, it was at first surprising that the inhabitants of one area felt the need and were able to treat those of the other as inferior to themselves and, to some extent, could make them *feel* inferior. There were no differences in nationality, in ethnic descent, in "colour" or "race" between residents of the two areas; nor did they differ in their type of occupation, their income and educational levels—in a word, in their social class. Both were working-class areas. The only difference between them was that mentioned before: one group was formed by old residents established in the neighbourhood for two or three generations and the other was a group of newcomers.

What, then, induced the people who formed the first of these two groups to set themselves up as a higher and better order of human beings? What resources of power enabled them to assert their superiority and to cast a slur on the others as people of a lesser breed? As a rule one encounters this kind of figuration in connection with ethnic, national and other group differences that have been

xvii

mentioned before and, in that case, some of their salient features tend to escape one's notice. But here in Winston Parva the full armoury of group superiority and group contempt was mobilised in the relations between two groups who were different only with regard to the duration of their residence at this place. Here one could see that "oldness" of association, with all that it implied, was, on its own, able to create the degree of group cohesion, the collective identification, the commonality of norms, which are apt to induce the gratifying euphoria that goes with the consciousness of belonging to a group of higher value and with the complementary contempt for other groups.

At the same time one could see here the limitations of any theory which explains power differentials only in terms of a monopolistic possession of non-human objects, such as weapons or means of production, and disregards figurational aspects of power differentials due purely to differences in the degree of organisation of the human beings concerned. As one came gradually to recognise in Winston Parva, the latter, especially differentials in the degree of internal cohesion and communal control, can play a decisive part in the power ratio of one group in relation to that of another—as, indeed, one is able to see in a great many other cases. In that small community the power superiority of the old established group was to a large extent of this type. It was based on the high degree of cohesion of families who had known each other for two or three generations, in contrast to the newcomers who were strangers in relation not only to the old residents but also to each other. It was thanks to their greater potential for cohesion and its activation by social control that the old residents were able to reserve officers in local organisations such as council, church or club for people of their own kind, and firmly to exclude from them people who lived in the other part and who, as a group, lacked cohesion among themselves. Exclusion and stigmatisation of the outsiders by the established group were thus powerful weapons used by the latter to maintain their identity, to assert their superiority, keeping others firmly in their place.

One encountered here, in a particularly pure form, a source of power differentials between interrelated groups which also plays a part in many other social settings, but which, there, is frequently overlaid for the eyes of an observer by other distinguishing

xviii

characteristics of the groups concerned, such as those of colour or social class. On closer inspection one can often discover that in these other cases too, as in Winston Parva, one group has a higher cohesion rate than the other and this integration differential substantially contributes to the former's power surplus; its greater cohesion enables such a group to reserve social positions with a high power potential of a different type for its members, thus in turn reinforcing its cohesion, and to exclude from them members of other groups—which is essentially what one means when one speaks of an established—outsider figuration.

However, even though the nature of the power resources on which is founded the social superiority and the feeling of human superiority of the established group in relation to an outsider group can vary greatly, the established—outsider figuration itself shows in many different settings common characteristics and regularities. One could discover them in the small setting of Winston Parva. Once discovered, they stood out more clearly in other settings. Therefore it became evident that the concept of an established—outsider relationship filled a gap in our conceptual equipment which prevented us from perceiving the common structural unity as well as the variations of this type of relationship and from explaining them.

One example of the structural regularities of established—outsider relationships may help readers to discover others for themselves as they go along. As the study of Winston Parva indicates, an established group tends to attribute to its outsider group as a whole the "bad" characteristics of that group's "worst" section—of its anomic minority. In contrast, the self-image of the established group tends to be modelled on its exemplary, most "nomic" or norm-setting section, on the minority of its "best" members. This *pars pro toto* distortion in opposite directions enables an established group to prove their point to themselves as well as to others; there is always some evidence to show that one's group is "good" and the other is "bad".

The conditions under which one group is able to cast a slur upon another group, the socio-dynamics of stigmatisation, deserve some attention in this context. One encountered the problem as soon as one talked with people in the older parts of Winston Parva. They were all agreed that the people "over there" in the newer part were a lesser breed. One could not help noticing that the tendency of one group to stigmatise another, which plays such a large part in relations between different groups all over the world, could be found even here in this small community—in the relationship between two groups who, in terms of nationality and class, were hardly different, and because one could observe it here, as it were, in a social microcosm, it appeared more manageable. It was easy to see in this setting that the ability of one group to pin a badge of human inferiority on another group and to make it stick was a function of a specific figuration which the two groups formed with each other. It requires, in other words, a figurational approach for its investigation. At present the tendency is to discuss the problem of social stigmatisation as if it were simply a question of people showing individually a pronounced dislike of other people as individuals. A well-known way of conceptualising such an observation is to classify it as prejudice. However, that means perceiving only at the individual level something which cannot be understood without perceiving it at the same time at the group level. At present one often fails to distinguish between, and relate to each other, group stigmatisation and individual prejudice. In Winston Parva, as elsewhere, one found members of one group casting a slur on those of another, not because of their qualities as individual people, but because they were members of a group which they considered collectively as different from, and as inferior to, their own group. Thus one misses the key to the problem usually discussed under headings such as "social prejudice", if one looks for it solely in the personality structure of individual people. One can find it only if one considers the figuration formed by the two (or more) groups concerned or, in other words, the nature of their interdependence.

The centrepiece of that figuration is an uneven balance of power and the tensions inherent in it. It is also the decisive condition of any effective stigmatisation of an outsider group by an established group. One group can effectively stigmatise another only as long as it is well established in positions of power from which the stigmatised group is excluded. As long as that is the case, the stigma of collective disgrace attached to the outsiders can be made to stick. Unmitigated contempt and one-sided stigmatisation of outsiders without redress, such as the stigmatisation of the untouchables by the higher castes in India, or that of the African slaves or their descendants in America, signals a very uneven balance of power. Attaching the label of "lower human value" to another group is one of the weapons used in a power struggle by superior groups as a means of maintaining their social superiority. In that situation the social slur cast by a more powerful upon a less powerful group usually enters the self-image of the latter and, thus, weakens and disarms them. Accordingly, the power to stigmatise diminishes or even goes into reverse gear when a group is no longer able to maintain its monopolisation of the principal resources of power available in a society and to exclude other interdependent groups—the former outsiders—from participation in these resources. As soon as the power disparities or, in other words, the unevenness of the balance of power, diminishes, the former outsider groups, on their part, tend to retaliate. They resort to counter-stigmatisation, as negroes do in America, as peoples formerly subject to European domination do in Africa and as a former subject class, the industrial workers, do in Europe itself.

That may be enough to indicate briefly why the type of stigmatisation—of "prejudice" between groups—which one encountered in the miniature setting of Winston Parva demanded an enquiry into the overall structure of the relationship between the two main groups which endowed one of them with the power to ostracise the other. It demanded, in other words, as a first step, a measure of detachment—of distancing—from both groups. The problem one had to explore was not which side was wrong and which was right; the problem was rather which structural charac-teristics of the developing community of Winston Parva bound two groups to each other in such a way that the members of one of them felt impelled, and had sufficient power resources, to treat those of another group collectively with a measure of contempt, as people less well bred and thus of lower human value, by comparison with themselves.

In Winston Parva this problem presented itself with particular force, because most of the current explanations of power differen-tials did not apply there. The two groups, as I have already said, were not different with regard to their social class, their nationality, their ethnic or racial descent, their religious denomination or their educational level. The principal difference between the two groups was precisely this: that one was a group of old residents established in the neighbourhood for two or three generations and the other was a group of newcomers. The sociological significance of this fact was a marked difference in the cohesion of the two groups. One was closely integrated and the other was not. Differentials of cohesion and integration as an aspect of power differentials have probably not received the attention they deserve. In Winston Parva their significance as a resource of power inequalities showed itself very clearly. Once one discovered it there, other cases of cohesion differentials as sources of power differentials came easily to mind.

How they functioned in Winston Parva was fairly obvious. The group of old residents, families whose members had known each other for more than one generation, had established among themselves a common mode of living and a set of norms. They observed certain standards and were proud of it. Hence the influx of newcomers to their neighbourhood was experienced by them as a threat to their established way of life even though the newcomers were fellow nationals. For the core group of the old part of Winston Parva, the sense of their own standing and of their belonging was bound up with their communal life and its tradition. To preserve what they felt to be of high value, they closed ranks against the newcomers, thus protecting their identity as a group and asserting its superiority. The situation is familiar. It shows very clearly the complementarity of the superior human worth—the group charisma—attributed by the established to themselves and the "bad" characteristics—the group disgrace—attributed by them to the outsiders. As the latter—newcomers and strangers not only to the old residents but also to each other—lacked cohesion, they were unable to close their own ranks and fight back.

The complementarity of group charisma (one's own) and group disgrace (that of others) is one of the most significant aspects of the type of established–outsider relationship that one encounters here. It deserves a moment's consideration. It provides a clue to the emotional barrier against closer contact with the outsiders set up by this kind of figuration among the established. Perhaps more than anything else, this emotional barrier accounts for the often extreme rigidity in the attitude of established groups towards outsider groups—for the perpetuation of this taboo against closer contact with the outsiders for generation after generation, even if their social superiority or, in other words, their power surplus diminishes. One can observe a good many examples of this emotional inflexibility in our own time. Thus, state legislation in India may abolish the outcaste position of the former untouchables, but the emotional revulsion of high-caste Indians against contact with them persists, especially in the rural areas of that vast country. In the same way, state and federal legislation in the United States has increasingly eroded the juridical disabilities of the formerly enslaved group, and established their institutional equality with that of their former masters, as fellow citizens of the same nation. But the "social prejudice", the emotional barriers set up by the feeling of their own superior virtue, especially among the descendants of slave-masters, and the feeling of lesser human worth, the group disgrace, of the slaves' descendants, have not kept pace with legal adjustments. Hence, the swell of counter-stigmatisation in a balance-of-power battle with slowly decreasing differentials becomes noticeably stronger.

The mechanics of stigmatisation cannot easily be understood without a closer look at the part played by a person's image of his group's standing among others and, therefore, of his own standing as a member of his group. I have already said that dominant groups with a high power superiority attribute to themselves, as collectivities, and to those who belong to them, as families and individuals, a distinguishing group charisma. All those who "belong" participate in it. But they have to pay a price. Participation in a group's superiority and its unique group charisma is, as it were, the reward for submitting to group-specific norms. It has to be paid for by each of its members individually through the subjection of his own conduct to specific patterns of affect control. Pride in the incarnation of one's group charisma in one's own person, the satisfaction of belonging to and representing a powerful and, according to one's emotional equation, uniquely valuable and humanly superior group is functionally bound up with its members' willingness to submit to the obligations imposed upon them by membership of that group. As in other cases, the logic of the emotions is stringent: power superiority is equated with human merit, human merit with special grace of nature or gods. The gratification received through one's share in the group charisma makes up for the personal sacrifice of gratification in the form of submission to group norms.

As a matter of course, members of an outsider group are regarded as failing to observe these norms and restraints. That is the prevailing image of such a group among members of an established group. Outsiders, in the case of Winston Parva as elsewhere, are—collectively and individually—experienced as anomic. Closer contact with them, therefore, is felt to be disagreeable. They endanger the built-in defences of the established group against breaches of the common norms and taboos upon whose observance depended both a person's standing among his or her fellows within the established group and his or her own self-respect, pride, identity as a member of the superior group. The closing of ranks among the established certainly has the social function of preserving the group's power superiority. At the same time, the avoidance of any closer social contact with members of the outsider group has all the emotional characteristics of what one has learned in another context to call "the fear of pollution". As outsiders are felt to be anomic, close contact with them threatens a member of an established group with "anomic infection": he or she might be suspected of breaking the norms and taboos of their own group: in fact he or she would break those norms simply by associating with members of an outsider group. Hence contact with outsiders threatens an "insider" with the lowering of their own status within the established group. He or she might lose its members' regard—might no longer seem to share the higher human value attributed to themselves by the established.

The actual concepts used by established groups as a means of stigmatisation can vary according to the social characteristics and traditions of the groups concerned. In many cases they are quite meaningless outside the particular context in which they are used, and yet they hurt the outsiders deeply because the established groups usually have an ally in an inner voice of their social inferiors. Often enough the very names of groups in an outsider situation carry with them, even for the ears of their own members, undertones of inferiority and disgrace. Stigmatisation, therefore, can have a paralysing effect on groups with a lower power ratio. Although other resources of power superiority are needed in order to sustain the power to stigmatise, the latter is itself no mean weapon in balance-of-power tensions and conflicts. It may, for a while, cripple the ability of groups with a lower power ratio to strike back and to mobilise power resources within their reach. It may even help to perpetuate for some time the status superiority of a group whose power superiority has decreased or disappeared.

In English-speaking countries as in all other human societies, most people have at their disposal a range of terms stigmatising other groups and meaningful only in the context of specific established–outsider relationships. "Nigger", "yid", "wop", "dike", "papist" are examples. Their power to bite depends on the awareness of user and recipient that the humiliation of the latter intended by their use has the backing of a powerful established group, in relation to which that of the recipient is an outsider group with weaker power resources. All these terms symbolise the fact that the member of an outsider group can be shamed because he does not come up to the norms of the superior group because, in terms of these norms, he is anomic. Nothing is more characteristic of a highly uneven balance of power in cases such as these than the inability of outsider groups to retaliate with an equivalent stigmatising term of the established group. Even if they possess such a term in their communications, with each other (the Jewish term "goy" is an example), they are useless as weapons in a slanging match because an outsider group cannot shame members of an established group: as long as the balance of power between them is very uneven its stigmatising terms do not mean anything to them, they have no sting. If they begin to bite it is a sign that the balance of power is changing.

I have already said that stigmatisation of outsiders shows certain common features in a wide variety of established–outsider figurations. Anomie is perhaps the most frequent reproach against them; one can find again and again that they are regarded by the established group as untrustworthy, undisciplined and lawless. This is how a member of the old Athenian aristocratic establishment—the so-called Old Oligarch—spoke of the *demos*, the rising Athenian citizens—free craftsmen, merchants and peasants—who, it seems, had driven his group into exile and established democracy, the rule of the *demos*:

> Throughout the whole world the aristocracy in a state is opposed to democracy; for the natural characteristics of an aristocracy are discipline, obedience to the laws, and a most strict regard for what is respectable, while the natural characteristics of the common people are an extreme ignorance, ill discipline and immorality . . . For what you consider

lawlessness is in fact the basis upon which the strength of the common people rests.[1]

The sameness of the pattern of stigmatisation used by high power groups in relation to their outsider groups all over the world—the sameness of this pattern in spite of all the cultural differences—may at first be a little unexpected. But the symptoms of human inferiority which a high-powered established group is most likely to perceive in a low-powered outsider group, which serve their members as justification for their own elevated position and as proof of their own superior worth, are usually engendered in members of the inferior group—inferior in terms of their power ratio—by the very conditions of their outsider position and the humiliation and oppression that go with it. They are, in some respects, the same all over the world. Poverty—a low standard of living—is one of them. But there are others which, in human terms, are no less significant, among them constant exposure to the vagaries of their superiors' decisions and commands, the humiliation of exclusion from their ranks, and attitudes of deference bred into the "inferior" group. Moreover, where the power differential is very great, groups in an outsider position measure themselves with the yardstick of their oppressors. In terms of their oppressors' norms they find themselves wanting; they experience themselves as being of lesser worth. Just as established groups, as a matter of course, regard their superior power as a sign of their higher human value, so outsider groups, as long as the power differential is great and submission inescapable, emotionally experience their *power* inferiority as a sign of *human* inferiority. Thus a glance at the most extreme cases of power inequalities in established–outsider figurations, where the impact on the personality structure of outsiders shows itself in all its harshness, may help to show in better perspective the related personality characteristics and experiences of outsiders in cases where the imbalance is less great and poverty, deference and the sense of inferiority are more temperate. By probing into the

---

[1] *The Old Oligarch: Pseudo-Xenophon's "Constitution of Athens"*, London, London Association of Classical Teachers, 1969; and in J.M. Moore, *Aristotle and Xenophon on Democracy and Oligarchy*, London, Chatto & Windus, 1975. The Greek text can be found in *Xænophontis Opera*, ed. E.C. Marchant, vol. 5., Oxford Classical Texts, Oxford, Clarendon Press, 1900–20.

experiential aspects of established–outsider figurations, one may reach layers of human experience where differences of cultural tradition play a lesser part.

Established groups with a great power margin at their disposal tend to experience their outsider groups not only as unruly breakers of laws and norms (the laws and norms of the established), but also as not particularly clean. In Winston Parva the opprobrium of uncleanliness attached to the outsiders was relatively mild (and justified at most in the case of the "minority of the worst"). Nevertheless, old families harboured the suspicion that the houses "over there", and especially the kitchens, were not as clean as they ought to be. Almost everywhere members of established groups and, even more, those of groups aspiring to form the establishment, take pride in being cleaner, literally and figuratively, than the outsiders and, given the poorer conditions of many outsider groups, they are probably quite often right. The widespread feeling among established groups that contact with members of an outsider group contaminates refers to contamination with anomy and with dirt rolled into one. Shakespeare spoke of a "leane unwash'd artificer". From about 1830 the term "the great unwashed" gained currency as appellation of the "lower orders" in industrialising England and the *Oxford English Dictionary* quotes someone as writing in 1868: "Whenever I speak of . . . the working classes, it is in the 'great unwashed' sense."

In the case of very great power differentials, and correspondingly great oppression, outsider groups are often held to be filthy and hardly human. Take as an example a description of an old outsider group in Japan, the Burakumin (their old stigmatic name "Eta" meaning literally "full of filth" is now only secretly used):

> These people are less well housed, less well educated, hold rougher, worse paid jobs and are more likely to take to crime than ordinary Japanese. Few ordinary Japanese will knowingly socialise with them. Even fewer would let their son or daughter marry into an outcast family.

> And yet the extraordinary thing is that there is no essential physical difference between descendants of the outcasts and the rest of the Japanese . . .

> Centuries of discrimination, of being treated as less than human, and of being made to believe that as Burakumin they are not good enough to take part in ordinary Japanese life has scarred the Burakumin mind . . .

This is an interview with a Burakumin conducted several years ago. The man was asked whether he felt he was the same as ordinary Japanese. Answer: "No, we kill animals. We are dirty, and some people think we are not human." Question: "Do you think you are human?" Answer (long pause): "I don't know . . . We are bad people and we are dirty."[2]

Give a group a bad name and it is likely to live up to it. In the case of Winston Parva, the most severely ostracised section of the outsider group was still able, in a surreptitious way, to hit back. How far the shame of outsiders produced by the inescapable stigmatisation of an established group turns into paralysing apathy, how far into aggressive norm and lawlessness, depends on the overall situation. This is what one found in Winston Parva:

> The children and adolescents of the despised Estate minority were shunned, rejected and "frozen out" by their "respectable" contemporaries from the "village" even more firmly and cruelly than were their parents because the "bad example" they set threatened their own defences against the unruly urges within; and because the wilder minority of younger people felt rejected, they tried to get their own back by behaving badly with greater deliberation. The knowledge that by being noisy, destructive and offensive they could annoy those by whom they were rejected and treated as outcasts, acted as an added incentive . . . for "bad behaviour". They enjoyed doing the very things for which they were blamed as an act of revenge against those who blamed them.[3]

And this in a study of the Burakumin:

> Such minority self-identities may involve social retreat into ghetto enclaves or, if contact with the majority is necessary or expedient, the assumption of deviant social roles vis à vis the majority group. These deviant roles often involve a great deal of covert hostility towards any form of authority exercised by members of the majority group. Such feelings are a consequence of one generation after another experiencing exploitation . . . . One finds that outcast children are more prone to aggressiveness and in a sense they do actualise the stereotypes attributed to them, at least in some measure.[4]

---

[2] Mark Frankland, "Japan's Angry Untouchables", *Observer Magazine*, 2 November 1975, p. 40 ff.

[3] See p. 129 below.

[4] Ben Whitaker, "Japan's Outcasts: The Problem of the Burakumin", in Ben Whitaker (ed.), *The Fourth World: Victims of Group Oppression*, London, Sidgwick & Jackson, 1972, p. 316. There is another parallel with the situation in Winston Parva: "It must be emphasised that deviant courses of action occur only among a minority of outcasts, although it is a significantly high proportion compared with the main body of the population" (p. 317).

One has got into the habit of explaining group relations such as those described here as a result of racial, ethnic or sometimes religious differences. None of these explanations fits here. The Burakumin minority in Japan come from the same stock as the majority of the Japanese. They appear to be descendants of low-ranking occupational groups, such as those associated with death, childbirth, animal slaughter and the products derived from it. With the advancing sensitivity of Japan's warrior and priest establishment, observable as an aspect of the civilising process in Japan as elsewhere and manifest there in the development of Shinto and Buddhist teaching, these lowly groups were probably subjected to some form of hereditary segregation, which was strictly enforced from about AD 1600 on.[5] Contact with them was felt to be polluting. Some of them were required to wear a patch of leather on their kimono sleeves. Intermarriage with the majority of Japanese was strictly forbidden.

Although the differences between the outcasts and other Japanese were the result of a developing established—outsider relationship and, thus, entirely social in origin, the outsider group has shown, in recent studies, many of the characteristics usually associated today with racial or ethnic differences. It may be enough to mention one of them: "Recent reports by Japanese psychologists demonstrate that there is a systematic difference between the scores achieved on IQ and achievement tests by majority and outcast children attending the same . . . schools."[6] This is part of the mounting evidence that goes to show that growing up as a member of a stigmatised outsider group can result in specific intellectual as well as emotional deficiencies.[7] It is in no way accidental that one discovers similar features in the case of established—outsider relationships uncon-

---

[5] *Ibid*, p. 310.

[6] *Ibid*, pp. 314—15.

[7] One of the factors that can modify the impact of their situation upon members of outsider group is the possession by such a group of a cultural tradition of its own. Such a tradition, especially if it embodies, as in the case of the Jews, a strong tradition of book-learning and a high value placed upon intellectual achievement, can probably shield the children of such a group to some extent from the traumatic effect on their development of exposure to perpetual stigmatisation by the established group—to the humiliation not only of themselves but also of their parents and the whole group whose image and value forms a vital part of their self-image, their individual identity and self-evaluation.

nected with racial or ethnic differences as in relationships connected with those differences. The evidence suggests that, in the latter case too, these features are not due to racial or ethnic differences themselves but to the fact that one is an established group, with superior power resources, and the other an outsider group, greatly inferior in terms of its power ratio, against which the established group can close ranks. What one calls "race relations", in other words, are simply established—outsider relationships of a particular type. The fact that members of the two groups differ in their physical appearance or that members of one group speak the language in which they communicate with a different accent and fluency merely serves as a reinforcing shibboleth which makes members of an outsider group more easily recognisable as such. Nor is the designation "racial prejudice" particularly apt. The aversion, contempt or hatred felt by members of an established group for those of an outsider group, and the fear that closer contact with the latter may pollute them, are no different in cases where the two groups differ distinctly in their physical appearance and in others where they are physically indistinguishable, so that the low-powered outsiders have to wear a badge to show their identity.

It seems that terms like "racial" or "ethnic", widely used in this context both in sociology and in society at large, are symptomatic of an ideological avoidance action. By using them, one singles out for attention what is peripheral to these relationships (e.g. differences of skin colour) and turns the eye away from what is central (e.g. differences in power ratio and the exclusion of a power-inferior group from positions with a higher power potential). Whether or not the groups to which one refers when speaking of "race relations" or "racial prejudice" differ in their "racial" descent and appearance, the salient aspect of their relationship is that they are bonded together in a manner which endows one of them with very much greater power resources than the other and enables that group to exclude members of the other group from access to the centre of these resources and from closer contact with its own members, thus relegating them to the position of outsiders. Therefore, even where differences in physical appearance and other biological aspects that we refer to as "racial" exist in these cases, the socio-dynamics of the relationship of groups bonded to each other as established and outsiders are determined by the manner of their bonding, not by any of the characteristics possessed by the groups concerned independently of it.

The group tensions and conflicts inherent in this manner of bonding may be quiescent (which is usually the case if power differentials are very great); they may come into the open in the form of continuous conflicts (which is usually the case if the balance of power changes in favour of the outsiders). Whichever it is, one cannot grasp the compelling force of this kind of bonding, and the peculiar helplessness of groups of people bound to each other in this manner, unless one sees clearly that they are trapped in a double-bind. This may not become operative if the dependence is almost wholly one-sided and the power differential between established and outsiders, therefore, very great—as, for instance, in the case of the Amerindians in some Latin American countries. In such cases, the outsiders have no function for the established groups: they are simply in the way and so, very often, they are exterminated or driven out and left to die.

But where outsider groups are in some way needed by established groups, where they have a function for them, the double-bind starts working more overtly and does so increasingly if the inequality of dependence, without disappearing, diminishes—if the balance of power goes some way in favour of the outsiders. To see it, one may once more consider the two quotations cited before—that of the Athenian aristocrat used to ruling and contemptuous of the common people, and that of the Buraku outsider who measured his own group and, thus, himself with the yardstick of the establishment. These two figures represent polar cases, the one wholly convinced on the superior value of his own group, the other of his own group's badness.

Power superiority conveys advantages to groups endowed with it. Some of them are material or economic. Under the influence of Marx, these have attracted particular attention. To study them is, in most cases, quite indispensable to an understanding of established—outsider relationships. But they are not the only advantages accruing to a high-powered established group over a relatively low-powered outsider group. In the relationship between established and outsiders in Winston Parva, the quest of the former for economic advantages played a minimal part. What other advantages incite established groups to fight fiercely for the maintenance of their superiority? What other deprivations do outsider groups suffer, apart from economic deprivations? It is by no means only within the small, suburban community with which this study is concerned, that one can discover non-economic layers of the conflict between established and outsider groups. Even in cases where the struggle for the distribution of economic resources seems to hold the centre of the stage, as in that of the struggle between the workers and the managerial establishment of a factory, other sources of dispute are operative, besides that over the relationship between wages and profits. In fact, the supremacy of the economic aspects of established–outsider conflicts is most pronounced where the balance of power between the contenders is most uneven—is tilted most strongly in favour of the established group. The less that is the case, the more clearly recognisable become other non-economic aspects of the tensions and conflicts. Where outsider groups have to live at a subsistence level, the size of their earnings outweighs all their other requirements in importance. The higher they rise above the subsistence level the more does even their income—their economic resources—serve as a means of satisfying human requirements other than that of stilling their most elementary animalic or material needs; the more keenly are groups in that situation liable to feel the social inferiority—the inferiority of power and status from which they suffer. And it is in that situation that the struggle between established and outsiders gradually ceases to be, on the part of the latter, simply a struggle for stilling their hunger, for the means of physical survival, and becomes a struggle for the satisfaction of other human requirements as well.

The nature of these requirements is still, to some extent, obscured by the aftermath of Marx's great discovery and the tendency to see in it the end of the road to discovery about human societies. One might rather regard it as one manifestation of a beginning.

Among the goals that clash in established–outsider relationships, the outsiders' goal of stilling their hunger, of satisfying the most elementary animalic or material requirements, together with that of defence against physical annihilation by human enemies, in short the simple goal of physical survival, takes priority over all others wherever its fulfilment is uncertain. To this date that remains the primary goal of large sections of humankind, partly because other more powerful sections consume too much, since generally the human population grows more quickly than its food supply and humankind is too divided to take any concerted action against the distress of less powerful outsider groups, partly because the growing interdependence of all sections of humankind has intensified their internecine struggles, and the lesson that in an increasingly interdependent world domination by one section of mankind over the others is bound to have a boomerang effect has not yet been learned.

Thus Marx uncovered an important truth when he pointed to the uneven distribution of the means of production and thus to the uneven distribution of the means needed for satisfying men's material needs. But it was a half-truth. He presented as the root source of the goal clash between the power-superior and power-inferior groups the clash over economic goals, such as that of securing a sufficient food supply. And to this day the pursuit of economic goals, elastic and ambiguous as this use of the term economic is, appears to many people as the real, the basic goal of human groups, in comparison with which others appear to be less real, whatever that may mean.

Without doubt, in the extreme case of human groups exposed to prolonged starvation, the craving for food or, more generally, for physical survival may indeed have priority over all other goals. People may humiliate themselves, may kill and eat each other, thus regressing to a near animalic level. We have seen examples. Food, the gratification of material needs is indeed basic. But if the quest for the satisfaction of this type of human goal predominates to the exclusion of all others, humans are likely to lose some of the specific characteristics which distinguish them from other animals. They may no longer be able to pursue other goals which are specifically human and whose gratification may also be at dispute in the power struggles between human groups. One has some difficulty in finding the right concepts to refer to them because those available have at present an idealising ring; they sound as if one were speaking of something not quite real—not as real and tangible as the human goal of satisfying hunger. Yet if one tries to explain and understand the dynamics of established—outsider relationships illustrated in this book one has to say quite plainly that they play a very real part in the goal clashes between human groups bonded to each other in this manner.

Take an example once more the statement of the member of the Burakumin group quoted before. One can assume that in Japan as elsewhere the outcast condition of this group went hand in hand with forms of economic exploitation. However, the Burakumin had a traditional place and function in Japanese society. Today it appears that some are poor, though not noticeably poorer than the majority of Japanese poor, and some are quite well off. But the stigma does not disappear. The principal deprivation the outsider group suffers is not deprivation of food. What should one call it? Deprivation of value? Of meaning? Of its measure to self-love and self-respect?

Stigmatisation as an aspect of an established–outsider relationship is often associated with a specific type of collective fantasy evolved by the established group. It reflects and, at the same time, justifies the aversion—the prejudice—its members feel towards those of the outsider group. Thus, according to the gossip tradition of the majority Japanese, the Burakumin bear upon their person an inherited physical sign of membership in the outcast group—a bluish birthmark under each arm.[8] That illustrates very graphically the working and function of establishment fantasies vis à vis their outsider groups: the social stigma that its members attach to the outsider group transforms itself in their imagination into a material stigma—it is reified. It appears as something objective, something implanted upon the outsiders by nature or the gods. In that way the stigmatising group is exculpated from any blame: it is

---

[8] Whitaker, "Japan's Outcasts", p. 337. A Buraku poet, Maruoka Tadao, has written a poem, quoted in that article, which refers to this belief. These are two of the verses:

I heard whispering
Like the flow of the wind from mouth to mouth
That under each armpit I am marked
The size of an open hand.

. . .

Who marked my sides? For what unknown cause?
Why such an unknown brand upon my very self and soul?
Even today my ebbing thoughts,
So pale and cold, transparent as glass,
Hold me awake.

not *we*, such a fantasy implies, who have put a stigma on these people, but the powers that made the world—they have put the sign on these people to mark them off as inferior or bad people. The reference to a different skin colour and other innate or biological characteristics of groups which are, or have been, treated as inferior by an established group has the same objectifying function in this relationship as reference to the imaginary blue stigma of the Burakumin. The physical sign serves as a tangible symbol of the assumed anomie of the other group, of its lower worth in human terms, of its intrinsic badness; like the blue-stigma fantasy, the reference to such "objective" signs has a function in defence of the existing distribution of power chances as well as an exculpatory function. It belongs to the same set of *pars pro toto* arguments, at the same time defensive and aggressive, as stigmatisation of outsider groups—the formation of their overall image in terms of their anomic minority. Nearer home the vision of nineteenth-century working classes as the "great unwashed" is another example.

An approach to an established–outsider figuration as a stationary type of relationship, however, can be no more than a preparatory step. The problems with which one is confronted in such an exploration come into their own only if one considers the balance of power between such groups as changing and works towards a model which shows, at least in broad outline, the human—including the economic—problems inherent in such changes. At present the complex polyphony of the movement of rising and declining groups over time—of established groups which become outsiders or, as groups, disappear altogether, of outsider groups whose representatives move as a new establishment into positions previously denied them or, as the case may be, which become paralysed by oppression—is still largely concealed from view. So is the long-term direction of these changes, such as that from limited local balance-of-power struggles between a great multitude of relatively small social units to those between an increasingly smaller number of increasingly larger social units. In a period in which movements of former outsider groups into positions of power multiply, and at the same time the main axis of tension at the global level is that between larger state units than ever before, the lack of an overall theory of changes in power differentials and of the human problems associated with them is perhaps a little surprising.

However, preoccupation with short-term problems of the day and conception of the long-term development of societies as an unstructured historical prelude to the present still today block the understanding of long sequences in the development of societies and of their directional character—of sequences such as that of the movement of rising and declining groups and the dialectics of oppression and counter-oppression of an established group's ideas of grandeur deflated by those of a former outsider group, which rises and carries its representatives into the position of an establishment on a new level. Also, the heritage of the old enlightenment plays a part in this blockage. Despite all evidence to the contrary, the soothing belief that human beings, not only individually but also as groups, normally act rationally still retains a strong hold on the perception of inter-group relations. The ideal of rationality in the conduct of human affairs still bars access to the structure and dynamics of established–outsider figurations and to the magnifying group fantasies thrown up by them, which are social data *sui generis*, neither rational nor irrational. At present group fantasies still slip through our conceptual net. They appear as protean historical phantoms that seem to come and go arbitrarily. At the present stage of knowledge one has got so far as to see that affective experiences and fantasies of individual people are not arbitrary— that they have a structure and dynamics of their own. One has learned to see that such experiences and fantasies of a person at an earlier stage of life can influence profoundly the patterning of affects and conduct at later stages. But one has yet to work out a testable theoretical framework for the ordering of observations about group fantasies in connection with the development of groups. That may seem surprising, for the building up of collective praise- and blame-fantasies plays so obvious and vital a part in the conduct of affairs at all levels of balance-of-power relationships; and no less obviously they all have a diachronic, developmental character. On the global level, there is, for instance, the American dream and the Russian dream. There used to be the civilising mission of European countries and the dream of the Third Reich, successor to the First and Second Reichs. There is the counter-stigmatisation of the former outsiders, for example, of African countries in search of their negritude and their own dream.

There is, at a different level, as we shall see in this book, the idea of the old residents in Winston Parva, who in the name of their own greater human worth reject association with newcomers and stigmatise them, more mildly, but nevertheless unrelentingly, as people of lesser worth. Why do they do it?

Many different issues can bring tensions and conflicts between established and outsiders into the open. Yet at the core they are always balance-of-power struggles; as such they may range from silent tugs-of-war hidden beneath the routine co-operation between the two groups, within a framework of instituted inequalities, to overt struggles for changes of the institutional framework which embodies these power differentials and the inequalities that go with them. Whichever is the case, outsider groups (as long as they are totally cowed) direct tacit pressure or open action towards the decrease of power differentials responsible for their inferior position, established groups towards their preservation or increase.

However, once the problem of the distribution of power chances at the heart of established–outsider tensions and conflicts is brought into the open, it becomes easier to discover underneath another problem that is often overlooked. Groups tied to each other in the form of an established–outsider figuration are formed by individual human beings. The problem is how and why human beings perceive one another as belonging to the same group and include one another within the group boundaries which they establish when saying "we" in their reciprocal communications, while at the same time excluding other human beings whom they perceive as belonging to another group and to whom they collectively refer as "they".

As we shall see, the first newcomers in Winston Parva did not perceive the old residents as in any way different from themselves. They tried to make contact with some of them, as one often does when moving to a new neighbourhood. But they were rejected. In that way they were made aware of the fact that the old residents perceived themselves as a closed group, to whom they referred as "we", and the newcomers as a group of intruders, to whom they referred as "they" and whom they meant to keep at a distance. If one tries to discover why they did so, one becomes aware of the decisive part that the time dimension, or in other words, the development of a group, plays as determinant of its structure and characteristics. The group of "old families" of Winston Parva (some of whose members were, of course, quite young) had a common past; the newcomers had none. The difference was of great significance, both for the internal constitution of each of the two groups and for their relationship with each other. The established group of old residents consisted of families who had lived in that neighbourhood for two or three generations. They had undergone together a group process—from the past via the present towards the future—which provided them with a stock of common memories, attachments and dislikes. Without regard to this diachronic group dimension, the rationale and meaning of the personal pronoun "we" which they used with reference to each other cannot be understood.

Because they had lived together for a fairly long time, the old families possessed as a group a cohesion which the newcomers lacked. They were bonded to each other by the ambivalent and competitive intimacy characteristic of circles of "old families" everywhere, whether they are aristocratic, urban patrician, petty bourgeois or, as in this case, working-class families. They had their own internal ranking and "pecking" order. Each family and, individually, each member of a family had, at a given moment in time, its set position on the ladder of this order. Some of the criteria are set out in this book; others are implied. Both the ranking order itself and its criteria were known, as a matter of course, to everyone who belonged to the group, especially to the ladies. But they were known only at the level of social practice or, in other words, at a low level of abstraction, not explicitly at the relatively high level of abstraction represented by terms such as social standing of families or internal status order of a group. Many social data are still today conceptually represented only at a level comparable to that which our ancestors reached when they were able to distinguish between four and five apples or ten and twenty elephants, but were not yet able to operate on a higher level of abstraction, with numbers such as three and four, ten and twenty, as symbols of pure relationships without reference to any specific, tangible object. Similarly, in this case, the members of the established group were able to communicate their estimate of each other's standing within the internal ranking order of their group in a face-to-face encounter directly by their attitudes and, in conversation about others not actually present, by little symbolic phrases and the inflection of their voice rather than by explicit statements about higher or lower rankings of families and persons on their group's internal ranking and pecking order.

Moreover, the members of the group of "old families" were bound to each other by bonds of emotional intimacy ranging from the intimacy of long-standing friendships to that of long-standing dislikes. Like the status rivalries associated with them, these bonds too were of a kind which develops only among humans who have lived together through a group process of some duration. Without taking them into account one cannot quite understand the boundaries that the members of the established group of Winston Parva set up when they spoke of themselves as "we" and of the outsiders as "they". As their bonds with each other, resulting from such a group process, were invisible, the newcomers, who perceived the old residents at first simply as people like themselves, never quite understood the reasons for their exclusion and stigmatisation. The old residents, on their part were only able to explain them in terms of their immediate sentiments, of their feeling that theirs was a superior part of the neighbourhood with leisure amenities, religious institutions and local politics which everyone liked and that they did not wish to mingle in their private lives with people from inferior parts of the neighbourhood, whom they regarded as less respectable and norm-abiding than themselves.

It is symptomatic of the high degree of control that a cohesive group is able to exercise upon its members that not once during the investigation did we hear of a case in which a member of the "old" group broke the taboo of the group against non-occupational personal contact with members of the "new" group.

The internal opinion of any group with a high degree of cohesion has a profound influence upon its members as a regulating force of their sentiments and their conduct. If it is an established group, monopolistically reserving for its members the rewarding access to power resources and group charisma, this effect is particularly pronounced. This is due partly to the fact that the power ratio of a group member diminishes if his or her behaviour and feeling runs counter to group opinion so that this turns against him or her. As competitive in-fighting[9] of some kind—whether subdued or open and loud—is a standing feature of cohesive groups, the lowering of a group member's ranking within the internal status order of the group weakens the member's ability to hold his or her own in

---

[9] See also p. 155 below.

the group's internal competition for power and status; it may, in severe cases, expose him or her to the pressure of whispered blame-gossip or perhaps to open stigmatisation within the group (without the ability to fight back), which can be as unrelenting and wounding as the stigmatisation of outsiders. Approval of group opinion, as we shall see in the study of Winston Parva, requires compliance with group norms. The penalty for group deviance and sometimes even for suspected deviance[10] is loss of power and a lowering of one's status.

However, the impact of a group's internal opinion upon each of its members goes further than that. Group opinion has in some respects the function and character of a person's own conscience. In fact the latter, forming itself in a group process, remains attached to the former by an elastic, if invisible cord. If the power differential is great enough, a member of an established group may be quite indifferent to what outsiders think about him or her, but is hardly ever indifferent to the opinion of insiders—of those who have access to power resources in whose monopolistic control he or she participates or seeks to participate and with whom he or she shares a common pride in the group, a common group charisma. A member's self-image and self-respect are linked to what other members of the group think of him or her. Though variable and elastic, the connection between, on the one hand, the self-regulation of his or her conduct and sentiment—the functioning of the more conscious and even some of the less conscious layers of conscience— and, on the other hand, the norm-setting internal opinion of one or other of his or her we-groups breaks down only with sanity. It breaks down, in other words, only if his or her sense of reality, ability to distinguish between what happens in fantasies and what happens independently of them, fades out. The relative autonomy of an individual person, the extent to which their own conduct and sentiment, self-respect and conscience are functionally related to the internal opinion of groups to which he or she refers as "we", is certainly subject to great variation. The view, widespread today, that a sane individual may become totally independent of the opinion of all his or her we-groups and, in that sense, absolutely autonomous, is as misleading as the opposite view that his or her

---

[10] See the case of the woman who invited in the dustmen, p. 39 below.

autonomy may entirely disappear within a collective of robots. That is what is meant when one speaks of the elasticity of the bonds linking a person's self-regulation to the regulating pressures of a we-group. This elasticity has its limits, but no zero-point. The relationship between these two types of regulating functions (often distinguished as "social" and "psychological") at different stages of the group process called "social development", deserves a special study. I have explored some aspects of this problem elsewhere.[11] Here, what stands out most graphically is the way in which the self-regulation of members of a closely knit established group is linked to the internal opinion of that group. Their susceptibility to the pressure of their we-group is in that case particularly great because belonging to such a group instils in its members a strong sense of their higher human value in relation to outsiders.

In an earlier period, the impact that the belief of a group in its exclusive grace and virtue vis-à-vis outsiders had upon the self-regulation of sentiment and the conduct of its individual members showed itself most prominently in the case of groups dominated by priestly establishments and thus united against outsiders by a common superhuman belief. In our age, this impact of group charismatic belief upon group members has its most exemplary form in the case of powerful nations dominated by party-governmental establishments and, thus, united against outsiders by a common social belief in their unique national virtue and grace. In Winston Parva one could observe in miniature a core group formed by members of the old families, a central establishment guarding the special virtue and respectability of the whole village, which as a lower-level establishment solidly closed its ranks against members of a neighbourhood that was regarded as less respectable, as inhabited by people of lesser human value. In this case, the control represented by group opinion could be all the more stringent as the established group was small and had the character of a face-to-face group. There was no single defection from the established group, no single breach of the taboo against closer personal contact with the outsiders, which shows how effectively in such a setting the self-

---

[11] See N. Elias, *The Civilizing Process*, Oxford, Blackwell, 1994 (originally published as *Über den Prozess der Zivilisation* in two separate volumes in 1939, Basel, Haus zum Falken).

regulation of individual members can be kept in line through the carrot-and-stick mechanism to which I have alluded before. It can be kept in line through the rewarding participation of the group's superior human value and the corresponding heightening of an individual's self-love and self-respect, reinforced by the continued approval of the group's internal opinion and, at the same time, through the restraints each member imposes upon himself in accordance with the norms and standards of the group. The study of the established group in Winston Parva thus shows on a small scale how individual self-control and group opinion are geared to each other.

We owe to Freud a great advance in the understanding of group processes during which men's self-controlling agencies grow into shape. Freud himself, however, conceptualised his findings largely in a manner which made it appear that every human being is a self-contained unit—a *homo clausus*. He recognised the specifically human capacity for learning to control and, up to a point, to pattern their malleable libidinal drives according to their experiences within a norm-setting group. But he conceptualised the self-controlling functions which he saw growing up with the help of these experiences as if they were organs like kidney and heart. In short, he followed a tradition which is still as widespread within the medical profession as it is within the lay public at large. He conceptually represented controlling and orientating functions at the personality level of a human organism, which are patterned through learning, as if they were organs at one of its lower levels, which are little affected by learning. He discovered that the group process of a father—mother—child relationship has a determining influence on the patterning of a person's elementary drives and the formation of his self-controlling functions in early childhood. But, once formed, they appeared to him to work on their own, quite independently of the further group processes in which every person continues to be involved from childhood to old age. As a result, he advanced the conception of human beings' self-controlling functions—an ego, a super-ego or an ego-ideal, as he called them—to the point where they have the character of functioning in what appears to be a total autonomy within the single individual. But the layers of personality structure that remain most directly and closely linked to the group processes in which a person participates, above all the person's we-image and we-ideal, lay beyond his horizon. He did not conceptualise them and probably considered them as part of what he called reality, in contradistinction to affective fantasies and dreams, which he probably saw as his proper concern. However much he contributed to the understanding of the bonds that link people to each other, his concept of men was still largely that of the isolated individual person. In his field of vision the *persons* appeared as structured, and the societies formed by inter-dependent persons appeared as backgrounds, as unstructured "reality", whose dynamic was apparently without influence on the individual human being.

A person's we-image and we-ideal form as much part of a person's self-image and self-ideal as the image and ideal of him- or herself as the unique person to which he or she refers as "I". It is not difficult to see that statements such as "I, Pat O'Brien, am an Irishman" implies an I-image as well as a we-image. So do statements such as "I am a Mexican", "I am a Buddhist", "I am working class" or "We are an old Scottish family". These and other aspects of a person's group identity form as integral a part of his personal identity as others which distinguish him from other members of his we-group.

Freud once remarked that a breakdown of the personality structure, as in the case of neurotic or psychotic illnesses, may enable an observer to perceive its interconnected functions more clearly than its normal working. *Mutatis mutandis* one may say the same of we-image and we-ideal. They are always compacts of emotive fantasies and realistic images. But they stand out most sharply when fantasy and reality fall apart. For in that case their fantasy content becomes accentuated. The difference is that, in the case of such personality functions as ego-image and ego-ideal, the emotive fantasies represent purely personal experiences of a group process. In the case of we-image and we-ideal, they are personal versions of collective fantasies.

A striking example in our time is that of the we-image and we-ideal of once-powerful nations whose superiority in relation to others has declined. Their members may suffer for centuries because the group charismatic we-ideal, modelled on an idealised image of themselves in the days of their greatness, lingers on for many generations as a model they feel they ought to live up to, without being able to do so. The radiance of their collective life as a nation has gone; their power superiority in relation to other groups, emotionally understood as a sign of their own higher human value in relation to the inferior value of these others, is irretrievably lost. Yet, the dream of their special charisma is kept alive in a variety of ways—through the teaching of history, the old buildings, masterpieces of the nation in the time of its glory, or through new achievements which seemingly confirm the greatness of the past. For a time, the fantasy shield of their imagined charisma as a leading, established group may give a declining nation the strength to carry on. In that sense it can have a survival value. But the discrepancy between the actual and the imagined position of one's group among others can also entail a mistaken assessment of one's power resources and, as a consequence, suggest a group strategy in pursuit of a fantasy image of one's own greatness that may lead to self-destruction as well as to destruction of other interdependent groups. The dreams of nations (as of other groups) are dangerous.[12] An overgrown we-ideal is a symptom of a collective illness. Much could be gained from a better understanding of the dynamics of

---

[12] The rigidity of the we-image and the consequent inability of groups to adapt it to changing conditions of life show themselves not only in the fortunes of large groups such as social classes and nations, but also in those of small groups. A telling example can be found in "De tragedie der Puttenaren" in a book by A. van Dantzig, *Normaal is niet gewoon*, Amsterdam, De Bezige Bij, 1974, p. 21 ff. The author describes the fortunes of a group of 452 people who had lived all their lives in a small Dutch village community, when in November 1944 they were suddenly uprooted and as a reprisal sent—as a group—to a concentration camp. They remained, as a matter of course, obedient to the old village norms, i.e., they worked as hard as before, took the pauses they thought justified, showed their indignity over several aspects of camp life, etc. In short, being together, they were unable to behave in a manner of which public opinion in their village would have disapproved. The automatic reciprocal control of the villagers did not allow them to adjust their standards of conduct to the completely different conditions of life in a concentration camp. Only 32 of them came back to Putten, where 3 more died. One can, of course, not be certain that their survival rate would have been greater if they had not been sent there as a still reasonably integrated group. What one can say, however, is that this fact—the fact that they were sent to a concentration camp as a group (which in other cases is often considered as a positive factor of survival)—in this case contributed to their very low survival rate. In short, as the author says: "Many inhabitants of Putten were unable to free themselves from the laws which for so long had determined the course of their lives and the structure of their community." Van Dantzig very rightly says: "Psychoanalysis and sociology could have found each other here." The case which he so graphically describes shows very clearly the need for considering the we-ideal together with the ego-ideal as part of the personality structure.

established–outsider figurations and thus of the problems involved in the changing position of groups in relation to each other, of the rise of groups into the position of monopolistic establishment from which others are excluded, and the decline or fall from such a position to another where they themselves are, in some respects, among the excluded outsiders. In this respect too, the ideal of "rationality", this heritage of the old Enlightenment, still blocks the way towards a better understanding of such problems. It perpetuates the notion that nations, and their leaders too, on the whole act "rationally", which in this context probably means realistically.

The concepts put forward here as part of an established–outsider theory, concepts such as group charisma and we-ideal, may help towards a better fitting assessment of these group relations. The example of powerful establishments such as national groups losing their great power status and sinking into the ranks of second or third level establishments shows once more the close connection between the power ratios of groups and the we-images of their members. To bring these connections into the open does not mean that they form an immutable part of human nature. In fact, the greater the awareness of the emotional equation of great power with great human value, the greater is the chance of a critical appraisal and a change. The leading groups of nations, or of social classes and other groupings of human beings, are given at the height of their power to ideas of grandeur. The self-enhancing quality of a high power ratio flatters the collective self-love which is also the reward for submission to group-specific norms, to patterns of affect restraint characteristic of that group and believed to be lacking in less powerful, "inferior" groups, outsiders and outcasts. Hence the traditional patterns of restraint, the distinguishing norms of conduct of an old superior group are apt to become brittle or even break down when the rewarding self-love, the belief in the special charisma of the once-powerful group falters with the decrease of their great power superiority. But again such a process takes time. It may take a long time before the reality shock sinks in. The rewarding belief in the special virtue, grace and mission of one's own group may for generations shield members of an established group from the full emotional realisation of their changed position, from the awareness that the gods have failed, that the group has not kept faith with them. They may *know* of the change as a fact, while their belief in their special group charisma and the attitudes, their behaviour strategy which goes with it, persists unchanged as a fantasy shield, which prevents them from *feeling* the change and, therefore, from being able to adjust to the changed conditions of their group image and their group strategy. Therefore, as realistic adjustment is a condition without which they cannot achieve, as a group with diminished power resources, anything that can prove their human value to themselves and to others, the emotional denial of the change, the tacit preservation of the beloved group charismatic image is self-defeating.

Sooner or later the reality shock breaks in; and its coming is often traumatic. One can observe groups—in our time above all national groups—many of whose members, without knowing it, appear to remain in a condition of mourning for the lost greatness that was. It is as if they were saying: if we can't live up to the we-image of the time of our greatness, nothing is really worth doing.

With the help of this reference to cases in which changes in a group's position among other groups increase the unrealistic aspects of their collective image and ideal, one may be better able to understand the working of an established group's we-image and we-ideal in the following study. In that case one encounters such a group while its superior position in relation to outsiders is still fully maintained. The very existence of interdependent outsiders who share neither the fund of common memories nor, as it appears, the same norms of respectability as the established group, acts as an irritant; it is perceived by the members of the latter as an attack against their own we-image and we-ideal. The sharp rejection and stigmatisation of the outsiders are the counter-attack. The established group feels compelled to repulse what they experience as a threat to both their power superiority (in terms of their cohesion and monopolisation of local offices and amenities) and their human superiority, their group charisma, by means of a counter-attack, a continuous rejection and humiliation of the other group.

The flow of blame-gossip and the stained they-image of the outsiders can be regarded as standing features of this kind of figuration. In other cases it becomes routinised and may persist for centuries. Among the most telling features of the strategy of established groups is that of imputing to the outsiders, as a matter of reproach, some of their own standard attitudes, which in their case often enough earn praise. Thus in an Indian village the untouchables had to remove their shoes while passing through the caste Hindu streets, since wearing shoes amounted to "showing off". Elsewhere male outcastes were not allowed to sport upward-pointing moustaches as this signified self-assertion.[13]

In the same way an American writer, not unconnected with the American establishment,[14] spoke in all innocence of negro intellectuals "lusting for a taste of power", quite oblivious of the long-lasting use of their own power superiority by white Americans as a means to exclude the descendants of slaves from participation in the power resources monopolised by them.

One of the most striking aspects of present approaches to established–outsider relationships with "racial" connotations is their widespread discussion in terms of a here-and-now problem. The exclusion of the long-term group process—not to be confused with what we call "history"—from the study of this type of established–outsider relationship tends to distort the problem. In discussing "racial" problems one is apt to put the cart before the horse. It is argued, as a rule, that people perceive others as belonging to another group because the colour of their skin is different. It would be more to the point if one asked how it came to pass in this world that one has got into the habit of perceiving people with another skin colour as belonging to a different group. This problem at once brings into focus the long process in the course of which human groups evolved in different parts of the earth, adapted to different physical conditions and then, after long spells of isolation, came into contact with each other often enough as conquerors and conquered and thus, within one and the same society, as established and outsiders. It was as a result of this long process of intermingling, in which groups with different physical characteristics became interdependent as masters and slaves or in other positions with great power differentials, that differences in physical appearance became signals of people's belongingness to groups with different power ratios, different status and different

---

[13] Report of the Elayaperumal Committee, 1960, quoted in Dilip Hiro, *The Untouchables of India*, Report No. 26, London, Minority Rights Group, 1975, p. 9.
[14] See Eric Hoffer, *The Temper of Our Time*, New York, 1969, p. 64.

norms. Once more one is reminded of the need for reconstituting the temporal character of groups and their relationships as processes in the sequence of time if one wants to understand the boundaries that people set up by distinguishing between a group of which they say "we" and another to which they refer as "they".

The development of the Indian caste—outcaste figuration can serve as an example. It is one of the longest group processes of its kind of which we have some written documentary evidence going back to the second millennium before our era. One can hardly understand and explain the many-levelled established—outsider relationships in India, ranging from high castes to outcastes as they are today, without reference to the long group process during which this figuration became what it is. The point of departure was the gradual subjection of earlier inhabitants of India by conquering invaders from the north. They apparently came from the steppes of southern Russia via Iran, spoke an Indo-European language and, in some documents, referred to themselves as light-skinned Aryans, clearly distinguishable by their physical appearance from the dark-skinned tribes whom they had subjected to their rule. Among these Aryans, in contrast to those other branches from the same stock that we know as Hellenic and Germanic tribes, the primordial struggle between warriors and priests had resulted in the victory of the latter. This, and the fact that, in terms of their numbers, the conquering groups were probably much smaller than the subject population and, in addition, perhaps short of women, led to a systematic policy of closure and exclusion on the part of the established group in their relationship with the subject people— apart from relations of the conquerors with subject women, which resulted over the generations in a steady decrease of the physical, the so-called racial differences, without resulting in a decrease of the exclusion. Hardened into a tradition, this policy resulted in a condition where every group closed its ranks in relation to any other regarded as of lower standing. All groups distinguished from others by their rank and their social functions became hereditary groups which, in principle if not always in practice, were inaccessible to those not born into them.

Thus, as Indian society became more differentiated, it assumed the character of a hierarchy of hereditary castes and, at the lowest levels, of hereditary outcastes. The rigidity of this tradition of group exclusion may have been due, in the first instance, to the fear of losing their identity as well as their privileged position on the part of the light-skinned invaders and especially of their priests. Thus, the conquerors forced the conquered people to live outside their own villages. They excluded them from participation in the religious ceremonies, sacrifices and prayers to the gods and thus from the blessings they conferred on participants. By denying them participation in their own group charisma and their own norms, they forced the conquered into the position of people who were in their own eyes anomic and, at the same time, despised them for not obeying the norms they themselves observed. The priestly establishment, the Brahmins, used their monopoly of the means of orientation and of the control of the invisible powers systematically as an instrument of rule and a weapon of exclusion. The tradition of established–outsider relationships which was initially connected with the policy of conquerors in relation to the conquered and which permeated in course of time the increasingly differentiated hierarchy of castes down to the outcastes at the bottom of the social pyramid, assumed its special rigidity in the Indian case because it was firmly set in a mould of religious beliefs and magical practices by a ruling establishment of priests.

In contrast to the traditional policy of religious establishments such as those of Christianity and Islam, which was directed towards conversion and assimilation of outsiders, the Brahmins were from early days on habituated to a policy of exclusion; their policy was directed towards strict hierarchic segregation of groups, as a condition of their own high power ratio. As in the early days the non-Aryan subject peoples were rigidly excluded from participation in the rites and prayers of the ruling groups, so later all functional divisions within Indian society, from those of priests to those of street sweepers, were conceived in terms of a religiously sanctioned exclusion, of a hierarchy of hereditary social divisions between higher and lower castes. The differences were explained in terms of "good" or "bad" deeds committed in a former life. Thus, according to Hiro, one of the holy books, the Manusmriti, states:

"In consequence of many bad acts committed with his body a man becomes in the next birth something inanimate; in consequence of bad acts committed by speech, a bird or a beast; in consequence of mental sins, he is re-born in a low caste." The Brahmanical establishment thus enjoined upon the lower castes to accept their station in life without question, and to remember that if they followed their assigned *dharma* (i.e. duty) in this life they would be rewarded with a better status in the next life.[15]

One of the standard devices of an establishment under strain is that of tightening the restraints that its members impose upon themselves, as well as upon the wider group ruled by it, and the observance of these restraints can again be used as a sign both of one's own group charisma and the disgrace of outsiders. Sometime between 100 BC and AD 100 the Brahminical establishment came under pressure from rival Buddhist missionaries, which had been increasing since the time of the Buddhist emperor, Ashoka. It was during that period that Brahmins themselves renounced the eating of meat, that the caste population came to abstain from eating beef and that cows assumed the full status of symbols of a deity and, therefore, could not be killed. As in Japan, occupational groups whose work was regarded as unclean, who thus were considered as socially polluting, had existed before. The strengthening of the taboo against eating and killing animals finalised their status as outcastes. Butchers, leather workers, fishermen, executioners, scavengers and similar occupational groups were regarded as humans whose contact polluted others. Throughout the centuries their members were treated as hereditary outcastes, as pariahs.

For someone living in a relatively wealthy industrial society it requires an exercise in imagination to represent to oneself the mode of existence and the feeling of human beings in that situation. But it is an exercise worth doing. Throughout the long period the stained we-image of a person dominated and coloured his or her self-image. It overshadowed his or her image as an individual person in a manner to which one may not readily have access in societies where the feeling of pollution by social outsiders is not sanctioned by the ruling beliefs. This nightmare world of the tainted we-image can easily appear as alien. Yet some of the children growing up in Winston Parva's rat alley (as it was called by the established group) probably suffered from a similarly tainted we-image and became deviants as a result. Wherever established–outsider relationships exist such feelings are never entirely absent. The deep uneasiness

---

[15] Hiro, *Untouchables of India*, p. 5.

1
50

aroused through contact with members of outsider groups may be less strong, but even without religious sanctions it has similar features. At its roots is the fear of contact with a group which in one's own eyes, as in those of one's fellow, is anomic. Its members break rules which one is oneself enjoined to observe and on whose observation depend both one's self-respect and the respect of one's fellows. On it depends too one's participation in the special grace and virtue, in the charisma of one's group.

Some of these features could be observed even in so small a setting as that of Winston Parva. It seemed useful to allow the microcosm of a small community to throw light on the macrocosm of large-scale societies and vice versa. That is the line of thought behind the use of a small setting as an empirical paradigm of established–outsider relationships, which often exist elsewhere on a different scale. Some details can be brought into better focus there than in a study of corresponding relationships in larger settings. Others stand out more clearly in these larger settings. Together they may help towards a better understanding of the socio-dynamics of established–outsider relationships. Because such a study brings under a single conceptual umbrella types of relationships which one traditionally perceives only as different, they all, one may find, stand out more vividly.

One may see, for instance, more clearly the part played in established–outsider relations by differences in norms and especially in the standards of self-restraint. The established group tends to experience such differences as an irritant, partly because their own observation of norms is linked to their self-love, to their group charismatic beliefs, partly because non-observation of their own norms by others is apt to weaken their defence against their own wish to break the prescribed norm. Interdependent outsiders, therefore, who are more lenient, or are merely suspected of being more lenient, in the observation of restraints whose strict observation is vital for members of the established group if they are to maintain their standing among their fellows, are experienced as a threat to their own standing, their special virtue and grace by the established group. That was one of the main reasons why in the case of Winston Parva the established hit back so sharply. Rightly or wrongly they, like many other established groups, felt exposed to a three-pronged attack—against their monopolised power resources, against their group charisma and against their group norms. They repelled what they experienced as an attack by closing their ranks against the outsiders, by excluding and humiliating them. The outsiders themselves had hardly any intention of attacking the old residents. But they were placed in an unhappy and often humiliating position. The whole drama was played out by the two sides as if they were puppets on a string.

March 1976   Norbert Elias
                                                        Amsterdam

1 | Considerations of Procedure

WINSTON PARVA * formed in 1959–60 part of a suburban development on the outskirts of a large and prosperous industrial town in the English midlands. It was separated by a railway line from other parts of the sprawling suburban growth ; a bridge over this line was the only link with Winston Magna and the rest of Winston. It had less than 5,000 inhabitants who formed a fairly compact community with its own factories, schools, churches, shops and clubs. And with its own divisions.

It consisted of three different neighbourhoods known and recognised as different by the inhabitants themselves. Zone 1 was what is usually called a middle-class residential area. Most of its inhabitants regarded it as such. Zones 2 and 3 were working-class areas one of which, Zone 2, housed almost all the local factories. In terms of income ranges, types of occupations and " social class " the inhabitants of Zones 2 and 3 seemed not markedly different. An observer used to assessing the social structure of a neighbourhood group in these terms alone might have expected to find that the two working-class zones had much in common, that the inhabitants regarded themselves more or less as equals and that the main dividing line in the communal life of Winston Parva in terms of the mutual ranking of the inhabitants and of the barriers to social relations and communications lay between the middle-class zone on the one hand and the two working-class zones on the other.

The configuration which one encountered in actual fact was different. A preliminary survey suggested that not only the middle-class inhabitants of Zone 1, but also the working-class inhabitants of Zone 2 regarded themselves and their neighbour-

* All recognisable names in this study have been changed.

I

hood as superior in social status to those of Zone 3 and that
the social barriers dividing the two working-class neighbourhoods from each other were at least as great, if not greater
than the barriers to social relations and communications
between working-class neighbourhoods and the middle-class
neighbourhood in the area. The residents of Zone 3 themselves
seemed to accept the status inferiority locally accorded to their
own neighbourhood by comparison with Zone 2 although
grudgingly and with some bitterness. One could not help
asking why they acquiesced. How did the inhabitants of
Zone 2 manage to assert and to maintain their own status
superiority ? What were the resources of power which enabled
them to do so ? Were the occupational differences between
the inhabitants of the two working-class districts greater than
they seemed and were they responsible for the differences in
the status attached to the two neighbourhoods ? Were there
marked differences in the income levels between the two
groups or in the size and rents of their houses ? If not, what
other factors could account for these status differences with all
that they entailed in terms of human relationships ?

A tentative answer was not difficult to find. Zone 2 was an
old, Zone 3 a new working-class district. The inhabitants
of Zone 2 were for the greater part members of families who
had lived in that neighbourhood for a fairly long time, who
were established there as old residents, who felt that they
belonged there and that the place belonged to them. The
inhabitants of Zone 3 were newcomers who had lived in
Winston Parva for a relatively short time and who remained
outsiders in relation to the older inhabitants. It seemed
worthwhile to examine such a relationship. New housing
estates often spring up in old neighbourhoods, and in addition
to migratory social mobility which is the normal concomitant
of increasing urbanisation and industrialisation everywhere,
wars and revolutions bring again and again armies of migrants
as potential settlers into the neighbourhood of older communities.

As a casual observation the fact that length of residence can
be a factor in the ranking of families and groups is quite well
known. In studies of upper- and middle-class groups particu-

2

larly allusions to old families and new families or to old wealth and new wealth are not rare and the existence of a Society with a core formed by a network of old families is well known not only on the national, but also on the local level as a powerful factor in the social stratification and the social structure of many communities.

The fact that similar distinctions may also play a part in the relations of working-class groups is perhaps less well known. And a case of this kind is well suited to bring into fuller relief the general problem linking all these phenomena to each other—the problem why under certain conditions " oldness " of a group is regarded as a prestige giving factor and " newness " as a reproach. One might expect working-class groups to be less prone to this kind of ranking because in other classes it is usually associated with the " oldness " or " newness " of wealth. But expressions like " old working-class district " do occur in the relevant literature though they usually remain at the level of a layman's casual observation without links to sociological theory. It is fairly clear that the epithets " old " and " new " applied to social formations point to differences in their lengths of residence or to the length of time during which their members and their families have been known. It is perhaps less evident that these terms point to specific differences in the structure of groups and that this type of structural differences plays a part in their ranking.

A small community such as Winston Parva seemed to offer a good opportunity for learning a little more about such problems. The question was whether and how far a more systematic enquiry would confirm the impression one had of the relationship between the three zones of Winston Parva, whether one could throw more light on the reasons for this configuration and could form a tentative configurational model for this type of relationship which might serve as a guide, and could be tested, in studies of similar or related phenomena.

Together with problems of substance such as these, one was confronted with certain problems of procedure. Winston Parva was a relatively small community. One of the authors had worked there for a number of years and knew it from close personal experience. He carried out interviews with members of every thirtieth household on the electoral register in each of the three zones. He interviewed the leaders of local voluntary associations and analysed the membership lists. He organised for a time a local youth club and taught at a school there. The authors were also able to make use of record cards showing the occupation and place of residence of all parents of school children in Winston Parva.

Interviews and record cards made it possible to bring together quantitative data and to present some of them in the form of statistical tables. But quantitative data collected in this manner could be regarded as only part of the evidence required for studies in problems of this kind. They could help to ascertain whether or not " structural " differences, of the type which one has usually in mind if one uses the term " structure " in this context, such as differences in occupations or incomes, were large enough to account for the status differences which were locally claimed to exist between two working-class neighbourhoods or for the different images the neighbourhoods had of themselves or for the relatively high exclusiveness of the members of the " superior " neighbourhood in relation to those of the " inferior ".

As it turned out, such claims, such images, such barriers to social communication could not be explained in terms of this or that quantifiable factor alone. It could not be explained by means of procedures aimed at measuring " factors " or " variables " as if each of them existed and could vary all by itself independently of the whole social configuration—by means of procedures, in short, based on the tacit assumption that social phenomena were combinations of variables comparable to the combinations of atomic particles which served natural scientists as one of their principal models.

Nor could they be explained on the assumption often implied in the present uses of statistical procedures that individual attitudes and beliefs, encountered for instance in the course of interviews, had been formed by the interviewed individuals, in the first place, independently of other individuals, as it were, in the stillness of their ivory tower ; and had come into contact with those of others only secondarily. Even less plausible in this context was another of these tacit assumptions underlying

4

many statistical enquiries into attitudes and opinions—the assumption that power was so evenly distributed between individuals that each of them was able to utter opinions independently of what others thought.

All these assumptions were well in the line of a procedure which confined its uses to a concept of societies as congeries or heaps of people, as " statistical populations " and which made them withdraw their attention from the specific configurations people formed with each other—from specific social structures.

In Winston Parva it soon became quite obvious that the answers which one received in interviews or elsewhere, particularly those concerned with configurations within and between the various neighbourhoods, were not the expressions of ideas formed in the first place by each individual separately. The individual answers formed part and parcel of common beliefs and attitudes maintained by various forms of social pressure and social control particularly in Zone 2 where neighbourhood cohesion was relatively high, and also by the pressures of a common situation particularly in Zone 3 where cohesion was less great. They represented, in other words, individual variations of standard beliefs and attitudes current in these neighbourhoods.

It may well be that some of the people who were interviewed held individual views which diverged from the standard ideas and beliefs of their neighbourhood. But interviews of the conventional type are rough and ready methods of ascertaining people's attitudes and opinions. They rarely do more than scratch the surface. In communities such as these one could expect people in interviews with relative strangers to produce more readily the dominant standard ideas than any individually formed opinions which deviated from these standards. It was quite clear that in a closely-knit community such as Zone 2 people were eager to present a common front and to make the best possible impression on a stranger. Even outsiders within Zone 2 (recognisable as such if one had more than a fleeting acquaintance with the zone) produced as a matter of course the standard answers current in the neighbourhood.

If one worked for a while in Winston Parva one was left in no doubt about them. One did not even need highly elaborate

5

statistical techniques to ascertain them. The idea that one's concept of the norms of a community were abstractions or generalisations from a collection of individual opinions was soon dispelled in this social setting provided the observer's eyes were not blocked by preconceived dogmas. Opinions about a person's own and about other related neighbourhoods were, in this setting as in many others, not formed first by each individual for himself; they were formed in connection with a continuous interchange of opinions within the community in the course of which individuals exercised considerable pressure upon each other to conform to the common image of the community in speech and behaviour; within this pattern of neighbourhood control the most highly respected family networks held a key position; as long as they had enough power they acted as guardians of the community image and the approved opinions and attitudes. Even without counting heads one could gain a high degree of certainty about the normative community image which the members of Zone 2 shared with each other because it was frequently mentioned in conversations, directly or indirectly, as something which everyone there took for granted. It would probably have created quite a stir if a person who belonged to the zone had failed to accept it. But as far as one could ascertain, no-one ever did. The uniformity of opinion in that respect was hardly less great than that of the language people used. In such a setting one could gain a very high degree of certainty about people's communal beliefs and attitudes without taking the traditional random sample of opinions, though for tradition's sake that was in fact done in this case.

Other aspects of the enquiry too indicated that in this social context inferences from the statistical analysis of interviews alone were of limited value without the knowledge acquired by means of a systematic enquiry by a trained participant observer. Here is an example.

By and large the inhabitants of the three zones of Winston Parva saw themselves and each other in fairly conventional terms. They saw Zone 1 as a "better-class area" or a "residential area", Zones 2 and 3 as "working-class areas" though the inhabitants of Zone 2 themselves saw their own zone as vastly superior. But if one took a close look, one soon learned that each zone had its own minority group. Zone 1 had a row of cottages inhabited by manual workers and in some of the middle-class houses lived working-class families who had acquired their house in Zone 1 with the help either of a saved war gratuity or of the combined earnings of husband and wife. They usually regarded residence in Zone 1 as a symbol of social rise and success. Zone 2 had a small group of middle-class residents; Zone 3 a small minority of particularly large and troublesome " problem families ", partly, but not wholly, living on unskilled labour.

Occupational statistics would have helped to bring out the rough outline of this configuration. But the precise role played by it in the images and in the relationships of the three zones could not have been ascertained alone by means of inferences from the statistical analysis. The minority of Zone 1 played no part in the image of the zone at all. Neither in conversations nor in interviews was it ever mentioned in connection with the reputation or the status of the zone. The minority of Zone 2 was occasionally mentioned by its residents, always with evident pride; it reinforced their claim to a higher status than their neighbours in Zone 3. In contrast, the image and reputation of Zone 3 was in a very great extent affected by the relatively small minority of " problem families ". The reputation of the " established " was enhanced by a sprinkling of " socially better " families, the reputation of the " outsiders " was decisively coloured by the activities of their " lowest " section.

Thus in this small setting one encountered and, to some extent, learned to understand an optical illusion characteristic of the making of social images in many other much wider social settings : the image which the " established ", which powerful ruling sections of a society have of themselves and communicate to others tends to be modelled on the " minority of the best "; it inclines towards idealisation. The image of " outsiders ", of groups who have in relation to the " established " sections relatively little power tends to be modelled on the " minority of the worst "; it inclines towards denigration.

It was possible to test this hypothetical model of a specific configuration as it emerged in the preliminary observations by means of interviews and more systematic observation. But the arrangements of interviews and the focussing of observations which made such a test possible presupposed the presence at the spot of an observer trained for the perception of configurations such as this—trained not only for statistical analysis, but also for configurational analysis and synopsis. Although the latter are widely practised among sociologists, one often conceptualises sociological procedures as if the only scientifically reliable and legitimate procedure were the former. One often seems to feel that only statistical analysis can provide the impersonal certainty expected of a sociological enquiry. Statements not based on measurements of quantifiable properties are frequently dismissed as " impressionistic ", as " merely descriptive " or as " subjective ". Other investigators before must have been troubled by the inadequacy of a conceptualisation which implied that any verbal statement which bears no direct reference to statistical data is necessarily unreliable, imprecise and scientifically suspect, that the only certainties one can have about social phenomena are those based on statements which tell us how more there is, or was, of phenomenon A than of phenomenon B. Yet statements of this latter type are often not very illuminating unless they are combined with other statements about the mode of connection between A and B—unless procedures aimed at certainties about quantities are enriched by procedures aimed at certainties about configurations.

In actual fact such procedures, configurational analysis and synopsis, form an integral part of many sociological enquiries. They play a part for example in the building of models on the largest as well as the smallest scale—models of bureaucracies as well as of villages, of balance of power systems as well as of families ; they can be found everywhere in the development, the making and revising of sociological hypotheses and theories. They play a part, but they are still insufficiently conceptualized as characteristic procedures of a science whose central task is the study of individuals as groups, of configurations of individuals as such. That individuals are to be studied first as isolates, and that the configurations which individuals form with each other

8

are derived from what they are without configurations, is an odd idea which profoundly confuses enquiries into these configurations. The impoverishment of sociology as a science which has resulted from the prevalent evaluation of sociological methods—from the assumption that it is enough to use statistical methods if one wants reliable answers to sociological problems, is obvious enough. It has led to a state of affairs whereby wide areas of sociologically relevant problems are either left unexplored or, if explored, may be protected from the slur of being " merely descriptive " (because they are non-statistical) simply by a great name (as is the case with the greater part of the empirical work of Max Weber), or else they are undertaken as non-statistical enquiries simply because they seem fruitful without explicit reflections on the nature of the procedure which makes them so.

Hence, the use of such procedures, of configurational analysis and synopsis, is still largely confined to the accidence of individual gifts. It does not yet form an integral part of the training of sociologists to learn to observe and to conceptualise systematically how individuals cohere, how and why they form with each other this particular configuration or how and why the configurations they form change and, in some cases, develop. Yet, to overcome the limitations of sociological enquiries centred on statistical procedures is possible only if enquirers trained to perceive and to manipulate single factors or variables join hands with, or are themselves qualified to act as, enquirers trained to perceive and, at least conceptually, to manipulate configurations as such—trained for accurate synopsis as well as for accurate analysis.

Models of configurations, of social patterns or structures can be no less precise and reliable than the results of quantitative measurement of isolated factors or variables. What they lack is the deceptive finality of inferences based on quantitative analysis alone which is often mistaken for precision. Like hypotheses and theories in general they represent extensions, advances or improvements of the existing fund of knowledge, but they cannot pretend to be an absolute terminus in the quest for knowledge which, like the philosopher's stone, does not exist. Models of configurations, the results of configurational

9

enquiries, form part of a process, of a growing field of enquiries, and in the light of its development they themselves are open to revisions, to criticisms and improvements, the fruits of further enquiries.

The apparent finality of each statistical enquiry and the openness, the developmental character of configurational enquiries as links in a chain are closely connected with certain basic differences between the type of thinking required for a purely statistical and that required for a sociological analysis. In both cases analysing means focussing attention on one element of a configuration at a time—" factor ", " variable ", " aspect " or whatever one may call it. But in a purely statistical analysis the study of such elements in isolation is treated as the primary and often as the principle task ; " factors " or " variables " and their quantitative properties are treated as if they were in actual fact independent of their place and function within that configuration, and statistical correlations, including statistical correlations of relationships, never cease to be correlations of isolates. Sociological analysis is based on the supposition that every element of a configuration and its properties are what they are only by virtue of their position and function within a configuration. In that case analysis or separation of elements is merely a temporary step in a research operation which requires supplementation by another, by the integration or synopsis of elements, just as the latter requires supplementation by the former ; here the dialectic movement between analysis and synopsis has no beginning and no end.

On the assumptions underlying the traditional forms of statistical analysis one might have been justified in thinking that it was enough to determine the numerical size or other quantitative properties of each of the three zones of Winston Parva and, among them, of the minority and majority groups, in order to explain the different part which minorities play in these three zones and in their respective images. The problems with which one was confronted in a configurational analysis and synopsis were such that the finding of quantitative relationships alone, however precise it might have been, could not lead to an adequate answer. These problems were centred on configurations such as " working-class-minority-in-middle-class-residential-area," "middle-class-minority-in-old-working-class-area," "problem-families-in-new-working-class-area," "old-families'-network-in-relation-to-newcomers," "established-power-*élites*-in-relation-to-outsiders." However many statistical correlations one might care to establish, they alone could not lead to a clear understanding of the way in which configurations such as these functioned and in which they affected the people who lived there. One could not infer from a mere quantitative analysis, for example, that for the people of a middle-class area, for their manner of life, for the images they had of their own and of other zones the existence in their own zones of a working-class minority was of no significance while for the conditions of life as well as the images of the new working-class area their minority was of the very greatest significance. In some cases quantitative differences and relations were extremely useful as social indices. That rents were generally lower in Zone 3 than in Zone 2 and in Zone 2 than in Zone 1 was certainly suggestive. But the actual configuration, the complex relationship between these three zones could neither be adequately presented nor adequately explained by other than verbal symbols. Without the use of words as instruments of research figures remain mute. The different roles of minorities in different configurations are an example. In the context of a neighbourhood such as Zone 3 a specific minority played a part quite out of proportion to its numerical size. The present use of statistics often seems to imply that the greater the numerical size, the greater is the significance. In the case of the minorities in Winston Parva as in many other cases sociological significance was in no way identical with statistical significance. They pointed to a fact known, though perhaps not sufficiently noticed, from other enquiries, that social data can be sociologically significant without having statistical significance and that such data can be statistically significant without having sociological significance.

The need for this distinction is strengthened by the fact that sociological problems can hardly ever be adequately framed if they seem to be concerned with social phenomena exclusively at a given point and time—with structures which, to use the language of films, have the form of a " still ". They approximate more closely to what one can observe, and lead to comprehensive explanations only if they are conceived as problems of phenomena which have the form of processes, which participate in a movement in time. The role played in this study by the relative " oldness " and " newness " of a neighbourhood is an example. It meant that the phenomena under review had a historical dimension and that the finding of quantitative indices, even if one included " length of residence ", was in no way sufficient to gain access to the configurational, the structural differences to which labels like " old " and " new " referred.

If differences in " oldness " and " newness " are still rarely perceived as properties referring to structural differences of groups, it is largely due to the fact that the ruling concept of social structure has a strong tendency to make people perceive structures as " stills ", as " steady state structures ", while movements of structures in time, whether they have the form of developments or of other types of social changes, are treated as " historical " ; and that often means in the sociologists' language as something apart from the structure, not as an indelible property of social structures themselves.

It was easy enough, in this case, to determine how old Zone 2 was by comparison with Zone 3, how much longer working-class families had settled there than they had here. Nor was it difficult to collect statistical data showing other differences between the two zones. But statistical methods by themselves could not lead to a clarification of the structural differences which resulted from their " oldness " or " newness ". The significance of numerical differences for the relationship between the neighbourhoods of Winston Parva, and particularly for the status differences between the two working-class zones, could be brought out and could be explained only if figures showing quantitative differences were treated as indicators of differences in the structure of the two zones which resulted from the manner in which Winston Parva and its zones had developed, and which could be expressed with precision only as configurational differences in non-quantitative, in verbal terms.

2 | Neighbourhood Relations in the Making

WINSTON PARVA was the foundation of an enterprising man, Charles Wilson, who in the 1880's formed a company in order to build houses, factories and shops on the meadow land between the old village of Winston Magna on the one hand, a railway line and a canal on the other hand. On this ground his company constructed in the course of seven years 700 identical brick cottages, a few engine sheds, several factories and a new church built in cast-iron.

Some of the old residents still remembered how Charles Wilson drove through the streets of the township he had created in his horse-drawn carriage raising his top hat to the new " villagers ". They remembered the ingenuity he had shown in placing his brickyard so that he had direct access to the railway sidings through a tunnel. One man, in an interview, mentioned the boisterous parties held at the legendary man's large house on the main road to celebrate a successful soccer game in which his sons participated. Such reminiscences would probably have pleased the founder of Winston Parva, but to ensure that his name would live after him he used the first letter of each of the streets south of the settlement's main road to form his name :

Ch...............	Chestnut Street
A	Acorn Street
S	Sycamore Street
W	Willow Street
I	Ilex Street
L	Lime Street
S	Sloe Street
O	Orchard Street
N	New Street.

The tale was handed down and told to newcomers. It was the son of a London evacuee who pointed out the significance of the street names in the first few weeks of the research. Charles Wilson's part of Winston Parva, its oldest part, corresponded to Zone 2. The 80 years of its existence were enough to give the families who lived and remained there a strong sense of belongingness. They all " knew each other " and could place each other. Although from the start an industrial settlement whose inhabitants had no agricultural occupations at all, this the oldest part of Winston Parva was called affectionately and somewhat proudly by its inhabitants the " village ".

Zone 1 to the north of the " village " was a later addition. The bulk of the houses there were built in the 1920's and 30's by small local builders. The houses were detached or semi-detached. They catered for the needs of professional and business people. And in course of time some of the prosperous skilled workers from Zone 2 and individuals from Zone 2 who had acquired some wealth as traders and shopkeepers moved there as an outward symbol of their success. As a result some families had branches in Zone 1 and Zone 2 and the former constituted a kind of upper class for the " village " and for Winston Parva as a whole.

Zone 3 was built in the 1930's by a private investment company on land between the main railway line and a branch line north of the canal. Old residents said this land had not been developed by Charles Wilson because it was marshy and rat infested ; and as one shall see, the " villagers " continued to call the zone " rat alley ". One informant, a member of the local council, remembered that the leading residents of the " village " protested to the council about the development of this land in their neighbourhood. They regarded it as below their local standard. Whatever the truth of the matter, the investment company began to build there in the 1930's several rows of small houses with gardens and advertised them for rental. As far as the informants remember hardly anyone from the " village " moved into the new houses although for a considerable time rents remained lower. Almost all the people who responded to the advertisements were newcomers. Many, apparently, came from the north of England attracted by the higher employment rate in the area. One of the immigrants, a man from Yorkshire, remembered that he was shown a box of keys from empty houses on the Estate and told he could " take his pick ". Some of the houses were occupied by the families of men who had recently joined a local regiment. But until 1939, according to the older residents, quite a number of houses on the Estate remained without tenants.

They filled up not so much because people were attracted by the rent, but as a result of the changing conditions of the country. After the Munich crisis more families of the men from the local military depot were brought in and in 1940 the pattern of development changed more drastically. When the bombing of England started in earnest the evacuees moved in. A London factory producing instruments for the armed forces whose building had been destroyed was transferred lock, stock and barrel to Winston Parva. Production was set up in a disused factory building near the canal. More than 100 Londoners were added to the small community of Winston Parva. This sudden " mass immigration " had a strong impact on residents and immigrants alike. People in the older part of Winston Parva recalled, in interviews, the distress in which the evacuees had arrived. They had lost their homes and most of their family belongings in the bombing. An appeal by a local manufacturer brought an immediate response in the form of clothing, cooking equipment and furniture collected by the " villagers ". The older residents, however, in telling of these events rarely failed to mention that some of the gifts which the immigrants had been given appeared in the pawn shop windows a few days later.

It may well be that these memories were selective. The first wave of Londoners and the majority of the other early immigrants were like the majority of the " village " residents skilled or semi-skilled workers. The wage levels of the newcomers were not noticeably below those of the resident working-class families. But the newcomers differed from them considerably in their customs, their traditions, their whole way of life. Moreover, with them came a minority of unskilled labourers attracted by the variety of war work who settled on the Estate and whose standards of conduct, as it appeared,

differed not only from those of the " villagers " but also from
those of the majority of Estate residents. The existence of
pockets of immigrant labourers of this type was certainly
one of the reasons for the lower status allotted to the Estate
as a whole in the ranking of the neighbourhoods of Winston
Parva.

There were, thus, considerable differences between the old
residents and the newcomers. It was not easy to find adequate
concepts to express them. They represented a distinct form of
social stratification. The immigrants formed a lower ranking
social cadre than the established working-class residents but one
could hardly refer to the differences between the two working-
class neighbourhoods as class differences. To speak of status
differences pure and simple could be misleading because the
term is often applied to differences in the ranking of families
within the same neighbourhood. What one found in Winston
Parva were differences in the social ranking of the three neighbourhoods themselves. They expressed themselves in frictions
which occurred as soon as the old residents and the newcomers
began to take stock of each other. An early example, still
remembered at the time of the research, was the distribution
of members of the two groups in the local pubs. As in other
English communities, the " locals " were among the central
institutions of Winston Parva community life. One of the two
pubs of Winston Parva, " The Hare and Hounds ", was
situated on the way between the instrument factory and the
Estate. Some of the " Londoners " and a few other immigrants
gathered there more or less regularly. Pub visiting " villagers "
showed their disapproval of the newcomers by withdrawing
from " The Hare and Hounds " and by reserving for themselves the other pub, " The Eagle " where new residents in
search of company were frozen out. Among the " villagers "
" The Hare and Hounds " soon acquired, rightly or wrongly,
a reputation for noisy behaviour and heavy drinking. The
drinking conventions which the " villagers " had established
among themselves and to which they were used were not known
to, and were often not observed by, the new residents. In the
eyes of the " villagers " the coming of strangers was an
unwelcome intrusion. And the segregation of the two groups

established at the beginning of the war soon after the arrival of a fairly compact immigrant group acquired in time the force of a local tradition ; it was still fully maintained almost two decades later during the period of the research.

One can see here how it originated. The initial " conquest " of one of the pubs by the newcomers was a symptom rather than a cause of the frictions between the old and the new residents. To reconstruct the initial situation of the two groups and the development of their relationship helped to understand the set pattern it had acquired at the time of the research. One needed some knowledge about the making of this relationship in order to understand how it came about that the inhabitants of Zone 2 could successfully claim for themselves a higher status than those of Zone 3 while conceding in turn a higher status to most residents of Zone 1 ; and without clarifying and explaining this status order, one lacked the key to the understanding of other aspects of the community life.

One may be tempted to put the blame for the tensions between the old and the new residents on one side or the other. In fact they were, at the present stand of our social techniques, the normal concomitants of a process in the course of which two formerly independent groups became interdependent. If one considers the configuration that resulted from the newly established interdependence, as neighbours and members of the same community, of groups who were strangers to each other one can see how difficult it would have been to avoid tensions. What happened in the pub is a good example. Members of each group wanted relaxation in the company and in the manner which they liked and to which they were used. The old residents might have accepted the newcomers as people in need of help if they had submitted to their patronage, had been content with taking in their status hierarchy the lower position usually allotted to newcomers at least for a probationary period by already established, more closely knit and status conscious communities. As a rule, such communities expect newcomers to adapt themselves to their own norms and beliefs ; they expect them to submit to their own social controls and, generally, to show their willingness to " fit in ".

But the newcomers on the Estate, and particularly the

" Londoners " who formed, at least at the outset, a fairly compact group, continued to behave in Winston Parva as they had behaved before. If one can judge from similar groups of Londoners, they themselves probably would not have objected if " villagers " had joined their circle at the pub and shared their noisy enjoyment. That was probably what they expected ; they were used to the easier camaraderie that often prevailed among the lower and middle ranks of metropolitan working-class groups whose norms and standards were less stringent than those of many groups higher up in the status hierarchy perhaps because they had not the same need constantly to restrain themselves in order to demonstrate and to assert their status superiority over others. Moreover, compared with the " villagers " the immigrants had relatively little cohesion among themselves. They were a fairly open and a not particularly exclusive group.

Already at that time the " villagers " evidently formed a relatively close group in a much greater degree. They had developed traditions and standards of their own. Those who did not comply with their norms were excluded as people of an inferior sort. Hence they withdrew from the pub which the immigrants had chosen as their meeting place And they took up the struggle against the intruders by using all the characteristic weapons available to a well established and fairly closely-knit community in its relations with groups of new-comers who, for one reason or another, did not adapt them-selves to their traditions and their norms and who therefore threatened, as they must have felt it, their communal status and identity : They closed their ranks against the newcomers. They cold-shouldered them. They excluded them from all posts of social power whether in local politics, in voluntary associations or in any other local organisation where their own influence dominated. Above all, they developed as weapons an " ideology ", a system of attitudes and beliefs which stressed and justified their own superiority and which stamped the people on the Estate as people of an inferior kind. Built around certain stereotyped themes their status ideology was spread and maintained by a constant stream of gossip which fastened on any event in the " village " that could help to

18

enhance the " village " community and on any event among the Estate people that could reinforce the negative picture of the Estate. It also helped to block perception of any event which might conceivably contradict it. That does not mean there was a concerted plan among the " villagers " to act in that way. It was an involuntary reaction to a specific situation in line with the whole structure, the whole tradition and outlook of the " village " community. Nor does it mean that there was personal enmity or even that there were constant personal frictions between all the individual members of the two neighbourhood groups. Many individuals of the two neighbourhoods were personally on quite good terms with each other. Quite a number of men and women from Zones 2 and 3 worked together in the same local factory often enough on the same level. No reference has ever been made in the course of the enquiry to difficulties which arose on the work floor between inhabitants of different zones. Individual members of the two neighbourhoods apparently accepted each other readily in their occupational roles as workers. In that capacity individual men and women from Zone 2 appeared to be normally on friendly terms with those of Zone 3. But they accepted them only within certain limits. Their exclusive attitudes and their status ideology came into operation primarily with regard to roles outside the boundaries of their occupational life ; they were always present, but they showed up less during working hours and more outside work in their leisure activities, less in their roles as individual workers, and more in those as members of families who lived in different neighbourhoods. Even at the time of the enquiry, twenty years after the arrival of the evacuees, the older residents of the " village " still spoke of people from the Estate as " foreigners ", saying that they " couldn't understand a word they say ". A local newspaper reporter could still remark : " Of course, they're Londoners, you've got to remember that, with different ways, so they are different to the older people round here." One old lady bluntly called the Estate " the cockney colony ". But in fact Londoners were by no means the only immigrants. Already during the war a number of newcomers who occupied houses on the Estate came from Durham, Lancashire, Wales and

Ireland ; and others came later. In the derogatory stereotypes of the established group they all were lumped together. At the end of the war the former London factory extended production. Some of the London families returned to the East End ; but the majority remained in Winston Parva. Exactly how many of them stayed on could not be found out. The owner of the factory said that " 100 workers and their families came up" after the bombing, but he had no record of the number who had gone back to London. Records of population movements, rents and housing allocation during the war were intentionally destroyed, according to the Assistant Clerk to the council, because post-war expansion of local government services created a demand for the available filing cabinet space.

However, although efforts to ascertain the precise number of those who came and those who left again were unsuccessful, the actual configuration, the distinguishing structure of the community on the Estate and its relation to the community of the " village " which resulted from this development was clear enough. An industrial community of a type which is gradually disappearing, living in relative isolation with a fairly high degree of self-sufficiency and cohesion so far as neighbourhood contacts were concerned and, perhaps for that reason, in the imagination of its members resembling a village was confronted by groups of immigrants from different parts of Britain ; they became their neighbours, often their fellow workers and administratively part of the same community drawn there partly as a result of war-time evacuation and direction of labour, partly in search of opportunities for employment or for better employment. The " villagers " had strong roots at the place ; all the immigrants were initially uprooted people, and the fact that many of them came from different localities in England and were strangers to each other made it difficult for them to develop a community life of their own.

The structure of the community as one found it almost twenty years later was in the main the result of the encounter of these two groupings of people and of the blend of interdependence and antagonism which resulted from it. One cannot understand the structure of the community of Winston Parva to which one refers if one uses terms like " old working-class zone " and " new working-class zone " without reference to its development.

In community studies as in many other sociological investigations, the exploration of the development of the organisation of people under review is often treated as extraneous to the exploration of its structure at a given time. According to the present conventions of thinking, history has no structure and structure no history. What has been said so far about the development of Winston Parva, and particularly of the two working-class neighbourhoods, therefore, can easily be misunderstood as such a " historical introduction ", as a " purely descriptive " and extraneous addition to the investigation of the structure of Winston Parva at the time of the enquiry—of the " structure " conceived as a " still ". However, without reference to Winston Parva's development its structure at the time of the enquiry would have remained incomprehensible. The outline of that development formed an integral part of the enquiry into the structure—into the configuration of the community at a given time. In particular, the status differences between Zone 2 and Zone 3 would have remained inexplicable without reference to Winston Parva's development as a community just as they would have remained inexplicable if one had confined one's enquiry to statistical measurements of single factors or variables and their correlations at the period of the enquiry.

One could not dispense with such measurements. Statistical tables and inferences to be drawn from them, had and have their place in developmental and configurational studies. Thus in the case of the two working-class neighbourhoods one could not exclude the possibility that occupational differences and other similar factors were sufficiently significant to provide by themselves adequate explanations for the status gradients in Winston Parva. As it happened, in this case, statistical differences were not significant enough to illuminate and explain the problem why in this community members of one working-class area ascribed to themselves a much higher status than to those of a neighbouring working-class area and were able to get away with it. This kind of problem required consideration for the " old-new distinction " as part of a process in time. It required the building up of a model of the structure of such a community as an aspect of its development which could explain why one neighbourhood had in relation to the other enough power to claim successfully status superiority over the other with all that it entailed. Once built up, one could examine how far such a model was consistent with the observable facts, could revise it or abandon it if it failed the test, and could hand it on for further tests, for revision or demolition, as the case may be, to others engaged in related enquiries.

That was the procedure which made it possible to explore and to explain structural characteristics which one at first encountered as " stills ", as characteristics of a community at a given moment in time, such as differences in delinquency rates, later as indicators of a configuration which represented a stage in a community development. The conceptual and methodological separation of enquiries into the structure of human groupings at a given time and enquiries into the structure of the processes in the course of which they became what they were, showed itself, in this case too, as wholly artificial. The encounter of old and new groups, the pressures which compelled them to live together as members of the same community were not haphazard events. They formed a small, but not uncharacteristic, episode in the long-term and large-scale processes to which one refers under such headings as " industrialisation ", " urbanisation " or " community development ". Without visualising them as episodes within such processes one could hardly do justice to them.

Processes of this kind took place and are taking place in many communities all over the globe. Again and again in connection with the increasingly rapid development of countries and the tensions, the upheavals, the conflicts thrown up by it, groups leave their homes, half-voluntarily in search of their livelihood, driven out by government regulations or perhaps by force of arms, and settle elsewhere often at the doorsteps of older groups or in their midst. But at present, it seems, the people who find themselves in that situation, as well as those who try administratively to deal with the problems which arise from the encounter between old and new groups, tend to think of each of these encounters as if it were unique. They reflect on

22

it and try to deal with it as if it occurred here and now and nowhere else. And they are not given much help in their task by sociological studies which deal with community problems as problems of a particular community here and now without clearly indicating the paradigmatic character of their particular case—without bringing out the regularities underlying the problems of their particular community which they share with other communities involved in similar processes as well as the features in which they differ from them. Thus it was not only a predilection for theoretical excursions which made it seem advisable to change from time to time the focus of this enquiry from the narrower problems of Winston Parva to the wider theoretical problems of which they were an example. Winston Parva has been presented here as a paradigm—as a model indicating how helplessly people may be trapped in a conflict situation by specific developments. By demonstrating, and to some extent, explaining the nature of the trap, the model may help us to learn gradually, if developed further, how to loosen the teeth of the trap and to cope with such problems better.

3 | Overall Picture of Zone 1 and Zone 2

WINSTON PARVA was a growing industrial area. About 4,185 people [1] lived there in 1958, not quite 5,000 in 1959. Administratively it formed two wards of a larger urban district. But it was cut off from the major part of this district by a railway line. A single bridge over this line was the only link between Winston Parva and the rest of the district. As has been shown, the division of Winston Parva into three zones was connected with its development. In 1958 Zone 1 had 456 inhabitants, Zone 2 2,553 and Zone 3 1,176. Zone 2 and 3, too, had fairly sharp boundaries. They were separated from each other by a railway branch line and were linked only by a level crossing on the main road and by a small tunnel near the canal.

Zone 1 was usually regarded as the " best part " of Winston Parva. In the main, rents were higher. It was largely, though not exclusively, a middle-class area.

A list of the occupations of people living in one of the main streets of Zone 1 gives a fair idea of the social composition of its residents.

---

[1] The total population of Winston Parva was slightly larger. In addition to the three zones which formed the basis of this research there were two small " pockets " of population which have not been included in this enquiry. The first belonged to a military establishment. It consisted of a group of houses attached to a local regimental depot and provided housing for married officers and N.C.O.s. They and their families usually did not stay long. They played hardly any part in the community life of Winston Parva and hence were not included in the research. The second " pocket " consisted of several rows of houses at one end of Zone 3. They were built by the Urban District Council during the early stages of the research. Apart from the fact that figures of population and length of residence under these conditions were difficult to assess, the impact of these new immigrant families on the communal life of Winston Parva, during the period of research, was still negligible.

24

TABLE I

Occupations of Residents in Acacia Road, Zone 1

Occupation	Number
Directors and Managers	8
Doctors and Dentists	3
Business Owners	3
Retired Professional	3
Schoolteachers	3
Office Workers	3
Engineering Workers	2
Hosiery Workers	2
Widows	4
Labourer	1

The presence of manual workers among the residents of Acacia Road was due to the existence of a small number of cottages at one end of the road. In them, and in an adjacent row of terraced houses, lived the 12.9 per cent of the population which were listed in a table of occupations as semi-skilled and unskilled residents of Zone 1. The other occupations listed in Table I indicate the predominantly middle-class character of the street. The results of this survey were in line with the information collected during visits to householders and leaders of local voluntary associations and by means of systematic observations at the spot over a number of years.

From them emerged a fairly consistent picture of the zone without which that of the relationship between the two working-class zones would have been incomplete. Many of the inhabitants of Zone 1 did not actively participate in the communal life of Winston Parva. They lived their own lives within the invisible walls which often enclose middle-class families in residential areas. Each family formed a fairly exclusive group in relation to others. It is likely that the circle of acquaintances whom they invited to their houses, and by whom they were invited, came mainly from outside Winston Parva and especially from the large midland town to whose suburban area Winston Parva belonged. The mobility achieved by means of cars, if one did not need to regard the cost of transport as a heavy burden, made it possible to form and to maintain fairly close relationships with people who lived outside one's own neighbourhood.

But a small and fairly compact circle of residents of Zone 1 had close links with Winston Parva itself and played a very active part in its communal life. Among them was one of the men who lived in Acacia Road, Councillor Drew, who took a very active part in the life of the community. He was perhaps its most prominent citizen.

At the time of the enquiry he was a man in his early sixties. His father, a Manchester engineer, had moved to Winston Parva in the 1880's—the Councillor could not remember the exact year—and had for a time managed a local foundry. Councillor Drew himself had built up a flourishing business as building contractor. He was a County Councillor and member of the local Urban District Council. He was also Chairman or President of several local associations and member of the Board of Governors of two local schools. His name was a household word in every part of Zone 1 and Zone 2. As the interviews showed, it was less well known in Zone 3. In council elections he stood as Independent. He relied entirely on his standing in the community and had no political organisation of his own. Members of the local Conservative Association said that they always helped him. But his election posters said simply : " Vote for Drew the old folks' friend ". It had its appeal not only for old people, but for all those who shared the common values and beliefs of the " village ", their pride in belonging to an old-established community and their satisfaction in " belonging ". Drew was a symbol of this community spirit. He symbolised the close ties which bound people from Zone 1 and Zone 2 to each other. In many ways he acted as Winston Parva's unofficial mayor. His house combined, in a manner which almost seemed to belong to a period that had passed, at least in urban and industrial areas, the functions of a centre of his business and communal activities with those of his home. In 1958 he still conducted his business and his communal activities from his house. A room there served as his office. It also served as a centre for all his activities in what he himself called the " village life ". Deliberately or not, he played in this urban and industrial setting a part not unlike that played in a more rural setting by the squire. His wife held regular " Bright Hours " in their house for the ladies of their church. His married son who worked with his father in the contracting business lived near by in Zone I. The attribute most frequently heard when his name came up in conversations was " kindly " ; and great stress was placed by the older residents in the " village " on the fact that he had been " born here ". He had some of the characteristics of a community leader described by F. Hunter in " Regional City " : [1]

> " His age and status in the community allow him to pronounce on the problems of youth or business conditions, whether they concern his business or not, population problems, the issues of war and peace and many other matters which he discusses with assured learnedness. The newspapers carry his word as being authoritative."

Councillor Drew was the prestige leader and the central figure of several informally interlocking circles formed by kinship networks and a variety of local associations which had their roots in Zone 2 rather than in Zone I and had hardly any connecting links with Zone 3. But he had in Zone I itself an " inner circle ". Not far from Councillor Drew's house in Zone I lived a number of other prominent residents who were chairmen of local associations such as the Old People's Club or members of committees. These people were on visiting terms with him. They called him and each other by their christian names. Together, and each of them in his own way, they played a leading part in Winston Parva's communal life.

Thus the overall picture of Zone I was that of a neighbourhood of middle-class residents of whom the majority did not actively participate in local affairs while a minority served as community leaders not only in relation to their own neighbourhood, but in relation to Winston Parva as a whole and particularly to the nearby working-class neighbourhood here called Zone 2. The semi-skilled and unskilled workers who lived in the cottages at the " bad end " of Acacia Road lived geographically in Zone I but did not count socially as residents of the

[1] F. Hunter, *Community Power Structure*, 1953, chap III, 27.

zone. So far as the image of Zone 1 was concerned the presence of this minority was ignored. The families of the men who formed the other minority, of the elite group who took a leading part in the community life of Winston Parva, in most cases, had initially come from Zone 2. Several of these men still had parents or other relatives living there and the fact that they were " old residents ", members of " old families ", was always mentioned with considerable pride. It showed that one " belonged ", that one had been " born here ". That people who initially came from Zone 2 moved their place of residence to Zone 1 was a symbol of social success. The process continued. Several families said that they had moved into Zone 1 since 1945 having " always wanted to live here ". In a number of cases the husband's war gratuity had been used to obtain a mortgage. Among those who had moved from Zone 2 to Zone 1 were a few families of skilled workers, occupied in local industries, whose children had left school ; in some cases the wives too worked part-time in a local factory. No-one in Zone 1 mentioned that he had relatives in Zone 3. Nor did any family ties of this kind come to light in interviews and conversations with residents of Zone 3.

Thus the ties created by long residence in a relatively old industrial community were not broken when a family could afford to move from a working-class district to an adjacent middle-class district. Those who remained in the working-class neighbourhood seemed to feel that their connection with the men who had risen socially raised their own status and seemed to enjoy the reflected glory. In that way " old residents " in the working-class neighbourhood of Zone 2 and " old residents " who now lived in the middle-class neighbourhood of Zone 1 were linked to each other. The reputation, the image of Zone 1 as a " better area " was in no way affected by the fact that some of its residents came from a working-class area or were known to be of working-class descent. Its status as the highest ranking of the three zones was frankly acknowledged in Zone 2, more grudgingly in Zone 3. The residents of Zone 1 themselves, as the interviews indicated, were very conscious of the superiority of their neighbourhood in relation to Zones 2 and 3. They spoke of this superiority, as people in twentieth-century democracies often do, in indirect and seemingly colourless terms which lacked the emotional directness with which people of higher status in less democratic ages spoke of their own superior status, but which, nevertheless, was quite unambiguous. The terms they used had the character of code words. Every person of corresponding status was expected to understand their significance. They said ·: " This is the better part, all our family live this side ", or " There is a difference. Don't think I am being snobby, but there is ! " or " Very nice just here. Different from the rest of Winston Parva, especially the Estate."

As one would expect, Zone 2 differed from Zone 1 in outward appearance. In Zone 1 people lived mostly in semi-detached houses with garages and the streets were fairly wide. Zone 2 consisted of hundreds of terraced houses with many narrow alleys and small back yards. In terms of social class, as far as it could be ascertained, Zone 2 like Zone 3 was a working-class neighbourhood. Table II gives an indication of the " class " distribution of the population in the three zones. It is based on a survey carried out early in 1958 by the School Attendance Officers of the Local Education Committee. The occupations of parents of every child aged 18 or under were noted on individual record cards and classified according to the Registrar-General's Index of Social Class.

TABLE II

Class Distribution of Parents of School Children in the 3 Zones

Zone	Numbers	Social Class									
		I		II		III		IV		V	
	Totals	No.	%	No.	%	No.	%	No.	%	No.	%
1	70	9	12·9	30	42·9	22	31·4	8	11·4	1	1·4
2	444	1	0·2	51	11·4	116	26·1	167	37·8	109	24·5
3	216	—	—	7	3·2	70	32·5	71	32·9	68	31·4
	730	10		88		208		246		178	

The figures give an intimation of the differences in the class distribution of the three zones. They indicate the existence of a

29

class IV minority in Zone 1 and of a class II minority in Zone 2. They show quite well the concentration of the inhabitants of Zones 2 and 3 in classes III, IV, and V with a stronger accent on class V in the case of Zone 3.

All the factories which provided employment for the inhabitants of the two working-class neighbourhoods were situated in Zone 2. They consisted of a variety of smaller firms mostly producing hosiery and footwear which kept to their traditional ways apparently without suffering unduly from any competitive pressure, of a medium-sized company producing instruments for the Armed Forces and a somewhat larger biscuit factory of a more modern type. Most of these firms employed less than 100 workers. Nearly all belonged to a larger national group. Their late nineteenth-century buildings had been outwardly modernised, with the exception of some of the smaller firms which had remained largely unchanged and looked a little delapidated. In many cases lighting was poor and machinery out of date, but as far as one could see, this did not impair the loyalty of the workers, at least of the older workers, who had been, as one locally said " fifty years in the Boot and Shoe ".

On the other hand, the largest factory in Winston Parva which produced a well-known brand of biscuit though originally a nineteenth-century building, had been externally and internally renovated and continued to expand. The firm had absorbed an adjoining footwear factory which had been partly rebuilt and extended to form an additional factory complex which dominated the skyline to the east. Conditions in this factory were strikingly different from those in the traditional industries. The nature of the work itself necessitated greater attention to cleanliness, but even beyond these hygienic requirements one noticed a definite trend towards modern techniques of production. Colour schemes were fresh and gay, rest and recreational facilities were good, wages were above the union rates.

One might have expected that the more modern character of this factory, compared with the relatively old-fashioned of others which were housed less pleasantly, would be in some way reflected in the local standing of the people who worked there. But that was not the case. Most of the work in the biscuit factory was unskilled, wages ranged in 1958 between £5 and £7 per week for an adult woman worker, while the same woman by taking a semi-skilled job in one of the more traditional industries could earn from £7 to £10 per week provided the factory was " on full-time ". During the period of the research some fluctuations occurred in the wages of the traditional industries due mainly, it was said locally, to foreign competition. One of the factories making footwear closed in 1958.

The prospect of having to " go on short-time every now and then " and of working in less congenial surroundings led to some uncertainty, especially among adolescent girls. They were faced with the choice between relatively high wages in the traditional industries with the possibility of " short-time " added to lack of modern amenities, and the lower but regular wages of the more modern biscuit factory. This uncertainty was one of the factors which made a number of young girls change their work several times in the first few months. It is relevant to what follows that the workers in the two types of factories were not firmly divided into groups of workers with different social and financial status. There was a good deal of labour mobility between the two types of factories in the area. Nor were they, in the majority of factories, divided according to their place of residence. Not only young, but also older, workers were frequently recruited from both working-class zones.

These factories represented the main source of factory employment in Winston Parva. The following table shows the number of local men and women employed in two local factories.

The " village " of Winston Parva where all local factories were situated acted as an industrial centre which provided work for local people while at the same time attracting workers from other neighbourhoods. In the two factories of Table III local workers were actually in a minority. That women went to work was customary in the whole area. The routines of married life were in many cases attuned to it. To have factories near one's home was of considerable advantage to married women. So was a family network which consisted of more than two generations. It enabled younger women to leave their children with " granny " or an elderly aunt while they went to work. Moreover, the fact that they as well as their husbands earned money strengthened their position within the family. It may well be that this custom had some connection with the formation of mother-centred family networks in the " village " though without examination of the conditions under which such networks formed elsewhere one could hardly decide the point.

TABLE III

Local and Non-Local Workers in Two Winston Parva Factories

Local and Non-Local Workers	The Biscuit Factory		A Traditional Factory	
	Nos.	%	Nos.	%
Total	270	100	166	100
Workers living outside W.P.	183	67·8	96	57·9
Workers living in W.P.	87	32·2	70	42·1
Of these :				
Men	35	12·9	24	14·5
Women	52	19·3	46	27·6
Married Women	39	14·4	43	25·9

The daily contact at work with workers who lived outside Winston Parva seemed to have singularly little influence on outlook and attitude of the workers who lived in the " village ". The pull of their own community on their sense of values and their goals was evidently much stronger than that of their place of work. Nor was their strong belief in the superiority of the " village " and its way of life over the Estate affected by the fact that they worked daily in the same factory and did often enough the same kind of work as workers from the Estate. Table IV gives examples of factories where workers from both working-class neighbourhoods of Winston Parva found employment.

The fact that workers from the two zones in these two cases as in others worked in the same factories did not lead to a lowering of the barriers which separated them outside work.

TABLE IV

Zonal Residence of Local Workers

Zone	The Biscuit Factory			A Traditional Factory		
	Men All	Women Single	Women Married	Men All	Women Single	Women Married
1	—	—	1	2	—	—
2	22	7	21	18	2	32
3	13	6	17	4	1	11
TOTAL	35	13	39	24	3	43

The picture shown in Table IV, the attraction of local industries for local workers, understandable particularly in the case of married women from both working-class zones, was fairly typical. However, there were some exceptions. The instrument factory, for example, which had been evacuated from London with part of its workers at the beginning of the war and whose workers had settled on the Estate still had few " village " people among its employees. Since the war it had become one of the leading factories in its field and had developed a flourishing export business. In 1958 the factory employed approximately 80 men and 20 women of whom 15 were married. According to the management about 50 workers, half their labour force, lived on the Estate. They were those of the original evacuees from London who had stayed in Winston Parva. Most of the other workers came from large Estates on the outskirts of the nearby town. Very few workers had been recruited from Zone 2. At the time of the enquiry, however, the management had just tried to attract more local labour. They had invited local school parties to visit the factory and as a result several boys from Zone 2 had been accepted as apprentices.

There were one or two other firms which had among their employees few workers from Zone 2 or none at all. And in their case, it seemed, the absence of " village " workers had some connection with the local ranking of these firms or perhaps of the people who worked there. In none of them was the level of wages markedly inferior to that paid by other local firms. But the work was heavy and made considerable demands on physical strength. One might take as an example a Concrete Supply Company and a small Foundry. Their combined labour force consisted in 1958 of some 150 men. A few women were employed in clerical and canteen work. Reliable information about their place of residence was unobtainable ; but according to a local estimate one quarter of the workers came from Winston Parva, almost all of them from the Estate. In terms of their occupational status the majority of them belonged to the lowest working-class stratum ; most of them ranked as unskilled labourers. But a few sample visits to their homes did not indicate any sharp dividing line between their manner of living and that of other residents of the Estate. Nor were they set noticeably apart as a distinct group in the opinion of other residents which had been consulted, not even in that of skilled workers. "Village" people, on the other hand, above all people from the "old families" tended to see in these heavy workers, particularly if they were a little noisy, simply "typical Estate people".

On the face of it, the "village" seemed to possess a high degree of uniformity. Particularly if one asked their opinion about the Estate the answers which one received from "villagers" were uniform. There was no doubt about the predominantly working-class character of the zone. The bulk of its inhabitants, approximately 80 per cent, were manual workers employed partly in local industries, partly in those of the nearby town. The dominant conventions, too, were characteristic of a particular type of working-class neighbourhood. The visiting ritual, for example, was markedly different from that prevalent among the middle-class families of Zone 1. There it was not the custom to call on other families without previous announcement. As a rule one used certain ritual formulas, spoken or written, if one wanted people to visit one's home and did not expect them to do so unless such an invitation was given. In the "village" people were not in the habit of inviting others formally to their homes except on very special occasions such as weddings or funerals. Their houses were probably too small for rounds of prepared visits and counter visits to develop as normal part of their social tradition. Incomes, too, were probably too small, or had been too small in the past, for such a tradition to arise among working men and working women. But in contrast to the dominant convention among middle-class people, that among working-class people allowed to a much higher extent informal visits. Women particularly were more apt just to " drop in " on neighbours for a chat at the back door or for a cup of tea. Convention did not give to people, and people did not expect to have, the same degree of family privacy which middle-class people expected to have, and which their convention gave to them in Zone 1. Doors were less firmly closed against others ; walls were thinner ; almost everything that happened inside the home was within reach of neighbours' ears and eyes ; little could be hidden away ; private and communal, " individual " and " social " aspects of life were less divided. News of any interest quickly spread through the gossip channels from house to house, from street to street. Housewives appeared to be their main carriers. Those who " belonged ", who were personally at one with the communal standards of their neighbourhood, did not seem to suffer from this relative lack of privacy. Those who did not " belong " often enough suffered.

But while compared with Zone 1 and Zone 3 Zone 2 possessed relatively open communications and a high degree of uniformity, as the enquiry progressed one became gradually aware of a kind of sub-stratification within the seemingly uniform working-class neighbourhood which provided some barriers to communications and social relations generally.

The " village " had no real centre, but a fairly large road cut it in two parts. The majority of its inhabitants lived south of this road in the houses built by Charles Wilson, in the streets immortalising his name. A minority lived to the north of it and a section of this part, adjacent to Zone 1, was widely regarded as the " better part " of the " village ", not only by its own residents but also, with rather less emphasis, by those of the other part.

In two of the streets of this northern part lived a " working-class *élite* ". It largely consisted of members of " old families "

35

and other families of skilled workers, active or retired. Here lived, in addition, the few middle-class residents of what was otherwise a working-class area. Most of the houses in these two streets were in no way better than those in the rest of the " village ". But among them stood a small number of houses which were slightly larger than the rest and whose rents were slightly higher. A minority of middle-class neighbours and of larger houses probably combined with the prestige enjoyed in the " village " by a number of " old families " to give these two northern streets the status of the " better part " of the " village ". Residents appeared to take great pride in living there. In the half-tones used for this purpose they often tried to draw the interviewer's attention to this distinction using expressions such as : " They are good people in our street, really nice." Yet in terms of occupation and social class, the actual differences between the *élite* streets and ordinary streets in the " village ", as Table V indicates, were small.

A few families who in the Registrar-General's classification would qualify as Class II people, but no women workers, lived in the " better " streets of Zone 2. One of the ordinary streets had a few women workers, neither had Class II residents. In statistical terms the number of middle-class residents in the northern streets of the " village " was small. As a factor in the configuration which endowed the two streets with their higher standing the minority of better class neighbours certainly played a larger part than their numbers might have suggested. They were almost invariably mentioned in interviews.

It was equally significant that the higher standing of the two streets was in no way affected by a minority of a different type —by a minority of lower status residents who lived there. One of these streets had what was locally known as the " bad end ". There, the Council had built in the 1930's a row of small houses which attracted a type of tenant a little poorer and somewhat less norm and status conscious, i.e. less " respectable ", than the inhabitants of the " *élite* " area and, in fact, than most of the residents of the " village ". In contrast to the resident middle-class minority, the inferior working-class minority, if people could help it, was never mentioned. Like a similar minority in Zone 1 it was generally disregarded in peoples' assessment of the status of their own neighbourhood and, as far as possible, " hushed up " in conversations with " respectable outsiders " such as the interviewer.

TABLE V

Occupations of Residents
in two " élite streets " and two " ordinary streets "
of Zone 2

Élite Street A		Ordinary Street A	
Number	Occupations	Number	Occupations
1	Journalist	—	—
1	Office Worker	—	—
2	Shopkeepers	1	Shopkeeper
3	Engineering Workers	3	Engineering Workers
—	—	1	Lorry Driver
2	Railway Workers	2	Railway Workers
5	Hosiery Hands	2	Hosiery Hands
2	Shoe Hands	5	Shoe Hands
3	Labourers	5	Labourers
—	—	5	Women Biscuit Factory Workers
5	Widows	3	Widows
24	TOTAL	27	TOTAL

Élite Street B		Ordinary Street B	
Number	Occupations	Number	Occupations
3	Office Workers	—	—
3	Shopkeepers	—	—
1	Garage Proprietor	—	—
1	Skilled Engineer	1	Skilled Engineer
1	Insurance Agent	—	—
1	Lorry Driver	1	Lorry Driver
1	Engine Driver	—	—
1	Railwayman	—	—
1	Bricklayer	—	—
1	Plumber	—	—
2	Hosiery Hands	2	Hosiery Hands
1	Shoe Hand	3	Shoe Hands
1	Labourer	7	Labourers
5	Widows		
23	TOTAL	14	TOTAL

Thus even this "closely knit" and seemingly uniform working-class zone of Winston Parva, the "village", had its internal status hierarchy. It had sub-zones which ranked higher and others which ranked lower though one could not assume that every single family living in the "*élite* streets" ranked higher than every single family living in the ordinary streets of the "village". The status ranking of families and individuals apart from the top and bottom layers defied here as elsewhere any attempt at a simple numerical representation. But by and large, the "best village families" lived or had at least a branch in the "better part".

If these status and power differentials caused frictions they remained largely underground. Open expression was made difficult by a mutual neighbourhood control which fostered and rewarded adherence to the common belief in the high value of the "village" as a community and of its way of life, and which discouraged open and direct expression of discontent, particularly in conversations with strangers. And among the incentives for "nomic" behaviour—for conformity, one of the strongest was the common need of almost all "villagers" to set themselves off from the other working-class neighbourhood at one's doorstep whose way of life according to "village" public opinion was less respectable and decent than one's own. In relation to the Estate the "village people" closed their ranks. It would have taken great courage or great foolhardiness on the part of a person living in the "village" to fall out of step with the ruling "village opinion" in any matter that concerned the people on the Estate. It rarely happened; in that respect individual inclinations appeared to agree with the dominant "village opinion". By and large it was probably more gratifying for individuals in such a community to share in the communal preenings and snubbings in assertion of the higher status of one's own community, or, sometimes, of one's *élite* group within one's own community, than to oppose them. And the social punishments that awaited anyone who in that context would have publicly uttered contrary ideas or who did not seem to conform willingly to the standards of the "old families", in a community such as this with its strong pressure for conformity and its tight neighbourhood control, would have been severe.

Instances of this exclusion of people whom ruling " village " opinion suspected of " non-conformity " could occasionally be found during the interviews although as a rule the " good people ", particularly the " good people " of the *élite* area tried to conceal the presence of a social " black sheep " in their own street. Thus, at the end of an interview in the " *élite* " area of the " village " a middle-aged housewife asked if she might know who was to be interviewed next. When told she said, " Oh ! I wouldn't go there. Oh no ! Go to number 15, they're nice but not there, she's a flighty one she is, only been here a year. Go to the Sewell's, they're nice." Newcomers who settled in the " good streets " of the " village " were always suspect unless they were obviously " nice people ". A probationary period was needed in order to reassure the established " good families " that their own status would not suffer by association with a neighbour whose standing and whose standards were uncertain. The ostracised " black sheep " was in this case a woman who had recently moved into the neighbourhood and who made the following comments when she herself was asked about her relations with her neighbours : " They're very reserved. They speak on the street but nothing else." She then told how she had asked the " dustmen in for a cup of tea one cold day ", soon after she had arrived in Winston Parva. " They saw it. That shocked them round here." It was not only that a newcomer had to observe the " village " standards, but he also had to make a point of showing that he observed them. Otherwise, he was given a low ranking in the status order of " village " families and treated as an outsider. This is an example of the frictions connected with the status and power differentials of a community, even of a relatively small and seemingly not strongly stratified community such as the " village". Frictions of this type were brought more openly and more directly to one's notice if one considered the more highly stratified community of Winston Parva as a whole. But one can see already from this overall view of Zone 2 alone the central position held in the structure of such a community by the ranking order of people.

In present day theories two problems posed by this communal status ranking which one could well observe in Winston Parva are often left unexplored. The first concerns the making of such a status order. One is apt to be satisfied with a set formula such as mutual status ranking which suggests that each family decides first on its own how to rank all others, and that the communal status order simply emerges from an exchange of views between individual families perhaps by a majority decision. Thinking about such matters often appears to proceed, not necessarily in full awareness of the fact, by analogy with the voting procedure : everybody, it seems to imply, casts its vote about the ranking of everybody else and the consensus about the ranking of families indicates the opinion of the majority. But the analogy is as fictitious as the assumption that society stems from a " social contract ". It neglects the question why people suffer themselves to be ranked below others. Moreover, in Winston Parva as in many other communities it was a minority of families who lived in those areas which ranked highest and the majority who lived in areas which ranked lowest. As elsewhere people allowed themselves to be ranked lower than others because they could not prevent it. They had not enough power. The good woman whom her neighbours in Winston Parva thought the interviewer should not visit and whom they treated with reserve when they met her in the street had not the power to make them behave differently. Nor had the people who lived at the " bad end " of a street or the Estate people of whom the " villagers " said they lived in " rat alley ", power enough to change the low place allotted to them in the status order of their community. In some cases greater power may go with greater numbers, with the " majority ", in others it may go with small numbers. Thus a closely-knit minority may exercise power over a less closely knit, less well-organised majority. The " old families " of Winston Parva were an example. They certainly did not form the majority of the inhabitants of Winston Parva. But the beliefs, the standards, the ranking of others current in this closely-knit *élite* group carried great weight with others largely because, as one will see, their members held all the key positions in the community.

The second problem, often overlooked, which observations in Zone 1 and Zone 2 helped to clarify, was that of the connection between status differentials and frictions. Terms like " status hierarchy " or " ranking order " are sometimes used as if they referred to normally harmonious configurations with which tensions and conflicts were connected only accidentally. In fact, as things are, tensions and conflicts form an intrinsic structural element of status hierarchies everywhere.

If one walks through the streets of a town or a village as a casual visitor, and even if one lives there for some time, one may not notice the status distinctions which the inhabitants make among themselves and the latent or open frictions connected with them. Even if one lives in such a community long enough to become aware of its internal status order, it is not always easy to match in one's own terms the intimate knowledge which the inhabitants themselves have of the standing of other families in their community. For normally the residents themselves do not express their ranking in general terms. They all, and particularly the married women residents, know implicitly the present market value of other families in their neighbourhood particularly in a closely-knit neighbourhood such as the " village ". The analysis of the structure of gossip in such a community which follows may help towards a clearer idea of the dynamics of ranking ; it shows the extent to which powerful minorities, as a kind of gossip leaders, can control the beliefs of a wider network of neighbours, can influence the allotment of gossip rewards and punishments and the yardsticks for the ranking of families. But the yardsticks are almost always implied as part of an axiomatic communal belief system and the ranking is usually expressed by means of simple value terms which have the character of communal code words, such as " better " or " not quite nice ", " all right " or " okay ". They can be used with sufficient gradations or undertones to make the actual position of a family in the status hierarchy quite clear to the initiated. By conceptualising the status order of a community as such, one extrapolates and verbalises a configuration which is never conceptualised and verbalised on the same level by those who form it. And yet it has at any given moment an exceedingly firm and definite pattern and so have the frictions which go with it.

The configuration which one found in Zone 1 and Zone 2 showed the significance of this specific communal order of superiority and inferiority and the peculiar type of tensions caused by it. One needed to know more about the structure of the " old families " and of the network they formed with each other in order to understand these status differentials better.

4 | The Mother-Centered Families of Zone 2

A LOCAL journalist, born in the " village ", summed up the impression which he had of the " village " when he said, " You don't know who's related to who. There's so many that although I've lived here all my life I still keep finding out relatives." It was a theme which cropped up again and again in conversations with people who lived in the " village ". The vicar spoke of the " strong family ties in the older part of the village ". A civil servant who lived in the " *élite* area " of the " village " repeated almost literally the words of the journalist, " There is so much inter-marriage here you don't know who is related to whom." None of these remarks could have been made with reference to the Estate. But there were also marked differences between the family pattern of the " village " and Zone 1. In Zone 1 families were small. They had seldom more than two children. In some of the homes the children had grown up, had married and had moved away from Winston Parva because it offered few posts of the kind to which they aspired. In homes with younger children it was noticeable how much more emphasis was laid on educational and recreational facilities. The people interviewed in Zone 1 quite often asked whether making such an enquiry was a full-time occupation and on learning that it was a part-time study and that the interviewer's main occupation was teaching, they immediately showed that they had given a lot of thought to the education of their children. Very earnest questions were asked about higher education, university places, youth clubs and a variety of cultural activities. Few people in Zone 2 and only one person in Zone 3 asked the interviewer about his own work. Usually they were people who had a child at grammar school. Quite evidently the families in Zone 1 in their semi-detached houses with garages, labour-saving kitchens and, at the most, one or two children were comparatively self-sufficient in relation to their neighbourhood and had much wider intellectual interests than the residents of the other zones.

In Zone 2 not only neighbourhood ties, but also kinship ties, were noticeably stronger than in the rest of Winston Parva. Both turned out to be closely connected. And the observation of this connection helped to correct an impression which one may gain from the sociological literature on families, the impression that the structure of families and the structure of the community where they live are totally unrelated to each other. In fact, the nature of family ties and the structure of families cannot be understood and explained as if families existed in a communal vacuum or as if the structure of families determined by itself that of the communities in which they lived.[1] The study of Winston Parva offered opportunities for comparing neighbourhoods of different types with each other. These comparisons indicated the extent to which the structure of families which one found in a particular neighbourhood was dependent on that of the neighbourhood in which they lived.

That was particularly noticeable in the case of the " village ". The closeness of family ties, especially among the " old families " of the " village " *élite*, could have been hardly maintained for long if neighbourhood ties had become looser or fallen apart. In fact it sometimes seemed a little questionable whether one could speak meaningfully of a " family structure " without reference to the structure of the relationships between families —to the structure of the neighbourhood.

In the " village " it was still a matter of pride among the old-established families to have a fairly large family. The family ethos, the strong identification of the individual with the extended kinship group and the relatively high subordination of individual members to their family was reinforced and preserved by the respect and approval which the individual member could expect not only within his own family, but also from members of other families if he conformed to the pattern. Close contacts between families supported and buttressed close ties within the family and made it more difficult for individuals to go their own way as long as they lived in the neighbourhood.

[1] See Appendix 3.

44

The closeness of family ties in the " village " became apparent first by the frequent references which were made in interviews either to the family collectively or to other members individually. On several occasions the introduction made at the beginning of an interview was cut short by a greeting like this : " Oh, come in ! You're the chap that was talkin' to mi mum and mi sister on Friday night, aren't you ? " It was quite striking to observe how often people visited in Zone 2 spoke of themselves as " we " including in this, if it was a woman, not only husband and children, but also her mother and, perhaps, her sisters and their families.

> " We came here about 60 years ago," said a young housewife, adding as an afterthought, " My mother and father that is. We were born here, all of us, and we're still here with our youngsters."

The influence of " mum " as a central figure of reference which has been observed by Young and Wilmott in East London[1] was also a feature of this zone in Winston Parva. Like the mothers of Ship Street studied by Kerr, the mothers of Zone 2 were the focus of many family activities—" living often in the house taken over from her own mother she manipulates the external world around her. She holds the rent book and deals with the rent collector, thus arranging for her daughters to come and live near her ".[2]

Although the relationship was sometimes a little ambivalent, some sons-in-law seemed to have become well integrated with their " extended family " headed by their mother-in-law. They had formed friendly relationships within the family circle. It was one of the characteristic leisure time patterns in the " village " that men from the same extended family group went together to the nearby public house for a quiet drink while their wives went " round to mum for an hour ".

Although one looked out for it not a single case could be observed in which the father played a similar part as the central figure of a kinship group. Elderly men were usually cared for by one of the daughters, as was the case with one of the

---

[1] Young, M., Willmott, P., *Family and Kinship in East London*. London 1962. Chaps. 3–6.
[2] Kerr, M., *The People of Ship Street*. London, 1958. p. 64.

best-known men in the Old People's Club, but the influence of such men was strictly limited. The preponderent influence of the mother as a kind of matriarch, the hub of a three-generation family group was probably connected with the fact that the main functions which this kind of grouping had for its members were largely women's and not men's functions ; they were primarily spare-time and person-to-person functions and only marginally specialised occupational functions centred on impersonal objects. It was part of a woman's role and inclination to look after children when daughters or daughters-in-law went out to work and generally to look after the personal interests of other family members whether male or female if they needed it. Many people interviewed in Zone 2 stressed that they saw at least one member of the " their family group " every day and in this way were able to hear the current family news. One male member of such a family said, " We see one another most days," and added, " we don't visit much, but if anything goes wrong somebody calls in to tell the others." Most of these people had no telephone, in contrast to the people of Zone 1 where telephones were frequently used as a means of communication, but the daily contact of the members of an " extended family group " ensured that information passed quickly in this relatively small neighbourhood. There was little evidence of whole families meeting in full strength for social purposes apart from weddings, christenings and funerals. The occasions on which the family was mobilised either in part or as a whole were well established and standardised, as was the manner in which it functioned, the routines of the family network in action.

Families were found co-operating in nursing their " mum " and in keeping her house clean ; in one such case a married daughter shared the " night duty " at her invalid mother's home with another married daughter. The wife's mother looked after the children of young married couples in their absence. Children of school age " went round to Gran's " after school. Babies were taken to their grandmother's house before work and called for in the early evening. Again one can see how closely this family pattern was connected with the needs of married women who went to work. Mothers, too, in most cases, seemed to have worked outside their homes at one or the other time of their lives. Their present role as guardians of the children in the absence of parents helped to strengthen and to extend the influence of the wife's mother. It often included decisions which had to be taken with regard to children. Even problems of grown-ups which required decisions were normally discussed with " mum " by their daughters and sometimes also by sons and sons-in-law.

Kinship networks of this type gave to their individual members considerable reassurance and security. If the wife's mother played a part in helping with her daughter's family, she herself could count on the help of her daughter's family when she needed it. Townsend observed in another old-established working-class district, in Bethnal Green, " how many women played a major part in rearing young children for as many as 40 or 50 years of their lives ".[1] One could observe the same pattern in Zone 2. Among those interviewed were eighteen elderly women who after their own children had grown up helped to look after their children's children or in other cases after the children of a sister or a sister's daughter.

The women of Zone 2 spoke with real affection of " our street ", or " mi mum's house " and of " our kids ", a term which referred to all children within the mother's family network. Such emotional ties prevented many of the married women from leaving Winston Parva and moving into the " unknown ". During the interviews several women said they had started married life away from Winston Parva but had returned there to be " near mum " because they felt lonely. Old people, too, found security as members of such a wide family network. They also derived from it day by day interests. Kerr observed in *The People of Ship Street* that " the fear of loneliness is an important factor in understanding this group. It is probable that their general lack of education and of opportunities to use their intellect restricts quite drastically the number of roles an individual can play."[2] In Zone 2, however, a large number of women were members of associations and clubs. They greatly enjoyed this extension of their interests

[1] Townsend, P. *The Family Life of Old People*, 1957, 34.
[2] Kerr, M. *The People of Ship Street*, 1958, 66.

even if their primary interest lay with the family. Membership of church or chapel groups, of political or other voluntary organisations, as shown later, involved women not only in roles other than those which they played within their own family group, they also served as links between several family groups.

The men were not quite so strongly involved in the circle of social activities and social interests centred on " mum " as were the women. The emphasis on extra-familial activities was in their case stronger than it was in that of the women. Nevertheless, the strength of the ties which bound men, too, to their " family group " was considerable. That one came across brothers helping with household repairs and met men of the same family group going together to the pub has already been mentioned. A study of membership lists of local associations, such as the Band, showed that brothers-in-law, fathers-in-law, sons and brothers often co-operated in the specific activities of the same voluntary association. In several cases men of the same family group participated in the same play, made music together, " tinkered " with cars together or occupied, in mixed as well as single-sex groups, some of the principle official positions. A few women, however, did not approve of their husbands' membership of any such extra-familial groups. Thus one wife when her husband was about to reply to an interview question about club membership said, " Club ! I tell him this is his club and he has to make the best of it." As far as one could see this husband accepted his role quite placidly.

Older male members of the kinship group often helped younger husbands, the fathers of small children, to improve the home in the evenings by some " do-it-yourself " work such as making furniture or fitting up a bathroom. A little less than 50 per cent of those interviewed in Zone 2 mentioned such work or a hobby for which they found time at home. The percentage ·in Zone 3 was 32 per cent. In the same way male members of the kinship group helped with " mum's " decorating, television repairs and household maintenance. If the men were members of the Band or took part in a church play, the women of the kinship group turned out to applaud their performance and to meet other women attending for similar reasons with whom they exchanged views. The ties between family members, in the

48

case of these " village " families, did not make for isolation. Links between family groups and local associations, which will be discussed later, were close. They were symptomatic of the firmness with which family groups in the " village " were embedded in their community. As one observed life in Zone 2 one could hardly imagine that any of these family groups could have continued to function as they did if all connections with other similar family groups in the neighbourhood had been cut off.

Comparison with the other zones indicated the advantages which the co-operation within a fairly large family unit had for its members. In Zone 1 most families could rely for many of the smaller and larger services which their own members could or would not perform to a larger extent on paid services from outsiders. In Zone 3 where families were smaller and neighbourhood contacts not very close the members of a small family encountered quite a number of difficulties because neither family help nor neighbourhood help was readily available if husband or wife fell ill or had to go away, and paid help was beyond their reach. Some " villagers " seemed to think this lack of neighbourhood co-operation might be due to " personal characteristics " of the people who lived there. In fact, it was due to the character of the neighbourhood itself. The people who lived there, compared with the " villagers ", were newcomers. Many of them hardly knew each other.

On occasions families are represented as self-sufficient entities or even as the basic elements—as the " bricks " of which societies are built. But even within the small compass of this study the differences of the types of family relations found in neighbourhood communities of different types were striking enough to suggest that the idea of " the family " as the basic, the primary unit of society, and as essentially self-sufficient and self-explanatory was a misconception. The family may appear as such from the standpoint of its own members. It is certainly the primary unit from a child's point of view. But if one observes that the configurations of people to which one refers as " families " greatly vary in structure and type and asks why they vary, one soon discovers that the forces responsible for these differences are not to be found within the families themselves. They can be found only in the larger units of which families form part. One cannot understand why the dominant forms of families were different in the three zones of Winston Parva without reference to the development and structure of these zones and of the community they formed with each other. It is hard to imagine that an extended mother dominated kinship group comprising three or even four generations could have formed itself or could have kept its cohesion for long in a neighbourhood of the type of Zone 3. In fact, one could hardly visualise one such family unit surviving for long in a community where no other family of the same type lived. The " village " had as its core a closely knit network consisting of a plurality of mother-centred family networks some of which formed a kind of " village " *élite* and helped to set the tone for others.

As the extensions of intra-familial activities into inter-familial activities indicated, the routines and conventions of kinship networks formed an integral part of the wider routines and conventions of the whole neighbourhood. One would form a rather distorted picture if one implicitly assumed that family characteristics were primary and neighbourhood character-istics derived from them. It was in this particular neighbour-hood that its mother-centred family networks grew into shape. The high degree of co-operation in the " village " was not due to the fact that accidentally a number of kind-hearted people had assembled there. It was a tradition which had grown up in the course of two or three generations among people who lived in a closely-knit neighbourhood of a specific type. The price which individuals had to pay for it, and which they were perhaps glad to pay, was submission and conformity to the communal norms. Help might be given in emergencies to complete strangers, but help and kindness were not readily extended to neighbours who did not conform, who remained outsiders ; they were given or withheld in accordance with " village " traditions and if they were given, they were not any less genuine and pleasant for that reason.

5 | Local Associations and the " Old Families' Network "

CLOSELY linked to the family ties were those created by membership in local associations of which Winston Parva had a considerable number. Almost all of them were centred on the " village ".

The network of old families which formed the core of the " village " community prescribed and provided most leisure-time activities for its own members and within this circle these activities were almost entirely communal : people usually spent their leisure time in groups, not alone and not even in enclosed dyads or pairs, but if in pairs still immersed in the communal medium—without walls in relation to third, fourth or fifth and perhaps to many more persons, and with very thin walls even in the case of courting couples. They spent their leisure time with members of their family or with neighbours, and local associations together with church and chapel provided the principle formal framework for " village " leisure-time activities, particularly in the case of middle-aged and older people.

In that respect, too, the " village " still showed features more characteristic of pre-industrial or of older relatively small industrial communities than of the larger urban type communities into one of which it was likely to be absorbed in a generation or two. The local nickname was not unjustified ; though completely divorced from agriculture it retained many characteristics of a village. A high degree of self-sufficiency with regard to leisure-time activities was one of them. The members of the old families' net-work found something reasonably interesting and for them apparently satisfying to do within their own community when their occupational or their housework was over and many less centrally placed " villagers " followed their lead.

Like members of fairly large working-class families elsewhere the ordinary " villagers " did not have a great deal of money to spend on spare-time activities. Their community, small as it was, offered few of the commercial diversions available in larger urban communities. Most of the time they provided each other with diversions, informally by means of gossip and other talk, more formally by such means as religious services and the varied activities of local associations. As far as one could see adult members of the old families' network and their associates in the " village " did not suffer from the peculiar " leisure time starvation " which appears to be the source of some discomfort in many more highly individualised urban societies ; they did not seem to suffer from the leisure-time boredom and emptiness quite often to be found in communities where people without much interest in the work which earns them their living, are left with insufficient opportunities for the use of their leisure time commensurate to their capacity for enjoyment and to their means, and with insufficient opportunities for increasing either of them.

Even in the " village " opportunities for a reasonably satisfactory mode of spending one's leisure time were by no means the same for all inhabitants ; and for people who lived on the Estate the chance to participate was minute. Because the diversions of the " village " were largely communal, they were closely linked to its social order. Like the gossip channels, neighbourhood activities, and particularly the activities of the leading local associations, were dominated by people who belonged to the old families' network including those who lived in Zone 1. Others who were willing to fit in were tolerated even if they came from Zone 3. But they were rarely in the centre of things ; they remained even in associations centred on places of worship more or less outsiders. And the feeling that one belonged was obviously an essential ingredient of the enjoyment provided by communal leisure time activities whether they had an informal character such as the meetings of neighbours on a shopping round and in a pub, or a more highly organised character such as meetings of local associations.

Among the latter, the most active centres of leisure time activities were associations grouped around churches or chapels. With one exception all places of worship in Winston Parva were situated in its oldest part, in Zone 2. The members of associations centred on them came from all three zones. The picture that emerged from the consultation of membership lists, for what it is worth, was this : the total of formally enrolled members of such associations was 385 ; of these 59 people came from Zone 1, 283 from Zone 2, 43 from Zone 3. More than half the members of associations centred on churches or chapels, about 200 people altogether, belonged to the Church of England. The centre of the Anglican community was St. Michael's Church situated on the main street of the " village ". Forty-four members of associations based on St. Michael's came from Zone 1, 163 from Zone 2, 37 from Zone 3, some of them not Anglican. The buildings of the church contained a hall and a number of pleasant meeting rooms. In many ways they had the function of a community centre. The hall was used by the Old People's Club which had strong ties with the Church of England. Together with other meeting rooms the hall provided regular accommodation for the Church Dramatic Society, the Ladies' Concert Party, the Scouts and a Youth Group. The activities of some of these associations extended to the mission hall which was used for Church of England services in Zone 3 and which was in that zone the only building available for public meetings.

The Dramatic Club produced and performed plays in the church hall regularly for the greater part of the year. Most of the plays were comedies or mystery murders of the type most popular with amateur groups. One of the most striking aspects of these performances was the obvious intimacy of the players and their public. Most members of the cast were well-known " village " people and their appearance on the stage in unusual and often amusing costumes immediately produced a lively reaction from the audience. The ability of " our Colin " was acknowledged vociferously by members of the audience, and by no means only by those who were related to the actors. The identification obviously extended to a whole network of families. Old ladies " laughed 'til they cried." Groups of

53

women moved their chairs around in the intervals so as to be able to talk to each other more comfortably. The christian names of the actors were on everyone's lips. And the same intimacy was to be found in other similar associations. Church and chapel committees and the various social activities organised by them were usually run by members of a few families or perhaps of one family for whom these activities were a direct continuation of those within their kinship group itself.

One could still see here, in a late form, what was probably the rule in European societies at an earlier stage of development, and what is certainly still the rule in many African and Asian communities today, that institutions which we call " religious " were not as sharply divorced from other communal institutions as our highly differentiated vocabulary suggests ; they were focal points within the network of communal relationships. Attending service was for a good many families in the community one of the most important and probably in many cases one of the most satisfying leisure activities partly, no doubt, because it ranked high in the value scale of the community *élites* and was another manifestation of communal intimacy for those who " belonged ".

Even in the choice of their residence families who belonged to the same religious group tended to cluster together. If one mapped out the places where members of St. Michael's lived one discovered a characteristic pattern. In Zone 2 they tended to live in small family clusters scattered through the " respectable " " village " streets. In a street which had once been " respectable ", but which had now for some time declined in reputation because the Council had recently bought some houses there for slum clearance, the St. Michael's people though small in numbers clustered together in the first twenty-eight houses nearest to the " respectable " part. It was as if initially a few " mums " of the same denomination had settled next to each other and had then asked the " rent man " to let their married daughters have other houses next to them when they became available.

The distribution of places of residence was noticeably different in the case of people from Zone 3 who were members of St. Michael's associations. They were far more dispersed ;

many streets had one single member and some none at all. And an analysis of membership lists of other churches in Winston Parva showed a similar pattern. In Zone 2, as in Zone 1, people with the same religious affinities tended to live in family clusters, in Zone 3 here and there as isolated individuals. Like the Church of England other denominations formed the centres not only of religious but also of many other leisure activities although, in accordance with their smaller membership, on a much smaller scale. Two of the chapels had dramatic societies and youth groups. There, too, as interviews, informal conversations and press cuttings indicated, certain families formed the core of the active membership of a particular place of worship and the same families played a leading part in their dramatic club, their choir and their youth club. Sunday worship, church and chapel committees, ladies' hours, dramatic societies, in short a fairly wide range of common leisure interests formed an integral part not only of an individual family group, but of clusters of families.

The picture of the self-sufficient small nuclear family as the archetype of a family did not fit the observations in the " village " community though it fitted part of the evidence from Zone 1. Closely knit as families were in Zone 2 they were " open " families and by no means self-sufficient. Activities within individual families and activities within clusters of individual families merged into each other and appeared quite inseparable. Common extra-familial tasks and goals of family members, such as those which were centred on religious or political associations, strengthened the intra-familial bonds. The former helped to maintain the latter partly as a result of the mutual control which the component families exercised upon each other in connection with the tacit rivalry between them—one dreaded laying oneself open to critical comments from friends more than from strangers, partly because they provided families with common aims beyond themselves. It is difficult to say how far that applied to those families which did not take a leading part in local associations—which were " followers ". Nor is it easy to convey a clear picture of the relationship between the various church or chapel-centred groups of families and between the associations to which they belonged. It evidently had a hierarchic pattern : some associations ranked higher in the esteem of the " villagers " than others. The prestige order of the associations was apparently linked to that of the families who played a leading part in them and vice versa. Every woman in the " village ", if not every man, appeared to know the status and prestige rating of every family and of every association in the community at a given time. As has been mentioned, they obviously had difficulties in communicating their rating which formed an implicit part of their communal conduct in everyday life, explicitly to outsiders. So far as the status differentials of their in-group, of the " respectable " families and associations themselves were concerned, they hardly ever spoke about them directly. They sometimes indicated these differences in ranking indirectly by shaking their head or by the tone in which they said " very nice people " or " quite nice people ". With regard to most of the finer shades of this internal status hierarchy the picture drawn here remained incomplete.

But there was no ambiguity about the highest and the lowest level of this status hierarchy in the whole of Winston Parva. Most of the highest ranking families of Zone 1 and of Zone 2 belonged to St. Michael's church and the associations centred on it. And not only this leading group but also those of other local associations were at one in the low status which they accorded to families from Zone 3. It was the leader of one of the non-conformist churches in the " village " who said of the residents of Zone 3 : " Let's face it, they're not like the village people. A few of them join the village life, but it is a few." The same phrases indicative of one's own superiority were used in interviews and in casual conversations with most " villagers ", phrases like " round here ", amplified by expressions such as " the old part " or " not the Estate, you know ".

The status order was not only reflected in the membership of religious, but also in that of secular, local associations. The " Evergreens ", the Old People's Club, was an example. It had 114 members and was one of the largest of the secular associations in Winston Parva. It was a welfare organisation characteristic of the manner in which an old industrial community, where traditions of previous generations had been kept alive to some extent, dealt with a problem which at a later stage of industrial development tended to become increasingly the responsibility of public authorities and dependent on public funds.

The regular meetings of the " Evergreens " took place every Wednesday afternoon at the church hall of St. Michael's. Organisational cross links and membership cross links with St. Michael's were close though the Club was open to old people of all denominations. Twelve members of the " Evergreens " were also members of St. Michael's, but according to the interviews many more attended the church on Sundays without being members. The secretary mentioned among the various aspects of her welfare work that " she got someone to call round to see if everything is all right " if a member was absent from a meeting and no-one had seen him or her for a little while. As the majority of the old people of Winston Parva lived in the " village ", it is not surprising that the " village " provided the greatest number of members. Fifteen members of the " Evergreens " came from Zone 1, 94 from Zone 2, 5 from Zone 3. Quite a number of old people from Zone 3, as the interviews showed, did not want to join. Some of them said they would not go because of the " clique ". Others scorned the " free teas " and " charity ". None of the old people from the " village " raised similar objections. And again, the 5 members of the " Evergreens " club who came from Zone 3 lived apart from each other in different streets while those from Zone 2, with regard to their place of residence, mostly belonged to family clusters.

Attendance at the Wednesday meetings of the " Evergreens " club was usually high. Some of the old people, as the secretary said, struggled against physical infirmities in order to attend. The hall was rather bare, but well able to accommodate 90 people or more. The atmosphere was very friendly. Most of the old people had lived in Winston Parva for more than 40 years and knew each other well, many of them were on christian name terms. Their in-group feeling strengthened by family ties and cross-associational membership must have presented a formidable social barrier to the old people from Zone 3. At a meeting the members were seated round the long tables. Some

57

played dominoes or cards. But the majority were just chatting. A pleasant volume of talk and laughter filled the room. From time to time an announcement read by the secretary produced a pause in their conversation ; she was always listened to with evident interest. The club organised several outings to historical buildings, or to the seaside during the year. At the end of the excursions " a free tea " was usually provided by the Working Men's Club. Refreshments during the weekly meetings consisted of a cup of tea, a slice of bread and jam, some cake and biscuits. Members paid a subscription of 1d each week towards the cost, and to help balance the budget local businessmen and a few local firms made generous donations. One of the men who helped most in this and in other ways was the President of the club, Councillor Drew, who also spent much time in visiting old people and in arranging measures for their welfare. The secretary, too, took great interest in her voluntary work. She was affectionately known by her christian name to many of the members. Each meeting ended with the singing of the " Evergreen Song ", written by one of the members. The song was mentioned in the course of several interviews both by members of the club and by non-members as a " lovely bit of music ". It ran like this :

THE DARBY AND JOAN SONG

Let us grow lovely growing old,
So many fine things do,
Old lace and ivory and gold
And silks need not be new.

But there's a beauty in old trees,
Old streets their glamour hold.
Why may not we as well as these
Grow lovely growing old.

Now in the twilight of our years
We all our memories hold.
So let us smile through all our tears
As lovely we grow old.

Another local association which had played a prominent part in the community for over fifty years was the Winston Parva

Prize Temperance Band. Its bandsmen's uniforms were to be seen at concerts in the nearby park at the Old People's parties, at memorial services and at Fêtes throughout the year. Rehearsals could be heard from the main road on a mid-week evening as the Band attacked " Poet and Peasant " or prepared some other pieces for a concert.

The history of the Band was yet another example of the role of kinship ties in the social life of the community. The founder of the Band was an old Winstonian whose name was a household word in the " village ". At the beginning of the century he had opened a music shop on the main street of the " village ". When the " old man " retired from the business his son managed the shop and conducted the Band. Occasionally, father and son appeared together on the concert platform and their appearance was usually given prominence in the local press. The Band had in the past won national championships and after a decline in the immediate post-war years had succeeded in winning further challenge cups. They all were exhibited in the shop window. The Band now admitted members from surrounding localities. But according to the conductor they all lived within three miles from the Band Room above the shop. They now formed the majority. Only twelve of the thirty-two members of the Band lived in Winston Parva. Six of these came from Zone 1 and six from Zone 2 ; no members came from Zone 3.

The members of the Band took their music very seriously. Rehearsals were usually well attended. The conductor was known as " Bob " and he in turn called the player by their christian names. An interval for tea was enlivened by small diversions such as a ritual " tea swindle " in which playing cards, coins and some good-humoured shouting produced money for the refreshments and a small profit. The membership fee was twenty-six shillings a year to which must be added expenses for the buying and maintenance of instruments. Four of the twelve members who lived in Winston Parva had fathers or sons there, two had wives and in-laws in Winston Parva, the rest, as the conductor said, were " members of churches and chapels of course ". The Vice-President of the Band was Vicar's Warden at St. Michael's church, the President for

59

1959–60 was Councillor Drew. The founder of the Band was an honorary " Evergreen ".

The Band still had a loyal following in the community although its great days belonged to the past. A local bus proprietor recalled how the Band used to march through the streets of Winston Parva at the head of the carnival procession before the " hospitals were nationalised ". The procession attracted great crowds and collected money for the hospitals. In interviews in Zone 1 and 2 the Band, like an aged relative, was often mentioned with affection though with undertones which implied that it was something of a relic of the past. Old people still liked to hear the concerts in the park. Many of them mentioned the old days when the Band led the procession. Interviews in Zone 3 showed very little interest in the Band. A few people ridiculed, none admired it, and the only musician interviewed in Zone 3 said it was " deadly ".

Thus, the Band formed a significant part of the tradition of the " village ". It was a small but prominent association which had strong ties with the old families and with other prestige-giving associations in Winston Parva. It reinforced the feeling of solidarity of the old residents and was ignored or rejected by the inhabitants of Zone 3.

Another association mentioned with pride in the " village " was the bowling club. Membership was open to both sexes and was drawn from an area wider than Winston Parva. Several residents of Zones 1 and 2 were prominent on the committee, in team lists and in press reports. The leisurely game on the greens in the park on a warm afternoon or evening attracted small groups of older people as spectators and the ladies' team was photographed from time to time in their white uniforms and straw hats. Membership lists were not available, but information by members indicated that no members of the club came from Zone 3. A similar pattern was found in an analysis of attendance at the Winston Parva evening institute. The variety of classes ranged from opera to metal work. Of approximately 100 people who attended one session only 34 were resident in Winston Parva ; of these 8 members came from Zone 1, 21 from Zone 2, 5 from Zone 3.

A small but very high-ranking group was the Benevolent

Committee. It consisted of ten members led by Councillor Drew. The Committee raised funds for distribution to older, less-fortunate inhabitants of Winston Parva. They raised funds with the assistance of local shopkeepers, businessmen and club officials. They were notified of cases in need of help. A member of the Committee was asked to visit the old person and to report to the Committee on the conditions. The Committee then decided on the most effective method of help. Usually a member would take food, comforts or money to the person in need. Sometimes the help was abused. In one such case an old lady who had received help was reported to be spending the money on " intoxicants ". The information was given to a member of the Committee " in conversation ". The member visited the old lady to check the report. He confirmed it and the help was withdrawn. Whatever its other functions the assistance given by the Benevolent Committee was also an instrument of social control.

Councillor Drew spent a great deal of his leisure time in this work. He frequently paid visits to old people, raised money for them, discussed their cases and gave talks to the " Evergreens " Club. One could often see his car parked near the house of one of the old people on whom he had called. The composition of the Committee showed the familiar pattern with a slight variation. The number of members from Zone 1 was higher than that of the other zones. Five members came from Zone 1, 4 from Zone 2, and 1 from Zone 3. The member from Zone 3 gave during an interview the following account of his election to the Committee. In the mid-1950's an open meeting had been called in order to discuss the welfare of old people in the area. The Benevolent Committee had existed for many years, but it had been run, as he said, " by the old clique some of whom were getting past it ". This group had been re-elected year by year and if anyone tried to get on the Committee " the other members withdrew their names so that no Committee could be formed ". At the meeting in the mid-1950's Councillor Drew apparently persuaded some of the old members to resign. The man from Zone 3 happened to go to the meeting and " stood for election ". He said : " Nobody else from the Estate bothered about charity." He was duly elected.

Like the activities of church and chapel-centred associations those connected with politics formed a specialised type of activity only in the case of a very small number of people. For most participants they were simply another form of social activity during their leisure hours. And the same was true of their political beliefs. In the case of most people they formed part and parcel of a more general belief system primarily determined by communal and only secondarily by national issues and situations.

The only political organisation in Winston Parva which functioned well was the Conservative Association. Its membership was small. The core was formed by 17 officials and active helpers of whom 5 came from Zone 1, 12 from Zone 2 and none from Zone 3. The Association had a club house on the main road of the " village ". But the Conservative Club was more a social than a political centre. It was mainly frequented by people who did not care to go to the Working Men's Club across the road. It was " a decent place to take the wife ", to " go for a quiet drink ", to " meet friends ".

For election purposes Winston Parva was divided into two wards, one formed by Zone 1 and part of Zone 2, the second by the other part of Zone 2 and Zone 3. The latter, during the time of the research was represented by Labour councillors, the former by Councillor Drew who was standing as Independent and had the backing of the Conservative Association. A woman shopkeeper, the Conservative candidate for the ward with a Labour majority at two recent council elections in which she had been narrowly defeated, explained that " there's not many interested in doing active political work ". Too many of her committee, she said, were 65 years and over, although among them were " good workers like Mrs. K " (an elderly Zone 2 widow). It was she who said of the residents of Zone 3 :

" They're a different class of people. . . . They don't belong to anything unless they can get something out of it."

Speaking of her defeat she said she was sure that it was largely due to the large Labour vote from the Estate.

Other members of the Conservative Association spoke more

enthusiastically of their committee. Using christian names they mentioned the " lovely bouquets " received from a successful candidate after the election—" and of course the good friends ". They often referred to Councillor Drew who stood as Independent. " We help Drew too," said one member of the committee, " even though he is not a Conservative, he's nice is Drew. . . ." But they all agreed in their critical attitude towards the voters of Zone 3, and the gist of their argument was almost always the same. They were reproached for not having any local loyalties and for only trying to get advantages for themselves :

> " They're Labour, out for anything they can get. They vote for anyone who says he's Labour, whether he is local or not."

One member of the Association said she had heard that the present Labour councillor " couldn't even write his name ". There appeared to be general agreement that if it were not for the Labour votes of the Estate, the Conservative candidate would get in every time. The Independent councillor himself thought the people on the Estate were " dead Labour " and " not intelligently aware " showing " no sense of responsibility, only want ". The political leaders of Zone 1 and 2 made no appeal for support from the voters of Zone 3. It was towards their own zones, particularly towards Zone 2, that their efforts at rallying people were directed. They were probably aware that Labour votes also came from the " village ". But in their case political leadership was still identical with social leadership in a wider sense. Councillor Drew himself had no political organisation of his own. He was so well known in Winston Parva that he virtually acted as unofficial Mayor of the community. That his election posters simply said—" Vote for the Old Folks' Friend " was significant. His conservative affinities, like those of many other members of the old families' network, did not require formal and explicit links with any party-organisation. They were self-understood and implicit ; they formed an integral part of his social position as member of an old Winstonian family and of the community of Winston Parva itself. It was not a piece of political propaganda, but the expression of a deep personal conviction when he said that the people from the Estate by voting Labour showed that they lacked intelligent awareness and a sense of responsibility ; this, to him, meant responsibility towards Winston Parva which as rejected newcomers they indeed lacked. This was one aspect of the trap in which they all were caught. It was the sincere conviction of the leading " village " families that everybody in Winston Parva ought to be conscious of his responsibilities towards his community and that he ought to prefer as his representatives local people to outsiders. That the Estate people did not act in accordance with the tenets of the " village " belief was one of the reasons why the " villagers " looked down upon them and excluded them as far as possible from their own circles. They could not detach themselves sufficiently from the demands of their own value and belief system to see that newcomers could not automatically feel the same attachment to Winston Parva, and all it stood for in the eyes of its older residents, as those who had grown up there. If at all, they might have acquired some affection for their new locality if the older residents, as it were, had eased them in. Instead the absoluteness of their value and belief system compelled them to demand implicitly that all residents of Winston Parva should share their own loyalty towards the place and to reject relentlessly those who did not. The Estate people on their part, and perhaps a number of rejected " villagers " as well, retaliated by rejecting the ruling political outlook and activities of Zone 1 and 2 as another example of the rule of the " cliques ", the " old fogeys ", the " snobs ". But their opposition was and remained almost wholly unorganised. Winston Parva had no functioning Labour organisation. The strong Labour vote in at least one ward of Winston Parva was due to informal situational factors unaided by any formal organisation. The Conservative Association of Winston Parva, on the other hand, small as it was, formed an effective organisational nucleus ; it was strong enough to mobilise the Conservative potentialities of the community when the need arose. It derived a good deal of support from other associations. Thirteen out of 17 people listed as members of the Conservative Association had ties with one or the other of the religious associations or the

64

" Evergreens " or the Band, and 6 of them had ties with all three.

The relatively high level of organisation in Zone 1 and Zone 2 and the relatively low organisational level of Zone 3 which one could observe here in the political field extended to many others. It was one of the basic structural differences between Zone 3 and the other zones, and, as one shall see, helped to explain the power differentials between them. The term organisational level does not only refer to the formal organisation of which the local associations were examples. No less important for the strong cohesion of the " village " were the informal ties which linked their members and particularly their leading members to each other and which accounted for the fact that a relatively small number of people, members of a small number of families, occupied most of the key positions in the high prestige associations of Winston Parva and wielded the power which went with them. Table VI gives an idea of these cross links.

Firmly established power *élites*, as one can see, can form rather quickly in a growing industrial settlement under favourable conditions. Already the second generation of an expanding though still secluded community near an industrial town could throw up its own local " aristocracy ". Table VI indicates some of the roots of its power. A common sense of belongingness, of responsibility and dedication towards their home community created firm links between people who had grown up and had probably become fairly prosperous there together. They may not have all liked each other personally, but they shared a strong feeling of their identity as a group. They identified themselves objectively as " old families " and subjectively as " we ". This closing of the ranks of a group of families in a community against those who did not or not quite belong allowed those of their members who were able and willing to spend part of their leisure time and some money on communal affairs to reserve for each other most of the leading positions in political, religious and other public organisations of the community and to exclude from them people whom they did not feel to be of their own kind. This monopolisation of associational and other local key positions by members of

65

Table VI

SEGMENT OF THE OLD FAMILIES' NETWORK

Distribution of some key positions
in Winston Parva

Councillor R. C. Drew
Member of second generation Winston Parva family
Local Contractor
Elected to the Council as "Independent" (the "Old People's Friend")
with support of Conservative Association

Chairman
Benevolent Committee

President
Old People's Club

Member of St. Michael's
Church

Chairman of
Board of Governors
of two local secondary
schools

Mr. D. D. Sterling
Member of second generation Winston Parva family

President of the Band

Committee member St. Michael's Church

Mrs. D. D. Sterling
Member of second generation Winston Parva family

Treasurer
Benevolent Committee

Secretary
Old People's Club

Member of St. Michael's
Church

Member of Board of
Governors of two
local secondary schools

President
Benevolent Committee

Mr. C. Lawson
Founder of a Winston Parva family
Founder of the Band

Honorary Member Old People's Club

Member of St. Michael's Church

Member of Board of
Governors of two
local secondary schools

Member
Benevolent Committee

Mr. D. R. Taylor
Member of second generation Winston Parva family
Chairman
Local Conservative Association

Member of Board of
Governors of two
local secondary schools

(*Councillor*) *Mrs. D. R. Taylor*
Secretary
Local Conservative Association

Member of local
Free Church

Member of Board of
Governors of local
secondary school

67

connected and like-thinking families, in this case as in others, was one of the most characteristic properties of the old families' network and one of the strongest sources of its power.

To some extent the development of such a power *élite* in Winston Parva was probably due to the uneven growth of wealth in the community. Some Winstonian families or branches of these families grew fairly prosperous and others not. Poorer or wealthier they retained a strong sense of belonging to Winston Parva and of belonging together, but individuals from the wealthier branches had the time and the money to take a lead in community affairs. Factors such as this, the immanent dynamics of a developing industrial community certainly played a part in this *élite* formation. However, it may also have been influenced by the traditions of England which offered many models for an aristocratic régime. In all likelihood both factors combined in this case, the dynamics of uneven growth providing the rough mould, the differentiated stream of England's tradition the finer pattern. For the specific institutions of Winston Parva which gave to members of leading old families opportunities of power were not invented in Winston Parva. The mode of electing community leaders, the local council itself, institutions such as political parties, churches, benevolent committees, bands and many others which developed in Winston Parva were modelled on precedents set by other British communities. The people who settled and lived in Winston Parva had learned and stored away for reference in appropriate situations specific ways of arranging communal affairs and of dealing with communal problems. They could draw on these stored images as models indicating how to do and how not to do things in community affairs. If they were flexible and inventive enough they could experiment with further developments. The manner in which second generation men and women in Winston Parva exercised power and assumed responsibilities as community leaders followed certain traditional patterns. Local contractor, owner of a local music shop or whatever their occupation, the roles they assumed as community leaders, their attitudes in relation to poorer people or to outsiders who did not conform were set in a highly specific mould. There was much to suggest that they were urban middle-class and working-class developments of roles which landowners, gentry and aristocracy in their capacity of leaders of rural communities had evolved before in a pre-industrial setting. This development of roles, the reflection of the macrocosm in the microcosm of Winston Parva, was all the more noteworthy as the community was, and remained, for the greater part a working-class community. Undoubtedly, the " village " was a working-class community of a special type. It was bound up with a relatively low degree of migratory mobility, with children staying and rearing their families at the same place as their own parents. During the early period of its growth the community, in terms of communications, was probably still fairly remote from the attractions of larger urban centres. Local industries were relatively small. They appeared to offer satisfactory employment, particularly to the more family-centred women. In this setting communal and family ties between people whose families had lived in the same neighbourhood for many decades, who had known each other from childhood, on, and, in many cases had grown up together, still proved stronger than the fact that some were prosperous and had middle-class occupations and others had remained comparatively poor and had working-class occupations. With the former in the lead they closed their ranks against newcomers and the principal social cleavage which developed in Winston Parva was that between old residents and newcomers. The former firmly established in all key points of the community organisation and enjoying the intimacy of their own associa-tional life tried to exclude strangers who did not subscribe to their community creed and who in many respects offended their sense of values. An analysis of the composition and leadership of some of the local associations gives some idea of the methods of exclusion. Residents in the *élite* area of Zone 2 were perhaps a little more emphatic in the expression of their pride than some of those who lived in the ordinary streets, but the feeling of superiority itself was shared by most of them. They had some characteristic forms of expressing this pride.

This is a selection of sayings which show them.

Residents of Zone 2 speaking of their own Zone.

HOUSEWIFE : " This is the old part you know where the older families live."

OLD LADY : " We still call this part ' the village '. There's a lot of us come from the original families round here."

THE VICAR : " There seems to be a great deal of inter-marriage between the families in this part, ' the village ' as they call it."

ENGINEER : " We're working class most of us, but decent working class, not like those on the Estate."

HOUSEWIFE : " Ours is a very nice street, good neighbours, nice people."

YOUNG MARRIED MAN : " These are good houses. They're old, but there's plenty of room and you can fit all kinds of improvements in."

YOUNG HOUSEWIFE : " I like it here. We're near my Mum and we can help one another."

WOMAN SHOPKEEPER : " We belong here. In a way it's our village and our families have built their lives round it."

6 | Overall Picture of Zone 3

THE Estate, at the time of the enquiry, had existed for about 20 years, the " village " for about 80. Its 797 inhabitants were working-class people. There was no sprinkling of middle-class people as in Zone 2. Differences in the proportion of skilled, semi-skilled and unskilled workers between " village " and Estate as has been shown in Table II, were relatively small. All three levels were represented in both neighbourhoods. But Zone 3 had 32.5 per cent skilled and 31.4 per cent unskilled workers, while Zone 2 had 26.1 per cent and 24.5 per cent respectively.

The Estate was owned by a private investment company to whom all the rents were paid. Each house contained two small rooms on the ground floor and two or three small bedrooms on the first floor. The houses were built very close together with small gardens dividing the rows. Many residents did their cooking in the living room, but a minority had constructed their own little kitchens at the back of the house in order to have more space in the living room. During the 30's when the houses were built, it was for a time not easy to find tenants. People from the " village " hesitated to move in the new houses although rents were then lower. People from outside came slowly. The houses filled up first when after the Munich crisis families of men stationed at a nearby regimental depot were brought in. Then with the bombing of London came the employees of the London instrument factory and from then on few houses on the Estate stood empty for long. People were attracted to Winston Parva first by a variety of war work, then by the employment offered locally by some of the expanding industries, and even the traditional firms concerned with hosiery or footwear though subject to some fluctuations offered wages high enough to attract workers from other parts of the country. A considerable number of those who migrated to Winston Parva stayed on, but the character of the Estate as a settlement of immigrants, and of immigrants of a specific type, showed itself even after a decade or two still clearly in the structure of the community. Most people migrated to the Estate as members of a small family group. Husbands and wives came together with or without children. As a result the proportion of people on the Estate who had relatives in Winston Parva was very much smaller than that of the " village " people, as Table VII indicates.

TABLE VII

*Number of Interviewed People with Relatives in Zone 2 and 3
and
the Total Number of their Relatives in Winston Parva*

	Interviews	Interviewed people with relatives in Zone 2	Interviewed people with relatives in Zone 3	Their relatives in Winston Parva
	Total	No.	No.	Total
Zone 1	12	10	—	61
Zone 2	64	42	5	128
Zone 3	25	3	6	15

All the 61 people mentioned as relatives by those interviewed in Zone 1 lived in the " village ". That confirmed the evidence from other sources which suggested a fair degree of local mobility, a steady flow of socially aspiring residents from Zone 2 into Zone 1. It helped to explain why so many close links could be observed between residents of a working-class neighbourhood and of a middle-class neighbourhood and why residents of both made common cause against those of another working-class neighbourhood. Forty-two of the 64 people interviewed in their houses in the " village " had 123 relatives in Zones 1 and 2 and only 5 relatives in Zone 3. By contrast, of the 25 people interviewed in their houses on the Estate only 9 had relatives in Winston Parva and only 3 of these had relatives who lived in the " village ".

The relative lack of local kinship ties contributed to the isolation of families on the Estate. It added to the problems of living there. The case of working women with small children has already been mentioned ; they had great difficulties in finding someone to look after their children while they were away. Several of them mentioned this problem during the interviews and asked if the research result might help to show the need for a day nursery in the neighbourhood. No problem of this kind was mentioned in interviews in the "village".

Migratory mobility, the type of social mobility which had thrown together on the Estate many relatively small family units who were strangers to each other created specific problems in almost every department of life. Asked about relations with neighbours quite a number of Estate families said " they were keeping themselves to themselves ", or used similar expressions. To some extent this tendency was due to the fact that unlike the " old families " of the " village " the " new families " of the Estate did not know what to expect of each other. The different local traditions which they carried with them on their migrations as part of their personal make-up created misunderstandings. To keep oneself to oneself was in part an attitude of self-protection against people who, although neighbours, had customs, standards and manners which were different from one's own, which, often enough, appeared foreign and aroused suspicion ; and there were neither social opportunities nor common traditions which could have helped to set in motion the rituals of mutual exploration which were a necessary prelude to closer neighbourhood relations. Perhaps their table manners were different and offended others' sensibilities. Perhaps they spoke with a different accent and a louder voice. Perhaps they came to ask for help without the right formulas, or borrowed things without bringing them back. Unifying norms of give and take more firmly established in older communities had not yet had time to grow among these newcomers. There was a lack of common customs of co-operation and of common rituals of social intercourse generally which in older communities served as lubricants of human relations. " When my washing blew down in her garden ", said a housewife on the Estate, "she didn't come and help. She just stood watching."

There were no people, community officers, clergymen, doctors or whatever their profession, who by training or good sense understood the sociological problems presented by such a community, who had authority enough and inspired enough confidence to help break down the walls of isolation and suspicion among people who though neighbours were strangers to each other and to build up institutional aids towards better integration. As is usual at the present stage of public thinking in such cases, one thought it enough to offer newcomers houses and employment. The rest of their problems, among them the whole of their leisure-time problems, were regarded as purely personal problems of minor importance. They were not yet perceived as sociological problems which arose from the specific nature of the community—of the configuration of individuals, not from that of the individuals who formed it. All local associations including church organisations were centred on Zone 2. All leading positions in the community were in the hands of people from the other two zones. And as families on the Estate could not rely for their social life on extensive kinship groups, the prospect for a satisfactory manner of living was for them not very bright.

It is not surprising that the majority of people interviewed in Zone 3, as Table VIII shows, said they did not like their neighbourhood or were indifferent, while the majority of people interviewed in Zone 2 said they liked their neighbourhood.

TABLE VIII

Attitudes towards their own Neighbourhood in the three Zones.

	People who said :					
	they liked their neighbourhood		they did not like their neighbourhood		it was not a bad neighbourhood	
Zone	No.	%	No.	%	No.	%
1	12	—	—	—	—	—
2	44	69	5	8	15	23
3	3	12	8	32	14	56

As the numbers were small one need not attach particular significance to the percentages as such, but other contacts and observations made during the years of work in Winston Parva confirmed the picture of these differences in the attitudes towards their neighbourhood in the three zones. Even people interviewed in Zone 3 who described the Estate as " not bad " usually mentioned several disagreeable aspects of life there before summing up their opinion in phrases like " We keep ourselves to ourselves " and " It's not bad really ". They tried to make the best of it but indicated at least by implication that they did not think very highly of their own part of Winston Parva. While many " villagers " were very proud of their neighbourhood, there was a complete absence of pride in their neighbourhood among the residents on the Estate.

The settlers on the Estate might have encountered considerable communal problems had they formed a community of their own. The fact that they became part of an older community greatly increased the difficulties of their situation. The wholesale rejection of the Estate people by the older, the established residents of Winston Parva who could have served as an integrating force made things worse. The difficulties started as soon as the immigrants arrived. A former Londoner remembered in the interview how he went at that time into one of the two " village " pubs, ordered his drink and moved over to a table to be "matey" with the people sitting round and was told, " This place is being saved for a friend ". And the fact that they were treated by the " villagers " as outsiders, as a lower status group, made it even more difficult for the newcomers to take an interest in their new community and to break down the barriers of their initial isolation. Another resident said he had visited "The Eagle " once or twice, but had been " cold-shouldered " and could speak to no-one as everyone else was " in groups and little bunches ". Other informants from the Estate told the same story. They had found the attitude of other guests in the pub unfriendly and had been " frozen out ". At the time of the research separation was almost complete. One of the two public houses, " The Eagle ", was almost exclusively frequented by " villagers ", the other, "The Hare and Hounds ", by people from the Estate.

When asked which public house the residents in the neighbourhood visited 50 of the 64 " villagers " interviewed in their houses mentioned " The Eagle ", 2 " The Hare and Hounds ". Of the 25 people from the Estate one mentioned " The Eagle ' and 19 " The Hare and Hounds ".

Slightly less strict though noticeable enough was the segregation in the case of the Working Men's Club. Although it had its premises on the main street of the " village ", men and women from the Estate formed the bulk of its members. Its weekend concerts, games of " bingo " and club outings attracted people whose own neighbourhood offered few opportunities for after work enjoyment. Some informants from Zone 3 said that having been " frozen out " of " The Eagle " they did not wish to take their wives into the bad atmosphere of " The Hare and Hounds." However, the Working Men's Club lacked the close familiarity which distinguished the clubs and associations formed by " villagers ". All three zones were represented on the committee but none of the members interviewed could name more than two members of the committee and those they named were always residents of Zone 3. Within this loose association, it must be noted, were some members from the " village " who enjoyed the Club because they claimed, " The games were better ", " The drinks were cheaper " or because " The wife enjoys it more than going to ' The Eagle ' ". The Working Men's Club, therefore, offered opportunities for families from the " village " and the Estate to come into closer contact after work and, perhaps, to form some kind of friendship with each other. But no such relationships were formed. Some members of the Club who lived on the Estate said that they met a few people from " the older part " at the Club and played occasionally dominoes or cards with them, but further questions always revealed that the acquaintance was limited to occasional meetings within the Club and never led to any other contacts. Although it was not possible to find out the exact number of Club members from each zone, " villagers " formed a small minority. While 14 of the 25 residents of Zone 3 interviewed in their houses said they were members of the Working Men's Club, only 3 of 64 people interviewed in Zone 2 admitted membership and many made scathing comments about the " din " and the " rough types " which the Club attracted. One man in Zone 1 admitted that he was a member, but he pointed out, somewhat apologetically, that he had agreed to accept the invitation to a place on the Club committee in connection with his business interests.

Part of this attitude was undoubtedly due to the fact that among the people who initially settled on the Estate were a considerable number of " rough types ". And although the rougher type of working-class people, at the time of the research, no longer formed more than a relatively small minority of the residents of the Estate, the memory lingered on. The first immigrants to the Estate were, above all, concerned with their own economic survival. The next had been uprooted by bombing from their homes and transplanted to the Estate by wartime necessity. At that time conditions had been rather grim :

" It is not so bad as it used to be ", said an older resident from the Estate. " Every house used to be taken on a Tuesday and by the following Friday they'd be gone again to avoid paying the rent. Sometimes, though, the landlord used to catch them and take their furniture. Then he would hold a sale in the house until the rent was raised."

Since then conditions had been greatly improved. Whatever else may be needed in order to allow a medley of workers uprooted among the eddies and gullies of war, economic dislocation, unemployment and, often enough, sheer poverty, to form with each other a reasonably settled community, it also needs time. The " villagers " proud of their own respectability and anxious to preserve the standards of decency in their own neighbourhood had been shocked by the rougher kind of people who settled at their doorsteps. They had formed their picture of the Estate people on the basis of these experiences. The fact that some of the " rougher types " continued to live on the Estate seemed to confirm again and again the picture of the Estate people which they had formed. The fact that the majority of the Estate residents no longer belonged to this " rougher type " of working-class people, that they were, by and large, no less decent and well behaved than they themselves,

77

could not prevail against the firm communal stereotype of Estate people which the " villagers " had formed and which was handed on from one generation to the other. They closed their ranks against the " whole lot ". Thus the people on the Estate were from the start excluded from the strongest integrating force in their neighbourhood. If one stayed for a while in Winston Parva one could not fail to notice that the " villagers " used with reference to the Estate certain standard phrases over and over again. It was part of their tradition. This was the kind of thing they said :

HOUSEWIFE : " They just haven't got the same standards."

HOUSEWIFE : " They have no control over their children."

HOUSEWIFE : " They're always fighting over there."

HOUSEWIFE : " That place—it's not like the village."

HOUSEWIFE : " They've got low morals."

HOUSEWIFE : " People round here don't fight and pull up the fences."

RETIRED MECHANIC : " They're refugees, a lot of boozers, that's what."

RAILWAYMAN : " People from the East End and used to nothing better."

LABOURER : " They are as different as chalk and cheese."

FOREMAN : " Let's face it, they're a different class of people."

SHOPKEEPER : " Slum clearance—Irish—Cockney, I don't know what."

From early days on the inhabitants of the Estate were stigmatised, in the public opinion of the " village ", as an inferior brand of people. And however conditions had changed the rejection and exclusion of Estate people remained an integral part of the " villagers' " image of Winston Parva and of themselves. It put the seal on their own superiority as members of the " old ", the " decent " part of Winston Parva. For the members of an immigrant community from different parts of the country this attitude of the " villagers " made it even more difficult than it already was to break down the barriers which existed between themselves as strangers and to develop some community life in their own neighbourhood. Closely connected with their lack of unity was the inability of the newcomers to assert themselves in relation to the older residents and to fight back. Instead, most of the Estate people seemed to accept, however grudgingly, the lower status allotted to them by the established groups. Although almost all inhabitants of the Estate were British, many regarded each other as foreigners. This was the kind of thing Estate people themselves said about their own neighbourhood :

> MECHANIC : " They're some rum ones down here. All sorts of foreigners, so I take no notice."
> HOSIERY WORKER : " They call us ' rat alley '."
> A YOUNG HOUSEWIFE : " I don't like it. I'am saving up to get away."
> A YOUNG HOUSEWIFE : " When I told the girls at work where I live, they gave me a queer look and said, ' Oh, down there '."
> A YOUNG HOUSEWIFE : " We'd like to move before the baby comes because we don't want it to grow up with the kids that do all the swearing round here."
> PRINTER : " It's the Cockneys, 50 per cent of the people on the Estate, and they cause all the trouble."

It may happen that residents of an area rank their Town neighbourhood as equal in social standing to that of a neighbouring district who regard it as inferior. But in the case of Zone 3 the ranking as a neighbourhood with a lower social standing was not confined to the inhabitants of Zone 1 and Zone 2. It was shared, by and large, by the inhabitants of Zone 3 themselves. They had a clear awareness that they, as Estate people, were set apart from the people in the " village ". A common way of expressing this awareness was the use, even among themselves, of derogatory terms commonly used in " village " gossip with reference to the Estate. All the people interviewed in their houses on the Estate mentioned the name " rat alley " as a generally accepted term for their own part of Winston Parva. A lorry driver said that bus conductors had been requested by their company officials not to call out " rat alley " at the bus stop at the corner of the Estate. Young people on the Estate showed strong feelings about the slur cast on their neighbourhood : " Have you heard what they call us over there ?" asked a 17-year-old girl, " rat alley ! The girls walk by with their noses in the air." Many of the Estate people behaved as if they secretly thought of one another : " You can't be much to shout about if you live here." There seemed to be little incentive for making or for keeping regular contact with one's neighbours. Young people often said outright that they planned to leave the Estate as soon as they could. Some of the older people mentioned sons and daughters who had married and left in order to live in a " nice house elsewhere ". While in the " village " a number of young women said they " liked to stay near their mum ", thus contributing to the growth of a network of old family networks, the uncomfortable feeling that the Estate was not a nice neighbourhood tended to drive many young people away. In that sense the specific configuration of the Estate as a loose community of immigrants and outsiders was self-perpetuating. People with any desire to get on who resented the slur cast on them because their place of residence was given a bad name in the neighbourhood tended to move out as soon as they possibly could thus making room for other immigrants some of whom probably went through the same cycle. Thus a housing estate which started as a centre for immigrants in a community with old established residents tended to retain characteristics of an immigrant community in spite of a sediment of families who stayed on. The dynamics of the Estate itself made it difficult to cast off the slur. Many residents clearly resented the air of superiority which people in Zone 2 assumed towards them. But what they said, and the manner in which they said it, indicated their resignation and helplessness. This was the kind of thing Estate people said about the " villagers " :

HOUSEWIFE : " They're snobby and snooty."
ENGINEER (London evacuee) : " They don't care for us and never have."
ENGINEER (London evacuee) : " Too smug, they've never tried to understand us."
LABOURER (Yorkshireman) : " Too damned stuck-up."
HOUSEWIFE : " A better class than round here, especially by the Church there."
EX-SERVICE MAN : " They're proud of their little place."
HOSIERY MECHANIC : " The old type, they call it the village and they freeze you out."

If one remembers that the proportions of people with the same occupational status and the same income levels were not very different in the two zones, the problem presented by the sharp distinction in their local ranking stands out more clearly. Their different position in the development of Winston Parva, the " newness " of the one, the " oldness " of the other zone, the lack of cohesion in the first, the high degree of cohesion in the second place, they all played a part in these status differences. In the case of the Estate people the awareness of the lower status attributed to them by the older residents did not increase their feeling of solidarity or induce any measures to foster it.

If one had listened to the views of the " villagers " about the Estate one might have expected to find there uniformly low standards of behaviour and cleanliness. In actual fact one could visit a good number of people on the Estate in their houses and find that neither the standards of cleanliness nor those of conduct were noticeably different from those of the people in Zone 2. Rooms were slightly smaller and rents a little lower than those of the terraced houses in the " village ". But the image of the " village " suggested that the Estate was a kind of slum inhabited by uncouth people who lived with hordes of uncontrollable children noisily in neglected houses. What one actually found there, the " reality ", differed considerably from this image. It took some time to determine clearly in what way and why the " village " image of the Estate distorted the facts. And as the research proceeded it became increasingly clear that such discrepancies between image and reality were of considerable significance for the understanding of the relationship between the older parts and the new part of Winston Parva. As so often, the image was a highly simplified presentation of the social realities. It created a black and white design which left no room for the diversities to be found among the Estate people. It corresponded to the " minority of the worst ". When one had visited a number of families on the Estate whose standards and manner of life differed little from those of the " villagers ", one might after a while come across a house whose inhabitants were exactly the kind of people which the " villagers " regarded as typical of Estate residents generally. They were of a rougher type ;

their houses were uncared for and much dirtier than any of the houses seen in the " village " and most of the houses seen on the Estate. The problem was how and why the behaviour of a minority came to dominate the image which the " villagers " had formed of the Estate community. The presence of this minority certainly made it more difficult for Estate people to defend their neighbourhood. " Villagers " could always shame them into acquiescence by pointing to one or the other activities of this minority as proof for the truthfulness of their image. Probably the poorest house encountered during the whole research was a labourer's house on the Estate. His wife, one was told, drank a lot and " worked in a pub ". If one looked further one found people who believed her to be promiscuous. There were two sons, aged 21 and 18, both working as labourers. The younger had attended a local secondary modern school, but he was already then quite notorious in the neighbourhood. At the time of the interview he was on probation and was later sent to prison. Two windows of the house were broken, the curtains at the bedroom windows had obviously not been washed for a considerable time, and the gate at the side of the house had been kicked so often that only the jagged upper half remained. There were only two chairs in the living room and kitchen, an armchair and a broken chair by the fireplace. The table was covered with unwashed pots and the remains of the evening meal. Although the room was lit by electricity, a gas fitting still hung from the ceiling and supported a long fly-paper covered with dead flies while the mother lashed out at more flies with an old newspaper. Over the fireplace was a cracked mirror ; round it the pictures of film-stars had been glued to the wall. Another rather neglected house was that of a man who had come to Winston Parva from another part of the Midlands. While on war service he had married an Italian girl. They had five children, aged between 5 and 17. The home was in a bad state of repair. The garden was completely uncared for. Neighbours said that the mother had left home several times since 1945 and this was confirmed in conversation with the headmaster of the school which her sons attended. The boys were members of one of the gangs from Zone 3. Their school records showed frequent breaches of school discipline and low educational achievement. The mother took no pride in her house or her family. She probably missed the security of kinship groups in her own country. The home of this family was the scene of an episode publicised by local newspapers as " The Battle of Winston Parva ". It took place one evening in the summer of 1958. The " Battle " was caused by the proposed marriage of the eldest daughter to an Irish labourer lodging nearby. When the young Irishman's father who lived in London heard of the proposal, he and two other sons came to Winston Parva evidently with the intention of preventing the marriage. But before calling on the girl's parents they went to a public house. After they had had a number of drinks they appeared before the girl's home, started shouting and finally forced their way into the house where they met with resistance by the inhabitants. In the course of several fights which ensued the girl was chased into the street by her fiancé, thrown to the ground and kicked for reasons which were not clear. At the same time the fights inside the house continued. Some of the furniture was smashed and windows were broken. The " Battle " was terminated by the arrival of the police and of an ambulance which took the casualties to the hospital. Vivid accounts of this family feud appeared in the newspapers of the nearby town and were illustrated with photographs of the people involved. But while the men were shown with their injuries, the girl was shown in her bathing costume. Commenting on this picture, a girl from a house in the same street was heard to say at the " Open " Youth Club : " She's common, she is ! Mi mum was talkin' to her mum last night and she's already had three letters about the photograph. Did yer see it ? In that bathin' costume ! Yes, three letters. One askin' her to go in for a beauty competition and two askin' her to be a model."

On the list of houses marked for interviews next to that which was the scene of the " Battle of Winston Parva ", one found an ordinary quiet working-class family with a fairly high level of aspiration, a good deal of foresight, and, as far as one could see, a relatively settled and uneventful family life. The parents had moved to the Estate during the war. The husband worked as skilled engineer in a local factory. The elder boy was in the sixth form of a local grammar school. The younger son was still at a junior school. The furniture was well worn and the home untidy. But the parents spoke with great pride of their sons and the educational opportunities available to them. They took obviously considerable trouble in encouraging their children to make full use of these opportunities and their level of ambition was high. During the interview the elder boy joined in the discussion and supplemented the parents' comments about the young people in Winston Parva. They said there were " nice people " on the Estate ; all the trouble, according to them, was caused by " the Cockney families ". The family referred to the poor amenities of Winston Parva. They especially mentioned the lack of recreational facilities and the husband suggested that a community centre would solve some of the problems for both the Estate and the " village ". Like many other people on the Estate, however, they found it best, as they said, not " to neighbour ", but to " keep themselves to themselves ".

Families who lived a relatively quiet and not very conspicuous life formed the majority.[1]   But the minority, parents and children, loomed much larger in the general picture of the community. As far as one could see, it did not consist of

---

[1] This majority-minority configuration is probably characteristic of many working-class estates. The following letter to the Editor appeared in a local newspaper with reference to another estate :—

ESTATE'S BAD NAME UNDESERVED.

" Decent folks as well as layabouts at B . . . "

There is a general impression in M., and apparently the B . . . parson was told about it before he went there, that all the worst crimes are hatched out at the B . . . estate. This is totally untrue. We have here as in all districts a minority who are petty thieves, layabouts and suchlike characters, but the majority of folk on this Estate are hardworking, decent, honest and respectable people who take pride in their homes, people who keep their children clean, tidy and honest, who bring their daughters up to be nice, respectable girls and not, as some folks think, immoral little tarts.

Oh, we have our share of wrong uns, but only our share, . . . Why do people judge an area by the few ? Why don't they use their common sense and judge us by the majority of folk and get their view in the right perspective and not make such misleading sweeping statements.

" One of the decent ones ".

September 1963

families which were poorer in terms of the income of the breadwinners. Their common characteristic was rather an inability to keep themselves and their affairs in order. Most of them had large families. Some were unable to keep their financial affairs in order. Most of them could not keep their children or their home in order. Personality weaknesses rather than economic distress appeared to be at the root of the trouble. They were essentially disordered families. In 1959 about 8 or 9 of them lived on the Estate. Their younger children formed the gangs of rowdy, poorly dressed youngsters whom one met roaming the streets of Winston Parva. During interviews in other houses one often enough saw or heard of youngsters who did their homework, listened to their record players or helped their mothers with the ironing. In the streets one saw, and particularly the " villagers " saw, mostly children from the small number of large problem families whom inadequate space at home and inadequate youth club facilities drove into the streets, who roamed around the " village " in the evening, visited the local cinema and often gathered in front of it night by night or who went, as one of them put it, " and hang around the park 'til we get shut out ".

The minority character of these problem families was brought out by a relatively small change of conditions which had the characteristics of an experiment *in vivo* once one had come to regard the role and nature of a minority in a communal setting as a significant question. While the research was in progress, the rents on the Estate were slightly raised. In connection with this rise in rents, as one will see, the 8 or 9 large problem families left the Estate although in most cases not because they could not afford to stay, but because they could get for the higher price better accommodation in council houses elsewhere. With their disappearance many of the disagreeable features attributed by the " village " to the Estate people as a whole faded from the picture. It would have required a prolongation of the research beyond its allotted time to investigate the long-term effects of this " experiment " on the relationship between the two neighbourhoods and especially on the traditional image which the established residents had formed of the outsiders. One of these effects which was accessible during the period of research, will be discussed more fully in connection with the incidence of delinquency.

But even as it was, the experience brought into focus a wider problem—the problem of the role of minority groups in a community, their role for the communal life itself as well as for the image which neighbours, or the inhabitants themselves, formed of a neighbourhood. As has been shown, a working-class minority in the residential middle-class area of Zone 1 had no significance at all for the social standing of Zone 1 in the eyes of its own middle-class residents or in that of their neighbours in other zones. The middle-class minority in the old working-class area of Zone 2 tended to enhance and to reinforce the relatively high ranking and the superiority which the inhabitants attributed to themselves in relation to more recent immigrants. A small minority of notorious families in the new working-class area, in Zone 3, tended to cast a shadow over the whole neighbourhood. It greatly disturbed the life of its inhabitants ; it depressed their self-esteem and their pride in their own neighbourhood and perpetuated their low standing in the eyes of the other residents of Winston Parva.

The tacit assumption, often implied in sociological studies, that greater numbers go naturally hand in hand with greater significance is not always born out by the evidence. Minority groups can have a sociological significance far surpassing their quantitative significance. One can say clearly why in the case of the Estate a minority of " notorious " families had an impact quite out of proportion to its numbers on the life and the image of a neighbourhood whose majority were ordinary respectable working-class families.

Had families of the same type settled in Zone 2 they would have come up against the solid power of a closely-knit community. They would have been subjected to all the pressures which such a community could exercise and, indeed, did exercise on deviants. They would have been cold-shouldered, ridiculed, slandered and humiliated by a constant stream of whispered or open remarks wherever they showed themselves. They would have been exposed to the full strength of the rejecting gossip which is one of the major weapons, and one of the pleasures, of a closely-knit community ; and if necessary they would have been brought to court. Their lives, in short, would have been made thoroughly uncomfortable until they either resigned themselves to the existence of disregarded outsiders or moved elsewhere. A loosely-knit neighbourhood of working-class families such as the Estate had no such weapons. A mass of neighbours who tended to withdraw, who denied themselves the pleasures of " neighbouring " and " kept themselves to themselves "—a neighbourhood without centre, without leadership, with little solidarity and cohesion was unable to bring any effective pressure to bear upon its deviant minority. They had no redress against the noise, the rudeness and the damage inflicted on them until they became a police matter ; and in accordance with the usual ding-dong of such a situation, by withdrawing into their shell, by trying to keep " themselves to themselves " in order to avoid close contacts with people they disliked, they made it less possible for themselves to close their ranks, to put pressure on the unruly minority and to exercise some control over them. The lack of cohesion, the relative isolation of families on the Estate made them powerless to stop unpleasant scenes. They felt helpless and resigned themselves to their fate while at the same time suffering under the low reputation of their neighbourhood and the rude behaviour of neighbours.

One of the interviews in Zone 3 was interupted by shouting from the house next door which became louder and louder. The couple which was interviewed at first tried to conceal the noise by talking louder. Then they began to look embarrassed. Finally, the conversation was interupted by a shriek from the woman next door : " It *is* my bloody business ", she cried, and there followed even louder bangs and the crying of children. The couple interviewed then explained that the people next door had been recently " in court " for fighting in the street while drunk. Another person interviewed in Zone 3 told how a friend had visited him one evening and parked his new car outside. When leaving the house, the friend discovered deep scratches along the side of his car. He questioned the children playing nearby and was told that the youngsters of the Cameron family had done the damage. When he went to see the family the mother after listening to the motorist's complaints said : " Well, what do you expect me to do about it ? You shouldn't leave the bloody thing there." Several people interviewed on the Estate said they felt sorry for youngsters who " got into trouble " and blamed the parents for neglecting their children. Again and again examples were given of parents who went out " drinking every night " and left the children to look after themselves. If one enquired more closely one found that the observation referred to the same cluster of 8 or 9 families.

However, although both " village " and Estate people had a fairly negative image of the Estate community, in one respect their images differed markedly. The residents of Zone 3 were to some extent aware of the fact that the bad reputation of their zone and its most unpleasant aspects were largely due to a minority, to a special group of families. The inhabitants of Zone 2 almost invariably spoke of the " bad family life " and the " low behaviour " in Zone 3 generally. They did not perceive the distinction between the majority of ordinary people whose manner of life and whose behaviour differed not very markedly from their own and the minority of disordered families whose deviant behaviour attracted all the attention. A characteristic statement made by a woman from Zone 2 was that " most of the residents on the Estate are foreigners and criminals ", the two being synonymous.

7 | Observations on Gossip

ONE of the gains of such a fairly intensive enquiry into a community divided against itself was a better insight into the nature and function of gossip. The " village " gossip about the Estate, as one saw, was based on a set belief about the Estate people which acted as a selecting agency : incidents on the Estate which did not fit the predetermined belief were of little interest to the " villagers ; " one hardly thought it worth one's while to feed them into the gossip mills. Incidents which corresponded to the set image of the Estate were taken up with gusto and kept the gossip mills going for a while until they got stale and were replaced by fresh gossip items.

Gossip, in other words, is not an independent phenomenon. What is gossip-worthy depends on communal norms and beliefs and communal relationships. The negative image of the Estate which made the " villagers " perceive as a welcome piece of gossip every incident which could serve as a confirmation was the reverse of the positive image which the " village " people had of themselves. Common usage makes us inclined to regard as " gossip " mainly more or less derogatory information about third persons communicated by two or more persons to each other. But structurally blame gossip is inseparable from praise gossip which is usually confined to oneself or to groups with which one identifies oneself. A comparison of the " village " gossip with whatever gossip there was among the Estate people showed very clearly how closely the structure of gossip is bound up with that of the community whose members are the gossipers. A closely-knit community such as the " village " required a healthy flow of gossip to keep the wheels turning. It had an elaborate system of gossip centres. After church and chapel, at clubs and at the pub, at plays and concert parties one could see and hear the gossip mills work-

89

ing. One could observe how the relatively high organisational level of the " village " facilitated the flow of gossip from mouth to mouth and made it possible for interesting items to spread through the community with considerable speed.

Every piece of news concerning people who were communally known formed tit-bits of gossip. In the " village " it happened several times that the interviewer was recognised when he entered a house before the introduction was completed as " the man who called at Mrs. Smith's the other night " or who had " visited the Old People's Club on Wednesday afternoon ". No similar incident happened on the Estate. The more closely-knit community had more ready-made channels through which news of public interest could flow and it had more interests which people shared. Whether a news item concerned strangers who came to the " village " or members of the " village " themselves it became soon public knowledge. Affairs of local families, often including personal details, were frequently discussed as a matter of course during interviews no less than at association meetings. Estate families, by comparison, spoke far less often of what happened in other families. A " village " resident, a prominent member of a church drama group, listed friends of hers who belonged to the group, during an interview. One well-known actress was omitted from the list and the interviewer mentioned the omission. " Didn't you know ! " was the surprised reply, " They're expecting a baby at Christmas so she is not taking part this time." At this stage the interviewer was already expected in the " village " to be fully included in the gossip circuits even though in fact he was not yet quite up to date. Most people in the " village " and by no means only members of the same kin group had known each other for a long time. An elderly lady recalled how she used to play with " Harry " 50 years ago, " when he chased me round the greens." In 1959 both were keen members of the Old People's Club. Long acquaintance, too, in a setting like that of the " village " deepened the common interest in everything that happened to members of the in-group and facilitated the flow of news. One knew where one stood with each other. There were few barriers to communications.

News about each other, about all publicly-known people made life interesting. Thus apart from blame-gossip mainly concerned with outsiders and from praise-gossip gaining kudos for oneself and one's group, the gossip stream contained simple in-group gossip, news items about friends and acquaintances which were of interest for their own sake.

In all its various forms gossip had considerable entertainment value. Had the gossip mills ever run dry in the " village " life would have lost much of its spice. The essential part of it was not simply that one took an interest in people, but that it was a shared interest. The people who provided gossip news were people about whom one could talk with others. In that respect, too, the differences in the structure of " village " and Estate helped to illuminate the nature of gossip. The " village " people appeared to have a much wider circle of common acquaintances about whom they could gossip than the Estate people. They always had at their disposal entertaining news items which they knew would be of interest to others. And the manner in which they talked about their common acquaintances was often hardly different from that in which they talked about film stars, royalty or, for that matter, about any person whose private affairs were " in the news ", who were known from newspapers, particularly from the popular Sunday newspapers which they all read. The " village ", as said before, was largely self-sufficient with regard to the after-work entertainment of its inhabitants. While entertaining gossip about its own members or those of the other zones of Winston Parva were constantly fed into the gossip channels, newspaper stories provided a good additional source of gossip, and the manner in which news from this or from that source were discussed was very much the same. They all were " personal interest stories ". If one heard someone tell the story of a play or a film to an acquaintance who had been unable to see it, it sounded exactly as if one heard them tell a story about neighbours in the " village " or people from the Estate. It had all the characteristics of a gossip story. The tone of voice and the vocabulary were the same, so was the simplification of characters and motives, the setting of highlights in terms of black and white and, of course, the underlying norms and beliefs. Particularly the women seemed to experience whatever they learned from communications about the outer world in terms of their own neighbourhood. In most cases the entertainment value of gossip items appeared to be bound up with ingredients which flattered the ego either of the teller or of the recipients or of both. That did not mean they always cast blame on others or had undertones of malice. There was no lack of compassion in the gossip of the " villagers " or of sympathy with the misfortunes of others.

The way they told the story of Mrs. Crouch was an example. She was widowed in the First World War and was left with three small daughters when she was still rather young. She went to work to keep her children and nursed one of her daughters through a serious illness. She joined an ex-service association to help with the welfare of other widows. A large photograph of her husband in uniform hung in her living-room. As the children grew up Mrs. Crouch joined several other associations. At club meetings, in casual conversations among neighbours people would refer to her story and to herself with great affection. They mentioned " dear Mrs. Crouch " or " nice old Mrs. Crouch " as a respected member of the " village ". Her activities for and in the community after the loss of her husband had obviously given her life new impetus and a purpose, and the " village " appreciated her loyalty to the dead husband, to the community and the accepted norms. In praising Mrs. Crouch they praised at the same time the decent, respectable life they led in their own neighbourhood in contrast to others one knew. The satisfaction they felt was that of people at one with their own community and their own conscience. Praise-gossip undoubtedly gave Mrs. Crouch considerable support, first in her early difficulties and now in her old age. In her case, as in others encountered during the research, a family unit in its difficulties and misfortunes derived great benefit from the support of the community. Supporting gossip was one of the vehicles for mobilising communal help. The word was passed in the streets, the clubs, the churches and through other gossip channels to shopkeepers and factory management that Mrs. X or Mr. Y was " having a hard struggle just now and deserved help ". The Benevolent Committee, as one has seen, both in giving and in refusing help, made use of gossip channels : "We keep our ears open," said a member, "and we ask shopkeepers to watch for any real case of hardship, especially among the old people, and then, when the names are passed on to us, we go along and investigate."

However, while supporting and praise-gossip played their part in the stream of gossip which never stopped running through the gossip channels in the "village", they were mixed with, and often inseparable from, gossip items with the opposite emotional colour, with rejecting and blame-gossip. On a rough estimate the latter seemed to play a much larger part as ingredients of the gossip stream than the former. One had the impression that news items about some breach of the accepted norms committed by communally known persons were savoured much more, that they provided more entertainment and more pleasurable satisfaction for tellers and recipients alike, than gossip about someone who deserved praise for upholding the accepted standards or support in his or her need. Although the latter, by proxy, also flattered the ego of the gossip carriers—our "nice old Mrs. Crouch" often had patronising undertones—the former, apparently flattered the gossip carriers' egos more strongly and pleasurably. Blame-gossip appealed more directly to the gossipers' sense of their own righteousness. But it also provided the pleasure of being able to talk with others about things which were forbidden, which one should not do. And the talk often sounded as if it tickled the imagination of the gossipers to think for a moment that they themselves had done what one should not do— "think of that ! "—had felt the shadow of the fear and the guilt they would have experienced had they done so, and had quickly come back to themselves gleeful and relieved with the feeling : "But it wasn't me ! " That one gossiped about it with others was proof of one's own blamelessness. It reinforced the community of the righteous. The group blame meted out to those who had broken the rules had a strong integrating function. But it did not stand on its own. It kept alive and re-inforced already existing group links.

In fact, it is hardly more than a half-truth if one stresses, as has sometimes been done, the integrating function of gossip. The facts, as this enquiry showed, are more complex even though basically the structure of gossip, the configuration of its functions in a community are simple enough. That gossip cannot be treated as an independent agent, that its structure depends on that of the community whose members gossip with each other, has already been said. Gossip played a different part and had a different character in the two working-class neighbourhoods of Winston Parva. In the closely-knit neighbourhood of the " village " gossip flowed freely and richly through the gossip channels provided by the differentiated network of families and associations. In the loosely-knit and less highly organised neighbourhood of the Estate the flow of gossip was on the whole more sluggish. Gossip circuits were shorter and often not linked to each other. Even neighbouring families quite often had no or only slender gossip links. There were more barriers to gossip communications.

Even within the " village " itself gossip had by no means only the function of supporting people of whom the ruling " village " opinion approved and of cementing relations between the inhabitants. It also had the function of excluding people and of cutting relations. It could serve as a highly effective instrument of rejection. If, for instance, a new resident in the " village " was felt to be " not quite nice ", stories about breaches of norms, often in a highly coloured form, were passed through the gossip channels as the case of the woman showed who had offered the dustmen a cup of tea one cold winter day. And the merciless hardness with which this formidable weapon was used communally by people many of whom seemed individually well-meaning and kind-hearted was not uncharacteristic of the peculiar effect which the working of the gossip mills and constant exchanges of news and views in closely-knit communities generally seems to have on communal opinions and beliefs.

One of the determinants of gossip is usually the degree of competition between the gossipers for the ear and the attention of their fellows which in turn depends on the competitive pressure, particularly the pressure of status rivalries, within such a group. One is more likely to get both attention and approval if one can outbid one's fellow gossipers, if one can tell, for example, when gossiping about outsiders something even more unfavourable, even more scandalous and outrageous than they, or can show, in other cases, that one is even more loyal than they in one's adherence to the group's common creed and more radical in one's assertion of the beliefs which strengthen the group pride. The distorting effect which the dynamics of competition within closely-knit groups have on group beliefs in general and on gossip items in particular is an aberration veering towards the most favourable, most flattering belief about one's own group and towards the most unfavourable, most unflattering belief about non-submissive outsiders with a tendency towards increasing rigidity in both cases. By and large one can say that the more secure the members of a group feel in their superiority and their pride, the less great is the distortion, the gap between image and reality likely to be, and the more threatened and insecure they feel, the more likely is it that internal pressure, and as part of it internal competition, will drive common beliefs towards extremes of illusion and doctrinaire rigidity.[1] In fact, one can often use the degree of distortion and rigidity of group beliefs as a yardstick if not for the actual danger at least for the felt danger of a group, and in that sense as a help in reconstructing its situation. The " villagers " though well entrenched and powerful in relation to the newcomers which settled on the Estate certainly felt that the new neighbours threatened their established way of life. They may even have sensed that they were the harbingers of new waves of urbanisation and industrialisation which threatened the old part of Winston Parva and its way of life at its very roots. The " villagers "

---

[1] One may well ask whether the position of a society in the long-term development of mankind does not also have something to do with the relative nearness or remoteness, congruity and incongruity of beliefs and observable facts. Seen all round, distance and incongruity seem to be greater, particularly in the case of beliefs about " nature ", in simpler than in more differentiated societies. But that is just the point. Simpler societies are also far more threatened and insecure because, partly as the result of such incongruities, they have less control over " nature ", over themselves and each other. And because they have less control, again, they are generally more insecure. In fact, this is one of the most fundamental of the human traps.

and above all the old families' network reacted to the threat with a strong emphasis on the old " village spirit " and a high degree of intolerance towards neighbours who did not conform.

" Village " gossip was patterned accordingly. Its intolerance, its function as a barrier to integration, strong enough in relation to nonconforming people within the " village ", were even more pronounced in relation to the Estate people, to the non-conformers without, although in the latter case they were less effectual as means of social control. The inability of most " villagers " to perceive that anything good might come from the Estate has already been mentioned. The catchwords used for Estate people, the stories told about them were all tilted so as to underline the exclusive superiority of one's own conduct, values and way of life and the total inferiority of those of the Estate people. One could not doubt that all that was done innocently and in good faith ; it had not the character of deliberate fabrication and propaganda. The ability of the " villagers " as a close group, by a mutual reinforcement of desirable views and a steady competition for approval, to shut out from their perception what they did not want to see about themselves and their neighbours and to accentuate sharply what they wanted to see was enough to explain the distortion. It was significant that after 20 years the older " village " people still underlined the social distance between themselves and Zone 3 people by calling them " evacuees ", " refugees " and " cockneys ". A church leader, member of a three-generation " village " family, summed up this kind of view by saying : " They're not like the village people. A few join in the village life, but it is only a few. I don't know what it is, but they are a cosmopolitan lot the other side of the railway." One can feel the genuine bafflement of the " villagers " that these new neighbours did not live up to their own, to the " village " standards which they implicitly assumed were the standards of all decent Englishmen. One can see once more the inability of the close group to see the other side and the paradoxical demands which followed from their innocent self-centredness : they rejected the other group as cosmopolitan outsiders and prevented them by their blame gossip from joining their own community life. They also blamed them for

96

not joining their community life. Children in the " village " heard the recurrent blame stories about the Estate from their parents and on their part took home from school any story about Estate children which was likely to confirm the belief in their inferiority. Thus during an interview with a " village " family, the topic of education and its importance to the younger generation was raised by the parents while their daughter aged 13 was present in the same room. The mother said that the benefit of a good education was wasted on some people and gave as an example " the woman from the Estate at the parents' evening last week. The headmistress was saying how nice the school uniform looked and this woman got up and said she " couldn't afford it as her husband was in jail ". The father gave a disgusted snort and the daughter laughed. The mother went on to say that it " was people like that from the Estate who spoilt Winston Parva ".

The understandable annoyance of people who did their very best to live up to their communal standards of decency and respectability with a minority of newcomers who did not live up to them crystallised into a tradition of wholesale condemnation of the neighbourhood on the other side of the railway line. Children learned the summary rejection of Estate people from their parents and being more outspoken and ruthless in such matters used it as a weapon against Estate children at school. Rejecting gossip and discrimination which at first may have been confined to adults hardened as one generation followed the other because children learned the discriminating attitudes and beliefs early in life. The relative " oldness " of the tradition, the fact that it was handed on from parents to children and again to their children when they grew up strengthened and deepened the effect which their communal character had on rejecting gossip, group prejudice, group discrimination and the beliefs which they embodied ; it increased their rigidity, their axiomatic character and their imperviousness to counter-arguments based on factual evidence.

Communally held beliefs are often impervious to any evidence which contradicts them or to arguments which puts them in the wrong simply because they are shared by many people with whom one is in close communication. Their communal character makes it appear that they must be true particularly if one has been brought up with them from early childhood in a closely knit group where the belief is taken for granted and even more so if one's parents and grandparents too have been brought up with it. In that case the feeling that the belief is true may become almost ineradicable ; it may persist as a strong feeling even if one has come to the conclusion, on a more rational level, that the belief is wrong and has come to reject it.

The belief which expressed itself in the " village " gossip about the Estate had evidently gained its rigidity in a process of this kind. The feelings at its roots had grown and hardened in the course of two or three generations. In the eyes of the " old families " who young and old lived behind the walls of their closely-knit community, they had become axiomatic and self-evident : everyone whom one knew well believed them. To shed, to oppose shared prejudices of this kind which assured and justified the superiority of one's own and the inferiority of another interdependent group and which was supported by the public opinion of one's whole community would have required extraordinary personal courage and strength on the part of a member. It would have meant incurring the disfavour of one's fellow members and risking all the pressures and penalties which closed groups can bring to bear upon non-conforming members. The " village " like every other closely-knit group-ing of men acted as a mutual admiration society. The exaggeration of its own good characteristics and of its neigh-bour's bad characteristics was one of the common symptoms. It accounted for the fact that many people in the " village " who in their role as individuals seemed to be kind-hearted, reasonable and fair, tended to be unkind, malicious, unrelent-ing and uncomprehending in their attitude towards outsiders when they spoke and acted in their role as representatives of their community. In that respect too " village " gossip reflected the structure and situation of the gossiping group. It was symptomatic of an old community with a high degree of cohesion. Although it helped to maintain cohesion and per-haps to reinforce it, it did not create it.

The same was true of the characteristics of gossip on the

Estate. As the Estate was a poorly integrated neighbourhood gossip was diffuse. There was little evidence of gossip as an integrating factor. The " notorious " families on the Estate provided ready topics of conversation for many of the " respectable " families. Their members often exchanged derogatory observations about the " notorious " families and passed on to each other news items of common interest. But they had less in common with each other than the " village " families and the tendency to " keep themselves to themselves " provided barriers for gossip exchanges. One of the recurrent gossip items during the years of research was the noticeable increase in the number of cars standing outside some of the houses in Zone 3. Under different conditions the increase might have helped to raise the prestige of the families concerned and perhaps of the neighbourhood. Instead, one could frequently hear sarcastic remarks about the owners of these cars made by other residents of Zone 3 : " It's the big families who have cars," commented a housewife, " they run them off their family allowances." Another said : " They're all on the H.P., you know. I ought to know. I work for a hire-purchase agency that deals with cars in this district."

But gossip about the " notorious " minority among members of the majority families in Zone 3 could not achieve by itself greater solidarity among the latter. It could not achieve anything which had not been made possible by other more basic factors in the situation. It could not act as an integrating factor in a situation which made most of the " respectable " families on the Estate hesitate to become too intimate with other Estate families. The absence of extensive family networks, of local committees and associations and of suitable buildings as meeting-places in Zone 3 hampered the formation of gossip centres and gossip channels comparable to those which existed in the " village ". The atmosphere of familiarity and often of intimacy based on long acquaintance which facilitated the flow of gossip in the " village " was completely absent on the Estate. There as in the " village " people told each other the most recent stories about drunkenness, violence, promiscuity and squalor at their doorsteps. But they spoke about it with greater reserve and often enough with some embarrassment. They could not gossip about this disorderly behaviour as freely and with the same feeling of superiority as the " villagers ", for it took place in their own neighbourhood ; their own lives and their own standing were far more directly affected by it. What mattered for the standing of a family in this as in other cases was evidently not only who you yourself were, but also who your neighbours were. It mattered for the ranking of others as well as for that of oneself. The low opinion which the " respectable " families on the Estate had of their own neighbourhood helped to prevent them from growing closer together. The fact that they too gossiped with each other did not materially alter the situation. It did not make for closer integration.

Thus the idea that gossip has an integrating function requires some qualification. It imputes to gossip the characteristics of a thing or of a person capable of acting on its own as a causal agent almost independently of the groups of people who gossip. In fact it is only a figure of speech if we say gossip has this or that function. For gossip is simply a class name for something people in groups do. And the term " function ", in this as in similar cases, looks suspiciously like a disguise for the older term " cause ". To ascribe to gossip an integrating function may easily suggest that gossip is the cause of which integration is the effect. One would probably be nearer the mark if one would say that the better integrated group is likely to gossip more freely than the less well-integrated group and that in the former case the gossiping of people reinforces the already existing cohesion.

Pattern and content of gossip vary with the structure and situation of the groups of people who gossip. That is what the comparison between the part played by gossip in the two working-class neighbourhoods of Winston Parva suggests. In the comparatively well-integrated neighbourhood of the " village ", gossip had an integrating function. It had no integrating effect that one could notice in the less well-integrated neighbourhood of the Estate. Without referring a class of group activities such as gossip to the actual group whose members act or produce it, and without explaining the former in terms of the latter the sociological task remains incomplete.

Gossip, however, has always two poles, those who gossip and those about whom they gossip. In cases in which subjects and objects of gossip belong to different groups, the frame of reference is not only the group of gossipers but the situation and structure of both groups and their relationship with each other. Without this wider frame of reference the crucial question why group gossip can ever be, as it was in the case of " village " gossip about Estate people, an effective device for wounding and humiliating members of another group and for ensuring one's ascendency over them, cannot be answered.

A good deal of what " villagers " habitually said about Estate families was vastly exaggerated or untrue. The majority of Estate people did not have " low morals " ; they did not constantly fight with each other, were not habitual " boozers " or unable to control their children. Why were they powerless to correct these misrepresentations ? Why could they be put to shame if a " villager " used in their presence a humiliating code word, symbol of their lower status such as " rat alley " ? Why could they not shrug it off or retaliate with an equally massive flood of insinuations and distortions ?

Some of the organisational explanations have already been mentioned. The " villagers " were more united than Estate people ; in relation to them they closed their ranks, and their unity lent strength and veracity to their statements about the Estate people however out of tune they were in relation to the facts. The Estate people could not retaliate because they had not the power. But in order to see the configuration in depth, one has to include in one's picture in addition to its organisational aspects, such as the monopolisation of key positions by members of the old families' network, also its personal aspects. The majority of the Estate people could not retaliate because, to some extent, their own conscience was on the side of the detractors. They themselves agreed with the " village " people that it was bad not to be able to control one's children or to get drunk and noisy and violent. Even if none of these reproaches could be applied to themselves personally, they knew only too well that they did apply to some of their neighbours. They could be shamed by allusions to this bad behaviour of their neighbours because by living in the same neighbourhood the blame, the bad name attached to it, according to the rules of affective thinking, was automatically applied to them too. In their case, as in so many others, blemishes observable in some members of a group were emotionally transferred to all members of the group. The rejecting gossip of the " village ", all the open or whispered expressions of reproach and contempt levelled against the Estate people had power over them, however decent and orderly they were in their own conduct, because part of themselves, their own conscience agreed with the " villagers' " low opinion of their neighbourhood. It was this silent agreement which paralysed their ability to retaliate and to assert themselves. They could be put to shame if someone called out a derogatory name applied to the group to which they belonged or accused them, directly or indirectly, of misdeeds and bad qualities which, in fact, could be found in their group only among the " minority of the worst ".

The attribution of blame or for that matter of praise to individuals who, individually, have done nothing to deserve it, because they belong to a group which is said to deserve it, is a universal phenomenon. People can often disarm or silence others with whom they disagree or fight by throwing in their teeth some disparaging and vilifying group name or pieces of shameful gossip which refers to their group provided they themselves belong to a group which successfully claims a superior status compared to that of their opponents. In all these cases the objects of the attack are unable to hit back because, though personally innocent of the accusations or reproaches, they cannot discard, not even in their own mind, the identification with the stigmatised group. Vilifications setting in motion the socially inferior group's own sense of shame or guilt feelings with regard to some inferiority symbols, some signs of the worthlessness attributed to them and the paralysis of their power to strike back which goes hand in hand with it, form thus part of the social apparatus with which socially dominant and superior groups maintain their dominion and their superiority over socially inferior groups. Individual members of the inferior group are always supposed to be tarred by the same brush. They cannot escape from the group stigmatisation individually, just as they cannot escape individually from the lower status of their group. One often speaks and thinks today as if individuals in contemporary societies were no longer bound to their groups as tightly as individuals were in former days when they were bound to clans, tribes, castes or estates and were judged and treated accordingly. But the difference is at the most a difference of degrees. The example of the Estate people in Winston Parva showed, in miniature, the extent to which the fate of individuals, through identification by others and by themselves, can be dependent even in contemporary societies on the character and situation of one of their groups. Merely by living in a specific neighbourhood individuals were judged and treated, and to some extent judged themselves, in accordance with the image which others had of their neighbourhood. And this dependence of individuals on the standing and the image of groups to which they belong, the profound identification of the former with the latter in the assessment of others and in their own self-esteem is not confined to social units with a high degree of individual social mobility such as neighbourhoods. There are others, such as nations, classes or ethnic minority groups, where the bonds of identification of individuals with their group and their participation by proxy in the collective attributes are far less elastic. The collective disgrace attached to such groups by other more powerful groups and embodied in standard invectives and stereotyped blame-gossip usually has a deep anchorage in the personality structure of their members as part of their individual identity and as such cannot be easily shaken off.

And an equally deep anchorage in the personality structure of individuals has its counterpart, the belief in the collective grace or virtue which many groups attribute to themselves and which may be attributed to them by other groups whom they regard as inferior. The mild form of such a group charisma which the " villagers "—which particularly the members of the old families' network felt they possessed is an example. It formed a focal point of the image they had of themselves—not as single individuals, but as a collective, as members of this

103

particular group. It helped to make their life together and their endeavour to preserve it more meaningful.

But the group charismatic claim performed its binding function—its function as group preserver—as in other cases, only by setting up sharp barriers against other groups whose members were, according to it for ever, excluded from participation in the grace and virtues attributed to those who belonged. By thus elevating the group's own members, the group charisma automatically relegated members of other interdependent groups to a position of inferiority. The group charisma claimed by the old " village " group had its sting. It did not simply help to define the boundaries between those who belonged and those who did not belong. It also had the function of a weapon which held outsiders at bay, which helped to preserve the purity and integrity of the group. It was a weapon of defence as well as a weapon of attack. It implied that it was a sign of disgrace not to participate in the grace and the specific virtues which the members of the distinguished group claimed for themselves. What one observed in the " village " was only a moderate small-scale example of a pattern which one can observe, often in a much more tense and virulent form, in the relation of many old established groups, nations, classes, ethnic majorities or whatever their form may be, to their outsider groups whether they are effectively kept in their place or are already rising. Everywhere group charisma attributed to oneself and group disgrace attributed to outsiders are complementary phenomena.[1] And, as in the " village ", everywhere these twin phenomena find their expression in stereotyped forms of praise for oneself and of blame, of group invectives and group abuse directed against the outsiders. Even the least " worthy " members of charismatic groups tend to claim for themselves by identification characteristics and values attributed to the whole group and to be found in practice perhaps only as attributes of the " minority of the best ".

Once more one can see how closely the structure of gossip

[1] The problems of " Group Charisma and Group Disgrace " have been discussed more fully in a paper read by N. Elias under that title at the 15th Deutschen Soziologentag (Max Weber Centenary), Heidelberg, 29th April 1964.

is bound up with that of the gossiping group. What has been observed before as " praise gossip " veering towards idealization and " blame gossip " veering towards stereotyped abuse are phenomena closely connected with the belief in one's own group charisma and the others' group disgrace. In old established groups, in groups where young people and perhaps their parents and parents' parents have absorbed such beliefs with the corresponding symbols of praise and abuse from childhood on, positive and negative group images of this kind deeply impregnate the individual's personal image. The collective identity, and as part of it the collective pride and the group charismatic claims, help to fashion his individual identity in his own as well as in other people's experience. No individual grows up without this anchorage of his personal identity in the identification with a group or groups even though it may remain tenuous and may be forgotten in later life, and without some knowledge of the terms of praise and abuse, of the praise gossip and blame gossip, of the group superiority and group inferiority which go with it.

8 | Young People in Winston Parva

LIKE other industrial areas Winston Parva had a number of young people who were near-delinquents or delinquents. In 1958 a few came from Zone 2, more from Zone 3, none from Zone 1. As everywhere else, it was only a minority of youngsters in Winston Parva who came before the courts. The figures for juvenile offenders in that year were 19 cases or 6·81 per cent of the children aged 7–16 in Zone 3 against 3 cases or 0·78 per cent of the children aged 7–16 in Zone 2. The difference between the delinquency rates of the two zones was considerable. Moreover, two of the three convictions of " village " youngsters concerned teenagers who had broken a technical rule, only one was convicted for an offence against property. The reverse was the case in Zone 3. There 17 of the 19 young offenders were brought to court for offences against persons or property. The other two were committed for technical offences such as riding an unsafe bicycle or playing on the railway. Some of the young people from Estate and " village " probably committed offences without being caught. Even though, by far the greater part of young people in both zones kept within the law.

Yet the chances for a satisfactory mode of growing up which the two zones offered to children were very different. The " village " had well-established communal standards. The fact that they were relatively uniform and were shared by many families made it easier for youngsters to live up to them and the well-developed network of social controls made it more difficult for them to slip up. On the Estate it was left almost entirely to the individual family to provide standards of conduct for their own children and the standards of one family were often not the same as those of its neighbours. The fact that they lacked communal reinforcement, that customs and norms of different families in the same neighbourhood differed widely and that youngsters of one family did openly what was strictly forbidden to those of another, made the growing-up process for young people on the Estate much more difficult than for young people in the " village ", and made disturbances much more likely. A closely-knit community such as the " village " was better able than the Estate to provide the steady adult control of children which is one of the conditions for the growth of a stable self-control. When both parents went to work relatives or neighbours were always ready to look after the children. On the Estate they often had to be left to their own resources. If " village " children played in the street they were among neighbours whom they knew and who knew them quite well ; their parents could always be sure that some neighbours would warn their children if they were about to hurt themselves or each other or to damage people's property. An adult who was annoyed by children would simply call out to them using one or the other of the standard phrases for such an occasion such as, " Stop it, or I'll tell yer mum ! " and that was usually enough.

The children of the Estate played among houses whose inhabitants in many cases were relative strangers, to whom they felt no obligation and who felt no obligation to them, who were often reluctant to interfere or to make contacts with them, who were indifferent and sometimes hostile to the playing children who reciprocated the feeling. One did not like to say, " I'll tell yer mum " if one hardly knew their parents or did not wish to know them. Moreover, complaints to some of the mothers in Zone 3 would have been answered, if at all, by a torrent of abuse.

A wide gulf separated the youngsters of working-class families on the Estate who tried to give their children a good education, urged them to " get on " and were intensely concerned with achievement and success, and other working-class families who let their children more or less fend for themselves, who had hardly the will and perhaps not the chance to better themselves and the lot of their children. Many of them did not know how to set about in order to " get on ". They lived from day to day, had no conception of a career and no long-term plans to speak of. While the majority of youngsters whom one met on visits to the Estate after school hours or after work were doing at home very much the same things as their counterparts in the " village " and were not particularly visible in the streets of Winston Parva, a minority seemed to have nothing else to do but to lounge around in the streets. It was always the same youngsters whom one saw there. They came from large families who lived in small houses. They had no other place to go to in Winston Parva. Most of them came from the 8 or 9 " notorious " families.

For a township of its size, the facilities which Winston Parva offered to young people were very poor. All the 6 church or chapel youth groups of Winston Parva met in Zone 2. Their membership was small. It was confined to young people who regularly attended service and was almost exclusively recruited from Zone 2. No youth club existed in Zone 3, although a small section of the Church of England organisation met in the mission hall on the Estate. All other youth organisations, with one exception, were fairly strict in their exclusion of young people from the Estate. Some of them tried to join, but in most cases they did not attend service as regularly as the " village " children and were then asked to leave. A church youth leader explained the situation to an area youth committee in the following manner :

> " We've got too many in our club. Well, it's not that alone, but there is a rule that only church members can be in the club. We've got over 40 on the books but only 14 go to church, so the committee says we have to chuck out some of the trouble-makers from the Estate that never come to church."

Such periodic purges kept all but a handful of Zone 3 youngsters away from the social activities and the training facilities provided by these clubs.

The only youth organisation which, as a matter of policy, kept its door open for youngsters from both the Estate and the " village " was the Open Youth Club organised by the County Education Authority. It was founded during the period of research. One of the authors took a hand in organising its activities. The need for such an organisation was great in a community such as Winston Parva. It also served as an " experiment *in situ* " which made it possible to study at close quarters some of the problems which arose from the segregation of the two working-class neighbourhoods for the younger generation.

In many of the aspects for which clubs are usually given credit, the Club was successful during the three years in which it was possible to participate in the Club work and to observe it. It continuously attracted fairly large numbers of young people from all parts of Winston Parva who appeared to enjoy its activities. It soon became the largest youth organisation of the community with about 50 members of which 20 lived on the Estate. It organised games, hobbies, competitions, dances and festivals. A committee chosen by the members themselves from their own numbers had a large measure of autonomy. The weekly meetings took place in a classroom of the secondary school which was put at the Club's disposal. The County Education Authority gave constant help. But the available means were limited. They fell short of the needs. In spite of many efforts, it was not possible to find larger and more adequate accommodation.

In trying to provide it one came up against certain peculiarities of the set of values probably current in many industrial communities which were of some relevance to the problems of the younger generation. In accordance with this value system, it was accepted that the schooling and training of young people —everything which involved, or was connected with, work, might be of public concern and could, therefore, be financed from public funds. But provisions for leisure-time occupation and enjoyment seemed to rank much lower in the scale of values of authorities and of the older generation generally. They had come to accept the fact that, in the majority of cases, individual families could not provide on their own schooling and training facilities for their children commensurate with the requirements of a highly complex industrial society. And the provision of such facilities, therefore, now ranked as an item of fairly high priority on the list of public expenditure. Provisions for enjoyable and fruitful after-school and after-work activities still ranked very low on that list. They were still evaluated largely as luxuries, not particularly essential for the well-being of the younger generation and often enough as private affairs which should be left to the individual families themselves.

Conditions in Winston Parva showed very clearly that the part played in the life of young people by their after-school and after-work activities and the degree of satisfaction they derived from them were far from inessential for their well-being and their conduct, including their conduct at school or at work. Their opportunities for spending their leisure time pleasantly and productively in the company of others were extremely limited. Apart from the older youth clubs and the Scouts neither of which attracted more than a small fraction of the younger generation, no special associations and no communal buildings were available where young people could meet. The schools offered some opportunities for sport, but they too were extremely limited. A rugby club meeting and playing at the fields of the boys' secondary school had a very successful record. But as the secondary school drew its pupils from a wide area around Winston Parva and as the members of the rugby club were largely recruited from its "Old Boys", most of them came from outside Winston Parva. It enjoyed high prestige in Zone 1 and 2 and was on occasions mentioned by Councillor Drew as an example of the "village" spirit, although the number of young "villagers" who participated in its activities was small.

One building opened its doors, at a price, to anyone. That was the local cinema. It was not surprising that many young people who could not or who did not like to stay at home spent their leisure time in and around it. The programmes concentrated on the lowest common denominator of the potential customers. The following list collected from advertisements indicated the type of films which were offered.

NUDIST PARADISE	GRIP OF THE STRANGLER
First British Nudist Film	
HOW TO MAKE A MONSTER	TEENAGE FRANKENSTEIN
RUNAWAY DAUGHTERS	BLOOD OF THE VAMPIRE

THE UNASHAMED
Filmed entirely in Nudist
    Camps

THE MATING URGE
Courtship and Love Customs in
    Strange Lands

DOLLS OF VICE

THE FLESH IS WEAK

THE SINS OF YOUTH
Can You Ignore This ?

SHE-DEMONS
Half Woman   Half Beast

THE NUDIST STORY
In Stunning Technicolor

BED WITHOUT BREAKFAST

THE WASP WOMAN   THE BEAST FROM THE HAUNTED CAVE
Grand Double Horror Sensation

The audience played up to this blend of nightmares and sex phantasies without taking it too seriously. Their behaviour as a crowd again showed how strong was the urge of many of the youngsters to demonstrate their defiance of the rules of established society and, if possible, to provoke their representatives. On the evenings when these films were shown, groups of adolescents, mostly in their late teens, came into Winston Parva not only from the Estate, but also from the surrounding villages and even from the nearby town. If the film had a sexual theme the first appearance on the screen of any female character was the signal for loud yells, whistles and stamping from groups of boys in the audience. Some boys from the Estate said at youth club meetings that they went to the cinema partly to enjoy the film and partly to enjoy the " racket " which they caused.

A member of a " racket "-making gang from Zone 3 gave the following description of an incident in the cinema which illustrates the situation :

" As there's nothing else to do we end up in the back row of the ' Regal '. I'm with the usual crowd, Dave, Doug, Lanky and Henry.

I and everyone else except Lanky are smoking and blowing out the smoke. We do this to annoy the others and soon we see nearly all the people turning round sneering and cursing us.

And then, when it was quiet the noise started, banging on the seats, shouting out, whistling and shooting peas, and all of a sudden above the racket there was a piercing crack and a thud and everyone turned round to see Lanky sprawled on the floor.

He was moaning ' To think I paid two bob for this, a crap film and a collapsible soap-box seat '."

The boy related then how the manager of the cinema and two assistants shone their torches on the boys and threatened to call the police if the gang did not leave. The boys therefore " trooped out " making as much noise as possible on the way.

Another boy from the Estate described how he had taken his girl friend to the cinema :

> " Me and Vera were sittin' in the ' Regal ' when I 'eard a kid behind me say a rude remark about Vera. So I goes up to 'im an' sez, ' Say that again and I'll smash yer head in.' ' Go on,' sez the kid, ' try it.' Well he was sittin' low in 'is seat like so I just slams 'im on top of the 'ead an' 'e starts yellin'. Then Wally the manager comes up an' asks what's goin' on. So I told 'im an' 'e asks the kid if it were right. ' Yes,' sez the kid, ' that's what 'appened.' ' Well,' sez Wally to me. ' Yer done right, you go back to your place,' and turnin' to the kid 'e sez, ' Any more remarks an' yer get chucked out see'."

At the end of the film show the young people drifted about the main street and one could observe that very few went to homes in the " village ". Several groups could usually be seen moving towards the Estate and other groups waited for buses back to town. Occasionally fights broke out between gangs who quarrelled on the " Monkey Walk ". Imposing a fine on two youths for such a fight a magistrate had said in December 1957 : " Fighting is peculiarly prevalent in Winston Parva. The magistrates are determined that this sort of thing shall stop." Evidence was given that the police were called to a fight outside the cinema and arrested the two culprits " who were surrounded by a gang of youths ".

Recurrent scenes such as these were symptomatic of a conflict situation which existed not only in Winston Parva but in societies with urban centres, and particularly with large urban centres, almost everywhere. They were symptomatic for the peculiar guerrilla warfare waged almost incessantly between established sections of these societies and socially produced outsider groups, in this case outsider groups of the younger generation. The cinema served here as a rallying point for crowds of adolescents who were particularly affected by the fact that their society did not provide clearly defined roles for adolescents. They had partially outgrown their childhood roles, but many of them did not yet fit, and some of them would probably never fit, into any of the prescribed adult roles.

The crowd at the cinema was not a chance assembly of " abnormal " youngsters ; it was representative of a phenomenon fairly normal in large-scale urban societies. They all produced and reproduced again and again groups of people who fit better and others who fit less well or not at all into the established order and its set roles. Many adolescents stood at the crossroad. Some were or would become delinquents, others would learn to fit into the set adult rules. But it is only in police records and the beliefs of many ordinary law-abiding adults that the dividing line between delinquents and non-delinquents is hard and fast. Classification of some young people as " delinquents " tends to make us forget that " delinquent behaviour " shades imperceptibly into non-delinquent behaviour. If one observes the conduct of children and adolescents in their actual communal setting, one can find many transitional forms of behaviour. Attempts to study, to explain and to make predictions about delinquents on the basis of individual criteria alone, by means of a psychological diagnosis unsupported by a sociological diagnosis are not likely to be reliable. For the conditions for the continued reproduction of delinquent groups of youngsters lie in the structure of a society and particularly in that of the communities in which groups of families with " delinquent " children live and in which these children grow up.

The crowd of adolescents converging on the cinema in the " village " of Winston Parva from the Estate and the wider urban neighbourhood was a good example of the communal character of the problems with which this section of working-class adolescents had to grapple. One could see them in better perspective if one compared the conditions under which the youngsters of the large problem families on the Estate and those under which youngsters of other Estate and of " village " families grew up, especially the conditions of their leisure time.

After school or work the former usually gathered for a time

in small groups near their homes. Occasionally one could see them playing a game of soccer. Mostly they seemed to be standing or walking around, looking as if they were waiting for something to happen without quite knowing for what. Sometimes the tension broke. They made something happen —by starting a fight, by getting a girl, by making a " racket ". They were left to their own devices with a great deal of life in them and little to use it on in a manner they could enjoy. Most of them seemed to suffer from leisure-time starvation. They did not know what to do with themselves after school or work. Their situation hardly agreed with the widely held idea that people need only be shown how to work, but need not be shown how to enjoy themselves. The unruly youngsters of Winston Parva suffered from both lack of opportunity and lack of ability to enjoy themselves in a manner which satisfied their own needs and which at the same time could be tolerated by the majority of their community without annoyance and revulsion.

This is a characteristic piece from a conversation with a seventeen-year-old boy from Zone 3 who was a member of the Open Youth Club. The subject under discussion was his latest appearance in court :

" This place is deadly. There's nowhere to go at nights. It's all right them sayin' go to the Youth Clubs, but if you go to them Church Clubs they kick you out. I told A . . . (the Probation Officer) last time I seen him—I says there's always trouble, the lads ain't got nowhere to go. He says—' Why don't you make a Club of your own ? '—so I says we 'aven't the money and there weren't no rooms anyway. There's only the Open Club I says and that's just one night of the week.

The police don't give you a chance, they're all after you if they see you on the street, glarin' at you. When they took me in they tried to get my finger prints, he says to me ' Pass that ashtray lad '—and I says get it yerself, I'm not so daft. They give you fags and that, but it's only to get you talkin'. They're after promotion that's all they care about. I tell the lads, I say if a cop comes after you—run, don't you stop and talk. If they get me again they'll send me away. They don't give you no chance. They're always watchin' for you."

Many of these wilder youngsters, even those who were not

caught, fined, sent to prison and labelled "delinquents", seemed to knock against the wall of an invisible prison in which they lived using up their energies in annoying and provoking all those whom they vaguely felt to be their jailers in an attempt to break out or to prove to themselves that the oppression was real. They even went to the "flicks" not merely for the sake of the film but for the sake of the "racket". There in the darkness of the cinema hall sheltering in the anonymity of the cinema crowd they could demonstrate their defiance against social rules they had not yet fully assimilated, particularly the rules curbing their still untamed sex needs, and could seek temporary relief from the fantasy nightmares within, in the fantasy nightmares without.

In the "village", too, young people seemed to suffer a good deal from leisure-time starvation. They, too, seemed to feel "shades of the prison house" closing in on them while growing up. But they were better able to cope with the experience thanks to the structure not only of their families but above all of their community. The patterns of the frustrations pressing down upon young people in the two working-class neighbourhoods were in some respects quite different. The pressures brought to bear upon young people in the "village" were perhaps more severe and more inescapable. But they were also more steady, more even and regular in their action and more clearly defined. They were linked to clearly intelligible social rewards and to recognisable social-individual goals—to rewards, that is, bestowed upon the individual by others and to goals selected by individuals themselves from a range of goals offered to them in their society according to their position within it. Moreover, in a community such as the "village" the frustrations of childhood and adolescence were compensated by a sense of belongingness and the pride in one's group which went with it. Youngsters were much better able than they were on the Estate to form for themselves a picture of how they stood and ranked in relation to others ; they were better able to form a picture of their own identity as individuals in their social setting, and the picture they could form was emotionally more rewarding ; it indicated their own worth as members of a community which, they were taught, was good and was superior to others, a community of which they learned to be proud. If they complied with the rules they could find help and guidance in their growing-up difficulties from the examples of the older generation. But they had to pay a price. The community in which they lived was firmly ruled by the elderly and the old. The ruled were in this case not outsiders but dependents who belonged to the same group as those who ruled. The youngsters were firmly encompassed by the in-group feeling of the older generation. The leisure-time arrangements were symptomatic of this distribution of power between the generations. While the "village" provided satisfactory communal opportunities for the after-work enjoyment of middle-aged and elderly people, few similar opportunities existed for the specific leisure-time needs of young people. One seemed to take it for granted that youngsters enjoyed the same things as their parents. Thus on the one hand the younger "village" people identified themselves with the code of their elders, took pride in it and looked down on the outsiders from the Estate as their elders did. On the other hand, they did not derive the same enjoyment as their elders from church and chapel clubs, ladies' concert parties and many of the other pleasant after-work activities which offered a great deal of satisfaction to adults. That was their dilemma. Most of the leisure-time organisations for young people were dependencies of adult organisations ruled by adult committees according to their norms. The young people in the "village" had to pay for the benefits which they derived from the relatively high stability and security of their community with an adult-centred, relatively empty social leisure life.

The young people on the Estate were not to the same extent exposed to the communal control of the older generation, but they also lacked the rewards of a firm network of adult controls—communal security and stability. In many cases stability was provided for young people by their families.alone. And the configuration of family stability in the face of relatively high communal instability and a high degree of status insecurity created problems for the youngsters on the Estate from which their contemporaries in the "village" remained free.

Even more difficult were the problems confronting Estate youngsters whose families too were unstable and disordered. They not only lacked stable communal controls, which they could absorb and which could help them to control socially unacceptable impulses, but also stable, socially approved models for their conduct set by their parents which could serve as a firm core for the development of their image of themselves and of their own value. Like other young persons of their age they had to grapple with the question, " Who am I ? " and " What is my value and standing as a person ? ". As in other cases, the answers were not only determined by what they themselves felt and observed in relation to members of their own families, but also by what other people in their neighbourhood felt and said about their own families and about themselves. One of the main characteristics of the situation in which children and adolescents of the disordered minority families from the Estate found themselves was that they had to grope for their own individual identity, for their own personal value and pride from the start as members of families who were treated as outsiders and sometimes almost as outcasts not only by the " village " people, but even within their own community. It was often immensely difficult for youngsters growing up in families of this type to escape from their outsider position. One cannot doubt that this position had a profound influence on the growth of their image of themselves, on their feeling of identity [1] and pride in relation to others, on their whole personality development.

Whatever affection they might find in their family, they could not find there stable and secure models as a crystalising core for the struggle with their own disjointed impulses. They were confronted early in life with a confusing situation when they began to sense that the rules and values implied in the experiences within their own families did not agree with those of the larger world outside. The voices and gestures of the orderly people around them, including those of the police, told them from childhood on of the low esteem in which they and their families were held. They could not derive much pride and much sense of direction from the knowledge that they were

[1] See Appendix 1.

identical and were identified with a family for which others had little respect.

That was the constellation which went into the making of the image they had of themselves. It was in many respects a negative and self-contradictory image. Like many other adolescents in societies with a prolonged schooling and adolescence period, their self-esteem remained highly vulnerable and unstable. Like others, they were uncertain as to their own worth, their own task and role in society ; they were not sure what others thought of them or what to think of themselves. But they had greater difficulties in forming a firm individual attachment, one boy with one girl, which in highly individualised societies is often the first great reassurance of an adolescent's individual worth and the first great accession of strength to his ego which he can find when he emerges as a person with his own identity from the childhood identification with his family group. In the case of these rougher Estate adolescents the common adolescent anxieties and insecurities about their own identity were aggravated by the instabilities of their families and the low esteem in which they were generally held. When they tried to branch out and to develop an identity of their own apart from their family identity, their self-esteem and their pride remained particularly vulnerable and unbalanced because they had always been and remained rejected outsiders. The weakness of their ego made it even more difficult for them than it was for ordinary adolescents to face the world in which they lived as single individuals when they emerged from the weak shelter of their families. Unsure of themselves and used to being treated with a good deal of contempt and suspicion by representatives of the authorities and the orderly world from which they were excluded, they tried to find help and support in temporary friendship alliances which they formed among themselves ; they found it easier to face a hostile and suspicious grouping of people towards which they themselves felt a great deal of hostility and suspicion, in groups of their own kind. Like their families, the successors in the life of these youngsters, the gangs they formed with each other were not particularly stable. But while they lasted they made it easier for them to face the world from which they were

118

excluded ; they acted as antedotes to the extreme vulnerability of their self-esteem. In groups of their own kind they could think more highly of themselves than they could have done alone, and could satisfy their need to prove to themselves how strong they were. They could find reassurance with regard to their own worth in the face of their own doubts constantly reinforced as they were by the attitude of the orderly majority. Gangs formed a rough-and-ready mutual admiration society for youngsters which were excluded from the mutual admiration and reassurance of the established groups. Successful gang fights, successful raids or challenges to the established authorities under a good gang leader appeared to provide for them the accession of strength to their self-esteem which other adolescents found, among others, in a successful individual love-attachment. The same was done for some of them by transient sex relations. But the accession of strength they gained in this way was comparatively short-lived ; it often left them as vulnerable and unsure of themselves as they had been before. These episodes, momentarily satisfactory as they were, contributed little towards their development as persons ; they did not help them to grow up.

There is much justice in the attention paid since Freud to the peculiar libidinal patterns and needs of adolescents. But unless the knowledge of these libidinal developments is linked to that of the development of a person's self and this in turn to that of the social configurations in which a person's self and self-image form themselves, the understanding which it provides of the problems of adolescents, in theory and practice, remains incomplete.

Ordinary youngsters in other social settings learned early to think of themselves in terms of a future. For most of the unruly Estate youngsters it was difficult to take any long-term view of themselves. They lived more than ordinary youngsters in and for the present moment. That was another difference which helped to build up barriers between them and the other youngsters. They did not understand how the people on the other side of the barriers felt, thought and lived and these in turn did not understand these unruly youngsters ; their reaction indicated only too clearly that for them they were almost literally " nobody ". The youngsters themselves, like others, wanted to be "somebody". But the only way they knew to show those who treated them as "nobody" that they were, in fact, "somebody" was wholly negative, like the feeling they had about their own identity—was that of rejected outsiders, who, with a dream-like compulsion and wholly ineffectually, rebelled against the rejection by a kind of guerrilla warfare, by provoking and disturbing, by attacking and, as far as they could, destroying the orderly world from which they were excluded without quite understanding why. The logic of their feeling and acting seemed to be : "We'll force you all to pay attention to us if not in love then in hatred." By acting according to this feeling they helped to reproduce the very situation from which they tried to escape. They induced the representatives of the orderly world around them again and again to reject them as outsiders and to treat them with contempt. They were born into a vicious circle from which it was hard to escape. By growing up in families which were rejected by the orderly families of their neighbourhood and excluded from closer social relations with them, they developed behaviour tendencies which attached the stigma of rejection and exclusion to themselves as individuals. And being rejected as outsiders of low standing, they on their part may well have set their own children, under the impact of the same social mechanisms, on the same course.

Tendencies of behaviour such as theirs are often studied in one generation only. If one considers a chain of generations at all, it is usually because one assumes these tendencies are due to some kind of biological inheritance. It is much more likely that they are, and were in this case due to a form of sociological inheritance. The specific pattern and particularly the mechanisms of transmission of sociological inheritance over generations have not yet been sufficiently studied, but this is an example : the behaviour of parents in disordered families such as these which led to their rejection and their low standing in the hierarchy of statuses engendered tendencies of behaviour in their children which led in turn to their rejection when they began to branch out on their own. Specific character patterns of one generation and the specific social configuration of which they formed part showed in this case a tendency to perpetuate themselves in the next generation—to induce in the children character patterns which sustained a similar social configuration.

Many contemporary writings on delinquency and related subjects seem to be based on the tacit assumption that offences against the law by children and adolescents have never been as widespread as they are now. And if one relies alone on delinquency figures for a relatively limited period of time this assumption may well be borne out by the available statistical evidence, although even then the influence on the number of cases brought before the court, of changes in the policy and efficiency of police forces and the attitude of the courts, have to be taken into account. The assumption hardly agrees with the overall evidence if one takes a long-term view. Reports from the earlier stages of industrialisation and the corresponding stages of urbanisation, such as Mayhew's studies of the London poor or A. Morrison's account of the *House of the Jago* and many others, suggest that during the earlier stages, at least in England, family disorganisation and law-breaking by young people were more common among the industrial working-classes than they are today and that these conditions were not only connected with the normal upheavals of industrialisation processes, such as the uprooting of families in quest of labour, but with the whole complex of high unemployment rates and low levels of wages. Throughout the nineteenth century one habitually spoke of the working masses in industrial towns as "the poor", and for the greater part they were poor. In all likelihood low levels and irregularities of income as part of a whole syndrome of factors which made life of the poorer classes highly insecure and unstable contributed in those days much more towards family disorganisation and lawlessness among the young than they do today.

That does not mean orderly and well-regulated home life was then unknown among the industrial working classes. There is a good deal of evidence to suggest that in England, as in other countries during the same stages of their development, sections of the working classes who, though poor, tried to live an orderly and respectable life within their means and capacities lived side by side, and were sometimes engaged in a tug-of-war with, other sections in their neighbourhood whose home life was more disordered and whose children had little respect for the laws and rules of the people who were better off. Strained relationships such as those between the working-class families of the " village " and the orderly majority of working-class families on the Estate on the one hand and the "notorious" minority of working-class families on the other hand are not an isolated case even in our time. They were probably much more frequent in the past, though in the past unstable and disordered working-class homes may often have formed the majority and the others a minority. Whatever the case may have been in America and in other industrial countries of Europe, in England the relatively high proportion of stable and well-ordered working-class homes in the large industrial towns of our time and the relatively low proportion of unstable and disordered working-class homes is the outcome of a long development, and this "civilising process", whatever else was involved, was certainly not unconnected with the rise in the standards of living of larger and larger sections of the working classes. If one considers this long-term development, one will probably find that part of the disordered working-class families, of the "problem families" of today, are the diminishing remnants of generations of such families—remnants who by a form of sociological inheritance of certain tendencies of behaviour have been unable to escape from the vicious circle which tends to produce in children of disordered families propensities for forming in their generation again disordered families. The number of people who were able to escape from the trap might have been greater if family disorganisation and disturbances of home life had not been constantly reinforced by other social conditions—by the disturbances of wars, unemployment, large-scale migratory movements, voluntary or involuntary, and the uprooting of families involved in them. The disordered families on the Estate of Winston Parva were a small sample of the backwash in our generation of the greater masses of disordered families in past generations. Their children showed some of the mechanisms of transmission. They showed how the conditions for the rejection of parents by their neighbours were perpetuated and reinforced by the behaviour of their offspring.

The majority of the Estate families tried to keep their distance from the minority. Their youngsters following the example of their parents spent a good deal of their leisure time at home. To loiter in the streets was regarded as a leisure-time occupation of the rowdy section of the Estate youths. " Respectable " parents on the Estate, as in the " village ", did not like their children to behave like the youngsters from the " notorious " families and to get mixed up with them. The Open Youth Club made an attempt at lowering these barriers. But soon after its initiation there, too, the full force of the communal divisions in Winston Parva made itself felt. Broadly speaking one could distinguish three groups of young people in the Open Youth Club corresponding to the divisions in their community at large : boys and girls from the " village " who formed the majority, " respectable " boys and girls from the Estate and boys and girls who came from the minority of disordered Estate families. The dividing lines were always noticeable even though marginal individuals particularly from the middle group occasionally crossed them in either direction. But efforts to overcome the segregation of these groups, to bring them closer together and to achieve a measure of integration were not successful.

The young people from the " village " had to live up to the firm standards and to the somewhat exalted communal norms of their elders if they wanted to retain the respect of their community. Councillor Drew who had a gift for expressing " village " opinion with authority on many subjects once summed up very neatly what one thought in the " village " about " the young people ". His statement was not uncharacteristic of the strongly norm-orientated view of the " village " realities and of the " villagers' " tendency to form a slightly idealised picture of their own kind :

> " The young people," he once said, " are basically good. They are good at athletics, etc. They get good school reports. They get a good education here. Most of the trouble is caused by those from the Estate who are of a different calibre and lack a decent home life. So the educated ones who built up the village spirit tend to draw away from the others."

Young " village " people could hardly escape from the implica-

tions of such " village " beliefs. The force of the injunctions
and prescriptions contained in statements such as these was all
the greater because they appeared in the guise of a simple
statement of fact. The belief of their elders that young people
were basically good greatly reinforced the individual young-
ster's need to appear good and to avoid any suggestion that
he or she had urges to do things of which parents and
neighbourhood would disapprove if they knew of them. And
" to be good " meant not to behave as young people from the
Estate were said to behave. It was not only the family but
the whole neighbourhood and its situation which had a strong
character-forming influence. The discipline to which young
people were subject by others and to which they learned to
subject themselves was firmly linked to the pride of the
" in-group ", the " village ", and the contempt for the " out-
group ", the Estate. One can easily discover instances of this
pattern elsewhere. External control and self-control bound up
with in-group pride and out-group contempt is a constellation
to be found in many groups, small and great.

The experience of the Open Youth Club where youngsters
from " village " and Estate met fairly regularly indicated how
strongly rooted this constellation was among the former. They
were well-behaved and orderly, but an attempt lasting approximately three years to bring about closer integration between
the two groups achieved very little. In the Club young people
from the " village " co-operated with those from the Estate,
as they were asked to do, in games and competitions. Beyond
that they hardly ever went. Although many of the Estate
youngsters were no less orderly and well-behaved than the
" village " youngsters, the odour of bad group names such as
" people from the Estate " or " rat alley " clung to them even
if no-one used them in their presence. To make friends across
the invisible barriers would have lowered a young " villager "
in the eyes of his fellows and probably in his own. The
segregation was strictly maintained even in the dating patterns
of the Club. To be seen out with a girl from the Estate would
have meant to invite scorn from other adolescents in the
" village " and possibly a rebuke from parents.

There were a few " village " boys who risked the rebuke.

They did " date " girls from the Estate who were regarded as good-time girls, sexually more easily accessible than others. They were girls who, as a rule, did not make regular " dates " with the same boy for any length of time, but were " passed round " a group of boys, thus confirming the worst suspicions of the " village " adults. One could observe them walking up and down the main street of the " village " until someone " picked them up " if the Open Club did not offer a sufficiently attractive selection of young males. In this sphere, too, the most deviant section of the Estate population determined the attitude of the " village " youngsters towards the whole group of Estate youngsters. The latter as a whole played for the young " villagers " the role of the " bad example " that appears to be in many societies an indispensable complement of the " good example " which the leaders wish their own group to follow.

There were always enough young people from the Estate who fitted this role. The main street of the " village " and to some extent the park between Zone 2 and 3 were used by adolescents and some younger adults as a promenade. It was called locally the " monkey walk " and was particularly crowded on summer evenings and on weekends. Young people strolled along in groups of the same sex trying to attract the attention of the other sex. " Village " parents strongly criticised the flamboyant dress of some of the adolescents of both sexes from the Estate. " If my lad came home with one of those things," said one of the parents pointing to a blue Edwardian suit lined with gilt thread, " he'd not be allowed to wear it." A woman shopkeeper told how she watched the girls in the main street from her window : " It's disgraceful ! They wear such revealing dresses and such heavy make-up that they look terrible, and you can see the men mentally seducing them ! " The shopkeeper added that she knew some of these girls were still at the secondary school and came from " that Estate ".

Thus by casting a group whom one stigmatised as socially inferior and contemptible into the role of a " bad example ", one associated the " bad urges " which young people might have with social inferiority. The scene of an individual's psychological conflicts and tensions was linked to that of social conflicts and tensions. " Low morality " was linked to " low social status ", loss of self-control to loss of social belongingness and identity, association with people from an outsider group with the fear of moral contamination and a weakening of one's own defences. And while the bad name associated with the whole Estate community made it almost impossible for individual " village " youngsters to distinguish between individuals from the Estate who shared their own standards and those who did not, there were certainly always enough Estate youngsters of the latter type in the public eye who enabled the guardians of the " village " morality to point a finger to their " bad example " and to say, " I told you so ".

Groups of boys from the Estate, aged between 15 and 19, could be seen going into the " Hare and Hounds " and drinking together. Younger adolescents had friends old enough to buy bottled beer and cheap wine which they drank together at street corners. Some groups of about the same age went to the side of the park by the railway embankment where they took part in sex games while older adolescents went there in groups or pairs to have intercourse. To speak about it was normally tabooed by a kind of " *esprit de corps* ", but the confidence of members of the Open Youth Club showed clearly that some of the young people knew and talked freely among themselves about what went on in the park. It also showed that they had begun to develop a sex ethos of their own which differed in some significant respects from that of the older generation. Petting was generally approved by Club members of both neighbourhoods though not by the parents. A minority of adolescents from the Estate, mostly known to the others, had full sexual relations. This, as far as one could see, was not in agreement with the proclaimed sex ethos of most of the " village " youngsters. However the " village " members of the Club who knew about what was going on and talked about it among themselves, as a rule, did not speak to adults about these matters. In that respect the verbal taboos with which respectable " village " adults in their communications with their own youngsters surrounded the sex act had their counterpart in corresponding taboos against open and direct communications about sex relations which "village" adolescents observed in relation to adults.

Among themselves the position was fairly clear. Two of the girls from the Estate who were members of the promiscuous group and who visited the Open Youth Club occasionally were ignored by girls from the "village" who made comments about them among themselves. Boys were more outspoken. Thus on one occasion a boy from the Estate called out to a girl called Gladys, "Hasn't anyone taken you down tonight, Glad!" The other was a girl still of school age who, one was told, could sometimes be seen in the "Hare and Hounds" where a group of youths would buy her drinks before taking her "to the embankment".

Some adults were aware of the "goings-on", but while young people talked about them with the Club leader quite openly once they had gained sufficient confidence in him, it was still hardly possible for adults to speak about such matters openly to an outsider. To break the verbal taboos which surrounded the whole sex sphere in the "village", except perhaps if the men were among themselves, was made difficult by a double barrier, by personal shame feelings and by the urge to keep the ideal image of the community, symbol of the communal charisma, free from any dark spots. One shop-keeper in the "village" hinted darkly at "immorality": "It's happening here, you know, by the Estate, but it's not been found out yet." A young man from the Estate said: "The things they get up to by the park, it'd make you blush if you went past." The majority of the "villagers" and of the Estate people probably concealed from outsiders what knowledge they had about these violations of their code and only discussed them in confidence with persons whom they knew intimately.

The "bad behaviour" of a minority of Estate youngsters which reinforced again and again the "villagers'" stereotyped image of the Estate was not confined to breaches of sex morality. One of the standard complaints of the "village" people was that about the bad behaviour of the "swarms of children" from the Estate. Tales were constantly repeated about the "masses" of children from Zone 3 who grew up to be delinquents and criminals and who destroyed the " old peace " of the " village ".

An attempt to ascertain the number of children per family in the three zones indicated that a considerably larger percentage of the total population in Zone 3 was under 18 years of age than in the other zones.

TABLE IX [1]

Number of Children in the Three Zones

Zone	Number of adult residents aged 21 and over	Number of children under 18 years	Children under 18 as a percentage of total zonal population
1	365	91	19·9
2	2039	514	20·1
3	797	379	32·2

As the following table indicates, the number of large families on the Estate was greater than in the " village ".

TABLE X [1]

Number of Families with three or more Children

Zone	Number of families with 3 or more children	Number of children in these families
1	3	9
2	23	86
3	28	107

Complaints about the " swarms of children " who disturbed the peace of the " village " were not entirely unjustified, but it was not so much the actual number of children on the Estate

[1] These figures are significant only in so far as they indicate differences between the zones. The absolute figures as the headings indicate are not conclusive because of the gap between the population figures for those under 18 and over 21. This gap, at the time, could not be accurately filled because figures for this age group included young men absent on National Service.

which mattered as the conditions under which they lived. The children which roamed the streets and disturbed the peace of the "villagers" came from the minority of "notorious" families which has already been mentioned. Living as they did in relatively small houses, children from these large families had nowhere else to go but the streets after school or work. Those who tried to join the older youth clubs were soon shown that they were not welcome. And attempts made to give them access to the Open Youth Club were not too successful. The majority of the young people from Zone 3 made few attempts to establish closer contacts with the young "villagers" once they became aware of the barriers which the latter put up between them. They had learned a certain reserve on the Estate and applied it, as it seemed, quite easily to their relations with "village" youngsters. But a minority of youngsters from the Estate, mostly children of the problem families, reacted differently. They enjoyed embarrassing the people who rejected them. The vicious circle, the see-saw process, in which the old and the new neighbourhoods, the established and the outsiders, were involved ever since they had become interdependent, showed its full force in the relations between their young people. The children and adolescents of the despised Estate minority were shunned, rejected and "frozen out" by their "respectable" contemporaries from the "village" even more firmly and cruelly than were their parents because the "bad example" they set threatened their own defences against the unruly urges within ; and because the wilder minority of younger people felt rejected, they tried to get their own back by behaving badly with greater deliberation. The knowledge that by being noisy, destructive and offensive they could annoy those by whom they were rejected and treated as outcasts, acted as an added incentive, and perhaps, as the major incentive, for "bad behaviour". They enjoyed doing the very things for which they were blamed as an act of revenge against those who blamed them.

Some groups of this type, mainly composed of boys aged between 14 and 18, "got a kick out of" trying to enter one of the church or chapel clubs. They would enter the club noisily, shouting, singing and laughing. When a club official

TABLE XI

MEMBERS OF THE GANG "THE BOYS"

Name	Age in 1958	I.Q.	Conduct at school	Employment	Official delinquency record	Zone of residence	Home conditions	Other points
Brian	16	70	Poor work. Frequent truancy.	Labourer. Frequent changes of work.	1957 Probation for theft. 1958 Sent to approved school. 1961 Fined for malicious damage.	ZONE 3	Very poor home. Mother " works in pubs ",—Father " beats him up ".	Number of offences kept dark considerably higher than official delinquency record.
Fred	16	90	Poor work. Emotionally unstable.	Machinist.	1958 Bound over for fighting. 1959 Fined for fighting. 1960 Fined for "Vandalism".	ZONE 3	Father absent from home for many years on Military Service.	Leader of " The Boys ". More cunning than Brian. Number of " dark offences " high. Many gang fights. Married 1961.
Harry	16	81	Poor work. "Sly."	Machinist.	1959 Fined with Fred for "Vandalism".	1958 ZONE 3 1959 Moved to Winston Magna.	One of the " notorious " families which moved in 1959.	Fred's friend. Number of " dark offences " high.

Name	Age							
Johnny	16	82	Poor work. Truant.	Labourer.	1957 Probation for theft (with Brian).	One of the "notorious" families which moved in 1959.	1958 ZONE 3 1959 Moved to Winston Magna.	1959 involved in gang fight. "Dodged the police."
Ken	15	90	Poor work. Unstable.	Labourer.	None.	One of the "notorious" families which moved in 1959.	1958 ZONE 3 1959 Moved to Winston Magna.	1958 found drunk in Zone 2 by Youth Officer. 1959 involved in gang fight. 1960 drunk in Zone 2.
Ted	16	70	Poor work. Deaf. Truant.	Labourer.	1957 Probation for theft with Brian.	Violent Father.	ZONE 3 Moved to Zone 2 by N.S.P.C.C.	Left Winston Parva 1960.
Phil	16	95	Fair. School athletic champion.	Labourer.	1959 Fined for insulting police. 1959 Fined for gang fighting.	Irish immigrant family.	ZONE 2	Married 1960.

approached them one of them would ask to join the club while the others stood around grinning. The boys knew beforehand that they would be asked to agree to attend church services regularly. When this provision was put to them they would begin to groan and to shout in protest. Then they were usually asked to leave, though in some instances they were allowed to stay for one evening in order to see what advantages club life had to offer them. The request that they should leave was the anticipated climax of the performance for the group. They expected to be asked to conform to the established standards of behaviour as laid down by the churches ; they expected to be rejected or to be accepted only on terms of their complete acceptance of " village " standards. When this stage was reached the group would leave noisily, shouting abuse, slamming doors and then gathering in the street to shout and to sing for a while. Sometimes a group might agree to stay for the evening and would then " make a nuisance " of themselves by knocking over chairs, by " being rough with the girls," or by making loud obscene comments about club activities.

In the early days of the Open Youth Club there was one group of youths who had become specialists in this type of performance. " The Boys ", as they called themselves, were a gang of six youngsters between 14 and 16, with one or two hangers-on of the same age. Table XI provides some of the relevant data.

Most of the boys came from disordered families and had been before the courts for a variety of offences. Their school work was usually poor, their I.Q. below average—which may have been another symptom of their antagonism against the orderly world to which the school belonged including intelligence tests, not necessarily its cause. Their raids against youth clubs formed part of the same pattern. They had a strong urge to arouse the anger and hostility of the people by whom they felt rejected and which denied them they hardly knew what. Their behaviour formed part of the vicious circle into which they were born as members of disordered families who were treated as outsiders and often as outcasts by the rest of the world they knew. They were rejected by their community because they behaved badly and they behaved badly because they were rejected. The gang was essentially a transient alliance of young outcasts. They tried again and again to provoke the anger and hostility of people who belonged to the world from which they were excluded, and revelled in their success when the hoped-for climax came and the provoked people attacked and punished them. At the beginning of the research they all were in their final years at the local secondary modern school and were without exception in the lowest grade " C " and " D " classes. They were frequently in trouble for " playing up " teachers, damaging school property, fighting and using obscene language. Three members of the gang were placed on probation during their last year at school for stealing from shops and houses in Zone 2.

In the evenings " The Boys " would leave their homes on the Estate and meet on the main road in Zone 2. There they would enter any of the youth clubs which happened to be open and do as much mischief as they could until they were made to leave. After a few weeks of their first raids a detailed and fairly accurate description of the gang and its behaviour had reached, through the gossip channels, all the youth club officials in the " village ". From then on they were usually met at the club doors by one of the club officials who told them he would call the police if they didn't go away.

When " The Boys " visited the Open Youth Club they were allowed to enter. At this stage there was still some hope that the Club might be able to help them a little and one could study them at close quarters. This is what usually happened. At first after their arrival " The Boys " sat close together, with a paper or magazine shared between them over which they laughed and jostled until the paper tore. Then they moved about the Club room as a group, knocking against chairs and benches. Fred, their leader, remarked, " Somebody's going to knock them chairs over, yer know," at which the gang laughed and looked around for the reaction of the Club members. Harry was the " clown ", the " stooge ", of the gang and sometimes " The Boys " pushed him against a line of chairs so that he sprawled across them falling to the floor. Ted tripped him as he got up and the gang laughed again,

Ted shouting, " What yer done that for ? Can't yer stand up proper ? "

At this stage the behaviour usually began to attract considerable comment from the other members of the Club. For a time the members' committee could be persuaded not to expel " The Boys ". When the gang had made several visits to the youth club and the boys had become acquainted with the hobbies of the various groups, they extended their role and began directly to interfere with group activities. Their urge to make the others angry, to provoke hostility and attacks against themselves, which had so far been frustrated, became stronger. They pushed a model aircraft from the table on which it had been painted ; they knocked over a box of toys which had been made for an orphanage, and broke some of them. They broke craft-knives or used the knives to damage chairs and books. One evening " The Boys " spent some time throwing darts at a small piece of wood which Harry held out until his hand was cut by a dart. At the Club Christmas party the contribution of " The Boys " to the festivities was noted as " uneaten cakes squashed on chairs and pressed against the walls, broken plates and two broken chairs ".

None of the gang attempted to dance although dancing formed a very popular and noisy part of the Club programme. They sat watching the dancers and the girls who danced defended themselves from the rude remarks made by the gang with effective sarcasm. Two girls from the Estate, however, Brenda and Val, encouraged " The Boys ", shrieked with laughter at their activities and accompanied them when the gang left the Club room. These girls allowed themselves to be " mauled " by any of the gang and encouraged " The Boys " by sitting on their knees, ruffling their hair and taking cigarettes from their pockets. Members of the Club committee complained that this group had used the cloakrooms for " crude behaviour " and that " it wasn't nice for decent members of the Club to go down there and see them carrying on ".

Adolescents from the " village " became increasingly incensed and disgusted by the way in which " The Boys " carried on. The " village " youngsters, too, broke the code officially set up by the older " villagers ", but, to some extent, as is often the case today in the sequence of generations, they had established among themselves, perhaps without being fully aware of it, a code of their own. It was upheld and controlled by " village " adolescents which formed the greater part of the youth club committee. Like other " village " members, the members of the committee enjoyed petting and other forms of mild sex play at the youth club. This was approved by the public opinion of the Club members and practised fairly openly. In some cases it was the prelude to firm attachments. Two members of the committee were engaged to be married and others " went steady ". Parents, though they might not have approved of petting, were either not told or closed their eyes and ears.

But " The Boys " broke not only the code of the " village " adults, but also that of their own contemporaries. And in this case, too, their behaviour had not simply the character of sexual licence. It had also, perhaps even mainly, the character of a demonstration, of a show of licence. The activities of the gang were meant to show that they went beyond what the others themselves accepted as the limits of their sexual conduct. They were obviously intended to shock the other youngsters whose complaints indicated clearly enough that the attempt was successful. The manner in which " The Boys " occupied the cloakroom and noisily rearranged the furniture was a thinly disguised attack against the " snobs " from the " village ". The two girls from the Estate were soon cold-shouldered by the other girls in the Club which included a 15-year-old girl who lived near them on the Estate. During the next few months the two " easy " Estate girls, Brenda and Val, would approach the Club and wait by the doorway for " The Boys ". The whole episode showed the strained relationship between the adult minority on the Estate and the adult " villagers " projected into the younger generation. It did not last long. In 1960 Brenda left Winston Parva with her parents, and Val, by then about 17, preferred the company at the public houses of the town to that at the youth clubs in the " village ".

" The Boys " themselves began after a while to visit the " Hare and Hounds " more frequently. Although they were legally too young to be served they succeeded for a time in buying beer and spirits there. At first they still came to the youth club after the visit to the pub bragging a little about their drinks, or left the youth club for the pub letting it be known by loud remarks and suitable gestures that they were " going to get some ale ". But in course of time they came less and less often to the Club. They found better entertainment in provoking directly the " village " adults. They liked to gather on the main road of the " village " where they could be seen by local shopkeepers and residents who bitterly complained about the noise, the " obscene language " and the rough play of " The Boys ". From time to time, the gang succeeded in starting a street fight. They had developed their own technique for doing that. Thus one evening " The Boys ", pushing and shouldering each other in the queue at the Fish and Chip Shop, knocked over a youth from a village nearby. Phil, the strongest member of the gang, " floored " the youth again as he was getting up. The police were called but the gang " melted " in the crowd around the Fish and Chip Shop and none of them were apprehended for their part in the incident. After another fight " The Boys " were refused entry to the public house and they began to buy bottles of cheap wine and beer from the stores. They met in alleyways and behind factories in the " village " or on the railway embankment, often persuading one of the girls from the Estate to join them. The Youth Officer for Winston Parva, returning from his office late one evening, saw " The Boys " carrying Ken ; when he stopped in his car to enquire if they needed help " The Boys " roared with laughter and told the Officer that " Ken has had too much tonight " so that they were helping him home. They all smelt strongly of alcohol and evidently regarded the Youth Officer's offer of help as a welcome addition to their evening's entertainment.

While the social significance of such incidents, its significance for the life of the community, was considerable, the actual number of young people involved in them was small. According to a rough estimate less than 10 per cent of the youngsters from the Estate, and perhaps not more than 5, formed gangs of this type. Stories about the wild behaviour of the " hooligans from the Estate " spread quickly through the gossip channels of the " village " where the youth club buildings were situated and along whose main street the intruders travelled. What the " villagers " saw supported their old belief that all the youngsters " down there " were of a different calibre and " lacked decent home life ". They had few contacts with the others and no desire to find out how they really lived. Rejecting gossip was the social weapon which they habitually used against people who did not conform to their own standards. But in this case it was a blunt weapon. To be rejected was what these children expected and expressions of annoyance and anger from those by whom they were rejected was what they enjoyed most. The " villagers " might have been more successful if they had made common cause with other Estate families who equally suffered from their minority. Together they might have been able to exercise stronger control over the disordered minority of the Estate. But the tendency to build up a stereotyped image of the outsider neighbourhood as a whole from their experiences with the minority of the worst made steps in that direction impracticable.

As has been mentioned, the minority faded away during the period of the research. The first evidence for the change was a change in delinquency rates.

TABLE XII

Zone	Year	Delinquents before the courts	Number of children aged 7–16	Delinquency rate %
1	1958	—	59	—
	1959	—	61	—
	1960	—	57	—
2	1958	3	388	0·78
	1959	4	379	1·06
	1960	2	401	0·49
3	1958	19	276	6·81
	1959	3	275	1·09
	1960	2	285	0·70

The figures were generally rather small. There was good reason to be undecided about their significance. The change

137

in the delinquency rates of Zone 3 might have been a freak. When the research began Zone 3 was widely regarded as a kind of " delinquency area " by the " villagers " and by most people in authority. And the relevant statistical data seemed to confirm this view. When the figures for 1959 became available, early in 1960, the situation had completely changed. The delinquency rate of 6·81 per cent had given way to a rate of 1·09 per cent and the next year produced a further fall to 0·70 per cent.

As it happened, figures for adult offenders before the courts, as far as they went, showed a similar pattern. No figures relating to Winston Parva alone were available. But a detailed study of cases reported by the local press, suggested by the County Police Office, proved of some help. The following table is based on it.

TABLE XIII

Number of Adult Offences Reported in the Press (1958–1960)

Zone	Year	Offences against Property	Offences against the Person	Offences against Technical Rules	Adult Population
		No.	No.	No.	No.
1	1958	—	—	—	365
	1959	—	—	—	351
	1960	1	—	—	359
2	1958	3	1	—	2039
	1959	3	1	3	2062
	1960	2	2	1	2051
3	1958	5	8	—	797
	1959	3	2	—	785
	1960	1	1	2	802

In 1958, 8 of the offences attributable to Zone 3 were concerned with personal violence. The figure included a case of violence against oneself, a double suicide of husband and wife who gassed themselves. Another of these 8 cases has already been mentioned ; it was reported in the press as " The Battle of Winston Parva " under headlines like : " He broke window

138

—punched me—girl ". All these cases aroused considerable comment in the press and in Winston Parva. The figures for 1958 suggested that the relatively high concentration of juvenile delinquency in Zone 3 was matched by a high concentration of adult offences in the same zone. They supported Morris's finding that " the greatest concentration of both adult and juvenile offenders occur in the same areas ". [1] The difference was greatest between the figures for Zone 3 and the middle-class area of Zone 1 with no recorded adult or juvenile offence in that year.

As in the case of juvenile offences, the figures for reported adult offences in Zone 3 fell in 1959 more or less to the level of Zone 2, if one considers the absolute figures, and in 1960 actually below it. 1960 was also the first year during the period of research in which a conviction was reported against a person from Zone 1. A widow was convicted of taking goods without paying for them from a self-service store. As in the case of adolescents, one can assume that a number of offences committed by adults went undiscovered. The Police Officer in charge of the whole area to which Winston Parva belonged had only 12 policemen and 1 policewoman at his disposal to supplement whatever neighbourhood control there was, and conversations in the Open Youth Club confirmed the impression that a number of offences remained " in the dark ". But this did not explain why the number of offenders declined. The police remained as watchful and efficient in later years as in the first year of the research. The police officer mentioned that it was usual for the police to " caution " a first offender rather than bring him before the courts, except in very serious cases. But this policy remained the same throughout the period in question. The use of the " caution " applied to the figures for 1958 as much as to those of the other years.

Some teachers and youth workers in Winston Parva were inclined to believe in a " swinging pendulum " theory of crime. Their theory was that 1958 was a " bad year " and a peak for delinquency in Winston Parva. They believed it would be followed by some years of decreasing crime par-ticularly in Zone 3 ; then the " pendulum " would swing back

[1] T. Morris, *The Criminal Area*, 1957, VI, 132.

and crime on the Estate would rise again. This was a type of theory, fairly widespread today, which appeared to give the explanation of an unexplained phenomenon without really providing one. The question why the incidence of crime should increase and decrease in this manner, even if it could be shown that the factual evidence agreed with the theoretical postulate, remained unanswered.

A fairly simple factual explanation was near at hand. In 1957 and 1958 Acts of Parliament ended rent restrictions which had been in force since before the war. Property owners were now in a position to increase their rent. As a result of this legislation rents on the Estate rose from 17s. 2d. per week in October 1957 to 24s. 9d. per week at the beginning of 1961. In Zone 2, where houses were generally larger and rents varied more widely, rents rose from about 18s. per week to about 35s. per week in the same period. During the same time a large Council Estate was completed in Winston Magna just over one mile from Zone 3. These houses had larger rooms, better bedrooms, a separate bathroom and other facilities lacking in the houses on the Winston Parva Estate. Several of the larger families on the Estate including some of the " notorious " families realised that instead of paying these higher rents for a small house without modern facilities they might as well " put their name down " for a Council house with better facilities as the size of their family gave them priority.

The " D " family was one of the " notorious " families which moved from the Estate in 1959. Mother, father and two of the 5 children worked in factories, and were therefore able to afford the new Council house rents. In previous years one or the other of the children had contributed their share to the discovered and undiscovered juvenile offences in Winston Parva with fair regularity. The condition of the house which this family vacated was described by the new tenants, a young couple with no children, as " terrible ! In a dreadful state, smelly, you know, and the paper hanging off the walls ". Another of these families, the " S " family, also left the Estate for a council house in Winston Magna. Two sons of this family had been leaders of gangs. One of them had been sent from the local secondary modern school to an approved school after a period of probation which did not help. These boys continued to commit offences after leaving the Winston Parva Estate, but their cases were no longer included in the figures for Winston Parva. The " N " family left the Estate for Winston Magna late in 1958. In that year their 16-year-old son was fined for smashing bus shelter windows as a member of a drunken gang. That offence, too, was no longer included in the figures for Winston Parva. Some of " The Boys ", as one saw from Table XI, belonged to the same group ; their families moved from the Estate during the later years of the research. According to information passing through the gossip channels at the time, the " landlord " of the Estate had put pressure on certain families in order to make them leave and to replace them by tenants of a better type. At the same time some families with delinquent children moved from the Estate into the poorer streets of the " village ". By and large one can say that changes such as these—a chain of events leading from the removal of rent restrictions and a rise in rents via the attraction of newer houses with somewhat better facilities at comparable rents for those who could afford it to a decrease in the number of problem families on the Estate—can account reasonably well for the decrease in the observable offences before the courts which Tables XII and XIII indicate.

They also throw more light on the characteristics of this minority group. The families who belonged to it have been described here by means of terms such as " problem " families or " disordered " families. The terms point to the fact that the home life of these families and the relations between their members fell below the fairly high levels of orderliness and regularity in the conduct of family affairs expected today in advanced industrial societies of families of all social classes. They fell below that level in one or the other of the many aspects of family life which demand considerable skills of management and organisational capacity, though one may not be aware of these requirements and take them for granted as gifts which everyone has, as it were, " naturally ".

In fact, the exercise of these skills required for family management, which includes the management of family income and expenditure, of conflicts and tensions between family members, of children, meals, health, comforts, cleanliness, leisure occupations shared or not shared and many others, is anything but a gift of nature ; it depends a good deal on the mostly informal training which people have received or have picked up from parents, relatives, neighbours and other acquaintances as they move along towards adulthood. In the past, the training in the rules and skills which enabled husbands and wives to manage their home relations, including relations between themselves, according to the standards of their community were often provided by a fairly concise tradition handed on from one generation to the other. But that manner of transmitting rules and skills of family management served its purpose well only as long as the conditions of life of the children were not too different from those of the parents. Today the tempo of change has greatly increased. Growing pressures for greater orderliness and regularity in the conduct of family relations, including the closer supervision of many aspects of family life by public authorities, as it were, from the wings, and the high degree of regularity and orderliness spilling over from many occupations into the home life, are counteracted by other factors which exert pressure in the opposite direction, among them the growing tempo of change which makes many of the rules and skills applied by parents to the ordering of their home life less useful for the children. Again and again, children in managing their home relations are confronted with problems which are different from those of their parents ; they are thrown back on their own resources and have to cope with them on their own as best they can. They may learn as much from examples set by people of their own generation as from those set by their elders ; they may even learn a little from films, plays, novels and television, and this wholly informal learning, in most cases, may work reasonably well.

But there are always a number of families who fail to manage their home relations in accordance with the established rules ; they fall openly below the standards of orderliness and regularity in the conduct of family relations which are prevalent in their community. It may be that they did not stand in the line of a family tradition where they learned the basic routines of an orderly home life. They may have lacked individual examples when they were young ; perhaps their parents themselves lacked the chance and ability of leading a reasonably well-regulated family life. It may be that upheavals or catastrophes in their family's position threw their home life out of gear when they were young or upheavals in society at large such as wars, unemployment, illnesses and others which have already been mentioned. In former days poverty and instability of employment as permanent conditions of life were in urban areas among the main factors of family instability and disorganisation in the working classes. It was significant that in the case of the " problem " families of Winston Parva neither of these factors—neither the smallness of the family income nor lack of opportunities for employment were any longer among the immediate reasons for their deviation from the approved standards of orderliness in the management of their family affairs. The immediate reasons, in most of these cases, were personality characteristics of the parent generation. And, as far as one could gather, sociological inheritance played a part in the making of these personality characteristics. A number of the " problem parents " were evidently the children of " problem parents " ; it appeared, from what little information one had, that they themselves came from families whose level of household management would have fallen short of that required as " normal " in communities such as Winston Parva, in their case quite often in connection with unemployment and poverty. They lacked a tradition, they often lacked the knowledge and self-control necessary for ordering their home relations in the manner approved by the majority of families in Winston Parva. It may well be that in the case of the neighbourhoods from which they came such deficiencies had been less conspicuous ; perhaps they had not been condemned there, to the same extent, to an outsider position on account of such deficiencies ; perhaps a lower level of orderliness in one's home life and of the skills of home management were less of a stigma there. On the Estate of Winston Parva, as on many other estates, where families from different parts of the country with different standards and patterns of home making were thrown together, differences in the level of orderliness, of the

" civilised " conduct of home affairs made themselves much more strongly felt. They assumed a new social significance there ; because the Estate formed part of an older community with a relatively high level of regularity and orderliness in the conduct of family affairs, newcomer families used to a lower level were at a distinct disadvantage. Within their new community their position had many of the characteristics of that of a lower social stratum. In fact, this group of disordered families ranked as the lowest social cadre in the status hierarchy of Winston Parva. They ranked low not because they were poorer than others. In fact, some of them probably had a higher family income than a number of families with a higher social standing ; and if they were poorer, as was sometimes the case, it was due more to their inability to manage their affairs or to keep a job than to any lack of opportunities for earning as much as the other families. On the face of it, the nature of their occupation might have been in some cases a reason for their low ranking. A number of the fathers in these families were labourers. But there were other labourers who led an orderly home life on the level of the majority and they in no way ranked among the " notorious " families as members of the lowest group on the ladder of statuses. That ranking was almost certainly not primarily due to what are often called " economic " differences, but to the inability or unwillingness of the members of certain families to conform in their personal conduct and in the conduct of their homes to the standards regarded as the norm by the majority.

The ranking, as one saw, was almost automatically extended from the parents to the children and affected the latter's personality development, particularly their self-image and their self-respect. The younger generation established and maintained among themselves in their own way the same social divisions as the older generation sometimes much more rigidly. Because the parents' consciousness of the differential ranking of families in Winston Parva and of their own position within the status hierarchy was communicated in a variety of ways, by words, by gestures, by the tone of one's voice, to their children and helped to fashion their consciousness of themselves from early days on, it created in them even stronger barriers between the various sections of the working-class neighbourhoods—barriers too deep-rooted to give way under the impact of short-term contacts such as those provided by a youth club. One could see there very clearly how deeply the consciousness of their standing among others had sunk into the children's consciousness of themselves. The pride of the " village " youngsters in their own status group and the corresponding contempt for the lower status groups on the Estate, particularly for the lowest group, the " bad example ", the " notorious " families and their offspring, had its counterpart in the rough and disorderly behaviour of the " low-status " youngsters who from early days on had been provoked by rejection and contempt into provoking and annoying those by whom they were rejected and treated contemptuously, while these in turn were understandably incensed at the constant threats to the orderliness of their lives.

In many respects attitude and outlook of the established and the outsiders, locked inescapably in the interdependence of their neighbourhood, were complementary. They had a tendency to reproduce themselves and each other.

9 | Conclusion

In studying a community, one is faced with a great variety of problems. The question is whether they are all equally central for the understanding of what gives to a grouping of people this specific character—the character of a community.

It is quite possible to divide the problems of a community into a number of classes and to go over them one by one. One might distinguish between economic, historical, political, religious, administrative and other aspects of a community, might study each by itself and in the conclusion indicate as best one can how these aspects are connected with each other.

But one can also reverse the approach and ask what is it that binds economic, historical, political and other classes of data together as aspects of a community. What, in other words, are the specific community aspects of a community? The answer to this kind of question, at first glance, is fairly simple and perhaps rather obvious. One evidently refers to the network of relationships between people organised as a residential unit—in accordance with the place where they normally live. People establish relations if they do business, if they work, worship or play with each other and these relations may or may not be highly specialised and highly organised. But people also establish relations when they " live together at the same place ", when they make their homes in the same locality. The interdependencies which establish themselves between them as makers of homes, where they sleep and eat and rear their families, are the specific community interdependencies. Communities are essentially organisations of home-makers, residential units such as urban neighbourhoods, villages, hamlets, compounds or groups of tents. It is difficult to imagine communities without women and children, though one can

146

imagine communities almost without men. Prisoner-of-war camps may be regarded as substitute communities.

In our times homes are often separated from the places where people make their living, in former days they were often not. But whether specialised or unspecialised, social units with a core of home-making families raise specific sociological problems. They are what one usually calls " community problems ". Business quarters where no-one lives, which are full of people without families on weekdays and empty on Sundays, raise different problems. So do families in a different configuration, for instance groups of families-on-holiday. If one thinks it appropriate one could call these groupings too " communities ". The word itself does not matter much. What matters is the recognition that the types of inter-dependencies, of structures and functions, to be found in residential groups of home-making families with a degree of permanence raise certain problems of their own and that the clarification of these problems is central for the understanding of the specific character of a *community qua community*—if one may continue to use the term in a specialised sense.

Among the central problems is that which concerns the distinctions in the value attributed within such a communal network of families to the individual family. Invariably some families or perhaps some groups of families in a community, as soon as they are linked to others by the invisible threads of a neighbourhood, come to regard themselves and to be regarded by others as " better " and, alternatively, as " less nice ", " less good ", " less worthy " or whatever word one may use. Academically we speak in such cases of the " order of ranking " of families or of the " status order " of a community, and as an approximation this conceptualisation is useful. But it does not indicate too clearly the central part played by such distinctions in the life of every community ; it does not indicate their wide functional ramifications, the wealth of personal associations of the people concerned and the tensions inherent in these distinctions.

Some of these ramifications have been indicated here. The " ranking of families " in Winston Parva, as one saw, played a central part in every department of the community life. It had an influence on the membership of religious and political associations. It played a part in the grouping of people in pubs and clubs. It affected the grouping of adolescents and penetrated the schools. In fact, " ranking of families " and " status order " are perhaps rather too narrow expressions for what one actually observed. They can easily make us forget that higher status requires for its maintenance higher resources of power as well as distinction of conduct and belief which can be handed on, and that it has often to be fought for ; they make us forget that lower status, to put it bluntly, can go hand in hand with degradation and suffering. Differences in status and ranking are often demonstrated as facts but rarely explained. One could see a little more clearly in Winston Parva how they came about, and what part they played in the lives of people.

What has been presented in this study is, seen from close range, an episode in the development of an industrial, urban area. Such a development entailed frictions and disturbances. Those who had already settled in the area and, under favourable conditions, had had time to evolve from the main stream of their national tradition a fairly set communal life, a parochial tradition of their own, were faced with the fact that more people arrived to settle near and among them who to some extent differed in their outlook, manners and beliefs from those customary and valued in their own circle. One cannot exclude the possibility that at first when new houses were built in their neighbourhood the established workers also felt that the newcomers might be potential competitors for employment and disliked them for that reason. If so, all tangible traces of this type of feeling had disappeared at the time of the research. During the war the largest group of the new workers arrived together with the factory where they were employed and, by and large, industry and chances of employment in the area were expanding.

The tensions between the old and the new residents were of a peculiar kind. The core of the old residents valued highly the standards, the norms, the way of life that had evolved among them. They all were closely associated with their self-respect and with the respect they felt was due to them from others.

Over the years a few of their numbers were prospering and socially rising. Roughly speaking, England's population can be divided into those who live in terraced houses—without a " hall " in the lower, with a small " hall " in the upper ranges —those who live in semi-detached and those who live in detached houses with a variety of sub-divisions. In Winston Parva, a small but steady trickle of people passed from the working-class level of terraced houses into a middle-class level of modest dimensions symbolised by semi-detached houses and still far from the world of large-scale industrial management or ownership of large enterprises and of the major professions whose representatives live in houses fully detached on both sides. The rise of this minority, some of whom exercised considerable power in the old community, was in terms of the public communal values a matter of pride for a majority of the older settlers.

The newcomers who settled on the Estate were felt as a threat to this order, not because of any intention they had of upsetting it, but because their behaviour made the old residents feel that any close contact with them would lower their own standing, that it would drag them down to a lower status level in their own estimation as well as in that of the world at large, that it would impair the prestige of their neighbourhood with all the chances of pride and satisfaction that went with it. In that sense the newcomers were experienced as a threat by the old residents. With the extreme sensitivity for anything that may endanger their own standing which people usually develop in a mobile social order full of status anxieties, they immediately noticed much in the behaviour of the newcomers that offended their sensibilities and appeared to them as a mark of a lower order. Gossip fastened quickly on anything that could show up the newcomers in a bad light and could confirm their own superiority in morals and manners, symbols of their own respectability, of their claim to a higher social status, of the existing social order.

That " oldness " is regarded as a great social asset, as a matter of pride and satisfaction can be observed in many different social settings. The study of the relationships between " old " and " new " families in Winston Parva may go some way towards the solution of the problem why "length of residence" and "age of families" can affect deeply the relationship between people. It may help particularly because here for once "oldness" was not associated with wealth past or present. The fact that in many other respects which are usually combined with "oldness" and "newness" the two groups of Winston Parva were almost equals made it possible to bring out certain chances of power available to "old" groups of people which are easily overlooked if others such as those derived from superior wealth, superior military strength or superior knowledge are also present.

The term "old" in this context, as one could see, was not simply a reference to the greater number of years during which the one neighbourhood had existed compared to the other. It referred to a specific social configuration which one can present without leaving much scope for uncertainty. In fact, one can set it out as a general model, a template of configurations of this kind. Summed up in this form one may hold it against other similar configurations. It may help to illuminate the new evidence and in turn be illuminated by it, or, if necessary, corrected or scrapped and replaced by a better model.

If the term "old" is used with reference to a number of families who have been residents of a certain locality for at least two or three generations, it has not the same meaning which it has if one refers to individual people as "old". It has no biological meaning, though people occasionally give it a pseudo-biological connotation by implying that "old families" are decadent or decaying like old people. In strictly scientific terms "old" in this context is a purely sociological category, and it is a sociological, not a biological, problem to which it refers. An old group of people need not be a group of old people.

If one speaks of some families as "old" one singles them out from others which lack this quality, and it is the reference to this contrast configuration with its specific status differences and tensions which gives to this use of the term "old" its specific social flavour. In a biological sense all families on earth are equally old. They all stem from "families" of ancestral apes or, if one prefers, from Adam and Eve. In its social context, in phrases such as " old families " the term " old " expresses a claim to social distinction and superiority. It has a normative connotation. The families who refer to their own circle of families as " old ", though not necessarily all their individual members, regulate their conduct so that it stands out from that of others. They fashion their behaviour in accordance with a distinguishing code which they have in common. Black sheep may occur among them. But the families as such are expected to disapprove of them, perhaps to cast them out. If not, they may indeed be regarded as decaying, not because of any biological changes, but because of their inability to keep up the higher standards and obligations expected of an " old family " in their own social cadre and often also in others.

The development of such standards is closely linked to that of the cadre itself. It requires a setting in which families have a chance to transmit distinguishing standards continuously for a number of generations. The chance to transmit such standards depends on others which though quite specific in their character may vary within a fairly narrow range from society to society. The transmission of distinguishing standards usually goes hand in hand with a chance to transmit property of one kind or the other, including offices or skills within the same family from generation to generation. Whatever specific form sociological inheritance may take in such cases, all these chances to transmit have this in common that they represent inheritable chances to exercise power in relation to others which, as a group, have only limited access to, or are excluded from, them. In the last resort old family networks can only develop where groups of families get the chance to transmit from one generation to the other sources of power which they as a group can monopolise to a fairly high degree and from which those who belong to other groups are correspondingly excluded. In many cases, no-one who does not belong to the circle of the monopoly holders can enter it without their consent. And as some form of monopoly is the source and condition of their continued distinction over the generations as a group of " old families ", they can continue to exist as such only as long as they have power enough to preserve it.

For a very long time groups of families could only acquire the sociological quality of " oldness " if they rose above the lower orders who had no or little property to transmit. The " village " of Winston Parva seems to indicate that property is no longer as essential a condition of sociological " oldness " as it used to be. Old peasant families based on the inheritance of land have of course been known in the past ; so have old craftsmen families whose " oldness " was based on the monopolised transmission of special skills. " Old " working-class families appear to be characteristic of our own age. Whether they are a freak or an omen remains to be seen. Because sociological oldness in their case is not noticeably connected with inheritance of property certain other conditions of power which are normally to be found in other cases too, but which in other cases are less conspicuous, stand out more clearly in their case, particularly the power derived from the monopolisation of key positions in local institutions, from greater cohesion and solidarity, from greater uniformity and elaboration of norms and beliefs and from the greater discipline, external and internal, which went with them. Greater cohesion, solidarity, uniformity of norms and self-discipline helped to maintain monopolisation, and this in turn helped to reinforce these group characteristics. Thus the continued chance of " old groups " to stand out ; their successful claim to a higher social status than that of other interdependent social formations and the satisfactions derived from them, go hand in hand with specific differences in the personality structure which play their part, positive or negative as the case may be, in the perpetuation of an old families' network.

That, in fact, is a general feature of " old families " : they stand out from others by certain distinguishing behaviour characteristics which are bred into the individual members from childhood on in accordance with the group's distinguishing tradition. Circles of old families usually have a code of conduct which demands, either in specific or in all situations, a higher degree of self-restraint than that usual among interdependent groups of lesser status. They may or may not be " civilised " in the contemporary European sense of the word, but in relation to those over whom they successfully claim status superiority they are as a rule *more* " civilised " in the factual sense of the word [1] : their code demands a higher level of self-restraint in some or in all respects ; it prescribes a more firmly regulated behaviour either all round or in specific situations, which is bound up with greater foresight, greater self-restraint, greater refinement of manners and which is studded with more elaborate taboos. The relationship between firmly-established clusters of " old families " and those who do not " belong " to them, like many other relationships between higher and lower status groups, is often marked by a descending gradient of self-restraint ; on the ladder of a civilising process the higher social formation usually takes up a position a few rungs above their own lower social formations. Relatively stricter morals are only one form of socially induced self-restraints among many others. Better manners are another. They all enhance the chances of a superior group to assert and to maintain their power and superiority. In an appropriate configuration civilising differentials can be an important factor in the making and perpetuation of power differentials, although in extreme cases it may weaken " old " powerful groups to be more civilised and may contribute to their downfall.

In a relatively stable setting a more articulate code of behaviour and a higher degree of self-restraint are usually associated with a higher degree of orderliness, circumspection, foresight and group cohesion. It offers status- and power-rewards in compensation for the frustration of restraints and the relative loss of spontaneity. Shared taboos, the distinguishing restraints, strengthen the bonds within the network of " better families ". Adherence to the common code serves their members as a social badge. It strengthens the feeling of belonging together in relation to " inferiors " who tend to show less restraint in situations in which the " superiors " demand it. " Inferior " people are apt to break taboos which the " superior " people have been trained to observe from childhood on. Breaches of such taboos are thus signs of social inferiority. They offend, often very deeply, the " superior " people's sense of good taste, of propriety, of morals, in short

[1] N. Elias, *Über den Prozess der Zivilisation*, Basle 1939, Vol. II, p. 163.

their sense of emotionally rooted values. They arouse in " superior " groups, according to circumstances, anger, hostility, disgust or contempt and, while adherence to the same code facilitates communications, breaches create barriers.

Thus people who belong to a circle of " old families " are provided by their common code with specific emotional bonds : underlying all their differences is a certain unity of sensibilities. In that respect they know where they stand with each other and what to expect of each other, as one often says, " instinctively " better than they know where they stand with outsiders and what to expect of them. Moreover, in a network of " old families " people usually know who they are socially speaking. That in the last resort is what " old " means with reference to families ; it means families who are known in their locality and who are known to each other for a number of generations ; it means that those who belong to an " old family " not only have parents, grandparents and great-grandparents like everybody else, but that their parents, grandparents and great-grandparents are known in their community, in their own social cadre and that they are known, by and large, as people of good standing who adhere to the established social code of that cadre.

Thus, while on the face of it " old " may appear as an attribute of an individual family, in fact it is an attribute of a network of families, of a social formation within which men, women and their offspring in the socially regulated order of descent to which we refer as " family " can be known to each other for several generations as in some way distinguished, as living up to certain shared standards in contradistinction to others. " Old families " in that sense never form singly ; they always come in clusters or groups as networks of families with their own internal status hierarchy and usually with a high rate of inter-marriage, as neighbourhoods, " Societies " with a capital S, patriciates, Royals and in many other forms. In this, as in other cases, the structure of families is dependent on that of specific social groups. Except as a remnant of a social cadre which has disappeared, an " old family " cannot exist singly ; it can only form in specific social situations as correlate of a specific social formation together with others of its kind.

154

That " old families " are known to each other and have strong ties with each other, however, does not mean that they necessarily like each other. It is only in relation to outsiders that they tend to stand together. Among themselves they may, and almost invariably do, compete, mildly or wildly according to circumstances, and may, often by tradition, heartily dislike or even hate one another. Familiarity produced by close acquaintance over several generations, intimacy born from a long sequel of common group experiences, gives to their relationships specific qualities which are as compatible with liking as with disliking each other. Whichever it is, they exclude outsiders. A good deal of common family lore is floating in the air of every circle of " old families " enriched by each generation as it comes and goes. Like other aspects of the common tradition it creates an intimacy—even between people who dislike each other—which newcomers cannot share.

" Oldness " in a sociological sense thus refers to social relationships with properties of their own. They give a peculiar flavour to enmities and to friendships. They tend to produce a marked exclusivity of sentiment, if not of attitude, a preference for people with the same sensibilities as oneself strengthening the common front against outsiders. Although individual members may turn away and may even turn against the group, the intimate familiarity of several generations gives to such " old " groups for a while a degree of cohesion which other less " old " groups lack. Born from a common history that is remembered it forms another strong element in the configuration of chances they have to assert and to maintain for a while their superior power and status in relation to other groups. Without their power the claim to a higher status and a specific charisma would soon decay and sound hollow whatever the distinctiveness of their behaviour. Rejecting gossip, freezing-out techniques, "prejudice" and "discrimination" would soon lose their edge ; and so would any other of the manifold weapons used to protect their superior status and their distinction.

Thus, concentrated in the form of a model, the configuration found at Winston Parva in miniature shows more clearly its implications for a wider field. The task is not to praise and to blame ; it is rather to help towards a better understanding and a better explanation of the interdependencies which trapped two groups of people in Winston Parva in a configuration not of their own making and which produced specific tensions and conflicts between them. The tensions did not arise because one side was wicked or overbearing and the other was not. They were inherent in the pattern which they formed with each other. If one had asked the " villagers " they would probably have said they did not want an Estate at their doorstep, and if one had asked the Estate people they would probably have said they would rather not settle near an older neighbourhood such as the " village ". Once they were thrown together they were trapped in a conflict situation which none of them could control and which one has to understand as such if one wants to do better in other similar cases. The " villagers " naturally behaved to the newcomers as they were used to behave to deviants in their own neighbourhood. The immigrants on their part quite innocently behaved in their new place of residence in the manner which appeared natural to them. They were not aware of the existence of an established order with its power differentials and an entrenched position of the core group of leading families in the older part. Most of them did not understand at all why the older residents treated them with contempt and kept them at a distance. But the role of a lower status group in which they were placed and the indiscriminate discrimination against all people who settled on the Estate must have early discouraged any attempt to establish closer contacts with the older groups. Both sides acted in that situation without much reflection in a manner which one might have foreseen. Simply by becoming interdependent as neighbours they were thrust into an antagonistic position without quite understanding what was happening to them and most certainly without any fault of their own.

This, as has already been said, was a small-scale conflict not untypical of processes of industrialisation. If one looks at the world at large one cannot fail to notice many configurations of a similar kind though they are often classified under different headings. Broad trends in the development of contemporary societies appear to lead to situations such as this with increasing frequency. Differences between sociologically " old " and

" new " groups can be found today in many parts of the world. They are, if one may use this word, normal differences in an age in which people can travel with their belongings from one place to another more cheaply under more comfortable conditions at greater speed over wider distances than ever before, and can earn a living in many places apart from that where they have been born. One can discover variants of the same basic configuration, encounters between groups of newcomers, immigrants, foreigners and groups of old residents all over the world. The social problems created by these migratory aspects of social mobility, though varying in details, have a certain family similarity. One may be inclined to fasten attention first on the differences. In studies of specific cases they always seem to stand out more clearly. One often hesitates to envisage the relation of specific episodes such as that which formed the subject matter of this study to the overall development of societies in modern times. One is more used to perceive the questions connected with them as a multitude of local social problems than as a sociological problem. The migratory aspects of social mobility are an example. Sometimes they are simply conceived as geographical aspects. All that happens it seems is that people move physically from one place to another. In reality, they always move from one social group to another. They always have to establish new relationships with already existing groups. They have to get used to the role of newcomers who seek entry into, or are forced into interdependence with, groups with already established traditions of their own and have to cope with the specific problems of their new role. Often enough they are cast in the role of outsiders in relation to the established and more powerful groups whose standards, beliefs, sensibilities and manners are different from theirs.

If the migrants have different skin colour and other hereditary physical characteristics different from those of the older residents, the problems created by their own neighbourhood formations and by their relations with the inhabitants of older neighbourhoods are usually discussed under the heading " racial problems ". If the newcomers are of the same " race " but have different language and different national traditions, the problems with which they and the older residents are

157

confronted are classified as problems of " ethnic minorities ". If social newcomers are neither of a different " race ", nor of a different " ethnic group ", but merely of a different " social class ", the problems of social mobility are discussed as " class problems ", and, often enough, as problems of " social mobility " in a narrower sense of the word. There is no ready-made label which one can attach to the problems that arose in the microcosm of Winston Parva because there the newcomers and the old residents, at least in the " village ", were neither of a different " race ", nor, with one or two exceptions, of different " ethnic descent " or of a different " social class ". But some of the basic problems arising from the encounter of established and outsider groups in Winston Parva were not very different from those which one can observe in similar encounters else-where, though they are often studied and conceptualised under different headings.

In all these cases the newcomers are bent on improving their position and the established groups are bent on maintaining theirs. The newcomers resent, and often try to rise from, the inferior status attributed to them and the established try to preserve their superior status which the newcomers appear to threaten. The newcomers cast in the role of outsiders are perceived by the established as people " who do not know their place " ; they offend the sensibilities of the established by behaving in a manner which bears in their eyes clearly the stigma of social inferiority, and yet, in many cases, newcomer groups quite innocently are apt to behave, at least for a time, as if they were the equals of their new neighbours. The latter show the flag ; they fight for their superiority, their status and power, their standards and beliefs, and they use in that situation almost everywhere the same weapons, among them humiliating gossip, stigmatising beliefs about the whole group modelled on observations of its worst section, degrading code words and, as far as possible, exclusion from all chances of power—in short, the features which one usually abstracts from the configuration in which they occur under headings such as " prejudice " and " discrimination ". As the established are usually more highly integrated and, in general, more powerful, they are able by mutual induction and ostracism of doubters to give a very strong backing to their beliefs. They can often enough induce even the outsiders to accept an image of themselves which is modelled on a " minority of the worst " and an image of the established which is modelled on a " minority of the best ", which is an emotional generalisation from the few to the whole. They can often impose on newcomers the belief that they are not only inferior in power but inferior by " nature " to the established group. And this internalisation by the socially inferior group of the disparaging belief of the superior group as part of their own conscience and self-image powerfully reinforces the superiority and the rule of the established group.

Moreover, the members of the established group and perhaps the newcomers too have been brought up often enough, as most people have today, with specific rigidities of outlook and conduct ; they have often been brought up in the belief that everyone does, or ought to, feel and behave in essentials, as they themselves feel and behave. In all likelihood they have not been prepared for the problems that arise when newcomers encounter old residents who feel and behave differently and who react negatively to their own modes of behaviour. They have not been prepared, in short, for the social problems of a world with steadily heightened social mobility, but rather for a past age in which opportunities for social mobility in the wider sense of the word were less rich. By and large, the threshold of tolerance for forms of behaviour and belief which are different from one's own, if one has to live with their representatives in close contact, is still exceedingly low. It seems to correspond to social conditions under which most people were likely to live for the whole of their lives within their native group, and were less often exposed to a shock, such as that which the " villagers " experienced, to the shock of a lasting interdependence with people of a different cast.

The situation is to some extent reflected in current sociological approaches to such problems. They, too, are perhaps more appropriate to these previous stages of social development. They are often strongly coloured by the implied assumption that " stable " or " immobile " communities are the normal, the desirable types of community, and others embodying a high degree of social mobility are abnormal and undesirable. Not a few of the current sociological concepts are fashioned as if the nearest approximation to the most normal, most desirable form of social life were some imaginary pre-industrial villages : there, it seems, people lived with a high degree of cohesion and stability, were fully adjusted, well integrated and as a result enjoyed a high degree of happiness and contentment. Industrialisation, urbanisation and similar processes, with the heightened mobility, the heightened tempo of life they brought about, seem to have changed that happy state. Confronted with the difficulties of a highly mobile and quickly changing world one is apt to seek refuge in the image of a social order which never changes and projects it into a past that never was. The current concept of adjustment itself, with its implied postulate of an unchanging, stable, balanced, integrated and cohesive social order to which one can adjust, seems a little out of place in twentieth-century societies which are rapidly changing and are anything but stable ; it appears itself as a symptom of an intellectual maladjustment. Empirical investigations such as those in " village " and Estate, may perhaps help, in time, towards the emergence of a more realistic picture. The former represents a more, the latter a less, cohesive type of community. Both, as one can see, have their specific difficulties and drawbacks.

A concept of social mobility which corresponds to the high degree and the manifold types of social mobility to be found as the normal feature in industrial societies has yet to be developed. The current concept of social mobility, useful as it is, focuses attention only on one of its aspects, on movements of people from one social class to another. It would probably create less misunderstandings if one referred to this aspect of social mobility as class mobility. One cannot easily avoid regarding as socially mobile, people who move from one neighbourhood, from one community, to another either inside the same country or between countries without necessarily moving from one class to another. In fact, people who move from one class to another almost invariably also move from one community, one neighbourhood, one social circle to another ;

they appear, at least for a time, in the role of newcomers and often enough of outsiders at the doors of an already established set. Whether one moves within the same class or between classes, certain basic features of social mobility recur. They may be less pronounced in the case of more highly insulated middle-class families whose rituals, sentiments, manners and customs, at least within one and the same country, tend to be less coloured by local differences and who are more used to specific forms of relatively loose, but highly regulated neighbourhood relations. They are pronounced enough in the case of working-class families, usually less insulated from each other and more used to, more in need of, local companionship and neighbourhood contacts. The relationship between " village " and Estate showed some of the characteristic problems created by increasing social mobility everywhere. The problem widely discussed under the heading " prejudice " was one of them. The relationship between the old and the new working-class community in Winston Parva showed, as it were, prejudice *in situ*, in its social setting, as normal aspect of the social beliefs of an established group in defence of its status and power against what is felt as attack of outsiders against them. It is more usual today to study and to conceptualise " prejudice " in isolation. The configuration in which it occurs is often perceived merely as a " background ". Here one encountered it as an integral element of a particular configuration. The difference may help to illustrate what is meant by " configurational approach ". It illuminates the unexamined selectivity and evaluation of most of the present approaches to prejudice which confine their concern—without saying why—to distorting beliefs, to profoundly emotional gossip schemes and perceptions of more powerful social formations which are used to keep down or to ward off less powerful formations with whom they live in some form of interdependence. One rarely discusses and one hardly conceives as " prejudice " the corresponding distortions and unrealistic perceptions embodied in the images which relatively powerless groups on their part have of established groups in whose orbit they live as long as they remain clearly inferior in power and status, although one may begin to classify their beliefs as

" prejudice " when they are half-way up. For as long as social cadres are relatively weak, their " prejudice " against the established has no sting ; they cannot in turn translate it into discriminatory actions except perhaps in the form of delinquency, vandalism or other breaches of the established law ; particularly among young people they are often the only means available to members of groups which are cold-shouldered, excluded and injured in their self-respect to get something of their own back from the established groups. What has been said about " prejudice " applies also to " delinquency ". It applies to many other topics which, because they can be classified under a separate heading, are often approached by those who set out to study them as if they existed in fact as a group of separate objects.

Another example worth mentioning in this context are the problems grouped together under the heading " anomie ". As one can see, groups of newcomers and outsiders are the groups most likely to be afflicted by that condition. It was once a concept with a reasonably precise meaning. When Durkheim coined the concept, it formed the core of an hypothesis designed to explain in sociological terms recurrent statistical regularities in the incidence of suicide. It became the symbol of one of the most fruitful and imaginative sociological hypotheses. But already Durkheim's own version of the concept " anomie " had specific evaluative undertones. The study of suicide marked in a sense the turning point at which Durkheim like many others before and after him changed from an attitude of confidence and hope in the progress of mankind to an attitude of increasing doubt about the progressive character of the development of society. Many events of his own time, among them increasing industrial strife, had shaken the firmness of Durkheim's belief in the inevitability of progress and had produced a measure of disenchantment. Instead of improving all the time, as one had hoped, the conditions of mankind, in some respects, seemed to get actually worse. One can see the change in the climate of opinion if one compares Durkheim's idea of society's development with that of sociologists of an earlier generation. Comte and particularly Spencer still seemed to perceive only the benefits which "industrial society" would bring to mankind. Durkheim belonged to a generation in which that belief was severely shaken. The immense difficulties, the tensions and conflicts which are the normal characteristics of industrialisation processes, became more apparent.

The sociological study of suicide appeared to provide clear scientific evidence for what had until then remained on the level of impressions. It showed unmistakably that seen over long periods the incidence of suicide as indicated by changes in suicide rates was on the increase. As, according to Durkheim, changes in social conditions alone could be held responsible for this increase, and as " anomie " was according to him one of these conditions, his whole argument implied that " anomie " itself was on the increase. Compared with the past, it seemed conditions had deteriorated in spite or perhaps because of the advances of industry. Thus from the start " anomie " had specific evaluative implications. It had undertones of disillusionment with the industrial urban society in which one lived. It contained a suggestion that conditions had deteriorated, a vague feeling that they were becoming worse than they used to be and that the past must have been better than the present. A whiff of this longing for a better past, now lost, in which " anomie " did not exist—for a past that never was, has clung to the concept of " anomie " ever since.

Moreover, the term had from the start definite moral connotations. Although a counter picture, a picture which showed what was the opposite to " anomie ", has never been firmly and clearly drawn, either by Durkheim or by those who used the term after him, it seemed to be generally understood that its essential feature was cohesion. With the usual concentration of research interests on difficulties by which one was assailed and the relative indifference to social phenomena which did not seem to present any difficulties, few studies, if any, were specifically devoted to non-anomic groupings because they were non-anomic. " Nomie " and social cohesion were often implicitly conceived simply as moral factors, as something positive and good to be set against " anomie ", and " lack of cohesion " which were, and probably still are, by many

163

people conceived not primarily as a specific social configuration, but as a moral reproach.

Perhaps more detailed enquiries into present and past communities, which, like Winston Parva's " village " are not " anomic ", may gradually lead to a more factual assessment of the conditions to which concepts like " anomie " and " lack of cohesion " refer and to an approach in which the search for connections and explanations takes priority over emotive evaluations and moral condemnation. In the case of the " village ", as one has seen, a relatively high degree of cohesion, whatever its other social functions, was also a significant factor in the superior social power and status of a community. High conformity to the established norms, the " nomic " character of life in the " village " was due to a blend of whole-hearted belief in the value of the " village spirit " on the part of a powerful core-group and coercive control exercised by the members of this leading group and many of its followers throughout the community over each other and over potential opponents and deviants. As far as possible opposition and nonconformity were suppressed or silenced. If the community leaders and their followers spoke of the " village " they often seemed to suppress facts not in keeping with their ideal image of the " village " even from their own consciousness. They spoke as if the " village " were in fact, as they thought it ought to be, a harmonious, wholly united and wholly good community. The concept of " anomie " is often used in a manner which suggests that people tacitly have in mind a counter image not unlike that which the core-group of " villagers " had of themselves.

With reference to suicide and related phenomena, the concept of " anomie " in spite of its strongly evaluative connotation has done good service. But in course of time the social conditions to which one refers under that name have become less and less specific. The term " anomie ", once fruitfully used by Durkheim as a leading term related to an explanatory hypothesis which could be tested by further empirical studies, is now often used as if it were the ultimate explanation of forms of social conduct or social relations of which one disapproves ; it is used, mostly, with open or hidden undertones of complaint or reproach. In the wide sense in which the term is often used today " anomie " itself seems to require an explanation.

There is thus a close connection between the ability to perceive and to study humans in configurations and the ability to keep out of one's enquiry evaluations alien to the subject matter at hand. The recognition that the concept and the problems of " anomie " cannot be clarified without clarification of the contrast configuration, of conditions which are not anomic is obvious enough. If the obvious is not clearly seen, it is because the selection of problems which one regards as worth studying or as not worth studying is often dictated by one's involvement in the immediate issues of society at large. " Anomie " referring to a form of social " malfunctioning " is felt to be a topical problem of considerable importance, and as such, appears worth investigating. Its counterpart, " nomie ", is regarded as " normal " ; it implies that " all is well " ; hence it doesn't seem to raise any problems. From the start the selection of topics for research is influenced by extraneous evaluations and, as one can see, what one regards as " bad " is apt to be given preference as a research topic to what one regards as " good ". One is preoccupied with all that creates difficulties, and does not bother so much about what seems to run smoothly. One asks questions about the former : " bad " things require explanations, " good " things apparently not. Thus, involvements and the evaluations derived from them tend to make us perceive groups of phenomena which are inseparable and interdependent as separate and independent. For phenomena which for the enquirer may be associated with diametrically opposite values can be functionally interdependent ; what is judged to be " bad " may follow from what is judged to be " good " ; what is " good " from what is " bad ", and unless one is able to stand back, unless one asks systematically for interdependencies, for configurations regardless of whether what one finds to be interdependent has different values for oneself, one is liable to separate what belongs together. The examples given have shown that clearly enough. It is because one evaluates crime and delinquency as " bad " and conformity to laws and norms as " good ", " anomie " as " bad " and close integration as " good ", that one tends to study the one independently from the other in an isolation which has no counterpart in what we actually observe. It is as if one would study and would try to find explanations for illnesses of persons without studying persons in good health. In terms of a scientific enquiry the framework of questions is in both cases the same : there is no justification for regarding sociological enquiries into what one judges to be forms of "malfunctioning", or, as it is sometimes put, of "dysfunctions" as a group separate from that formed by what one judges to "function well". As the example of "village" and Estate show both can be equally relevant sociological problems. In terms of what one actually observes the division of research topics according to whether they concern "dysfunctions" or "functions" is wholly artificial. It means separating research problems which are, in fact, closely connected and often inseparable on account of the different values attributed to them. One cannot expect to find explanations for what one judges to be "bad", for a "malfunctioning" of society, if one is not able to explain at the same time what one evaluates as "good", as "normal", as "functioning well", and vice versa. The same is true of many other divisions based on evaluations which are extraneous to the subject matter. It is true of the evaluation of majorities as sociologically more significant than minorities. In some cases the assumption may be correct, in others it is not. Which is the case, as the enquiry showed, depends on the whole configuration. It is true of distorted beliefs about out-groups. If those who hold such beliefs are powerful and can act on them by excluding the out-group from chances accessible to themselves, we call it "prejudice" and think it well worth investigating, perhaps in the hope that one will be able to do something about it in the end. But it is quite certain that one will not be able to do anything about it if one studies "prejudice" in isolation without reference to the whole configuration in which it occurs. That one usually does not regard as "prejudice" the distorted beliefs about out-groups of relatively weak groups which cannot act upon their beliefs is another example of the need for a configurational framework as a basis for separate classifications.

It is true, finally, of the overall picture of Winston Parva as it gradually emerged. Once people have become inter-dependent, research is bound to be sterile if one studies them in isolation and tries to explain their grouping as if they were separate things. The aim of a configurational study, as one has seen, was not to put praise or blame on one side or the other or to study what one might regard as " dysfunctioning ", for example the minority of disordered families on the Estate in wholly artificial isolation. In that case, too, the aim was not to evaluate but, as far as possible, to explain—to explain humans in configurations regardless of their relative " good-ness " or " badness " in terms of their interdependencies. The configuration of people on the Estate would have been incomprehensible without a clear understanding of that of the " village " people and vice versa. Neither of these groupings could have become what they were independently of the other. They could have grown into the roles of established and outsiders only because they were interdependent. It is because connections in social life are often connections between phe-nomena which in the observer's world carry different or even antagonistic evaluations that their recognition requires a fair degree of detachment.

There is no need here to go further into the problems of involvement and detachment [1] which, as part of N. Elias's configurational theory, have been discussed elsewhere. Im-plicitly and sometimes explicitly the theory has played its part in the conduct of this enquiry. There is nothing new in perceiving and presenting social phenomena as configurations. Familiar terms like " pattern " or " situation " point very much in the same direction. But they resemble coins which have gone from hand to hand so long that one uses them without bothering much about their content and weight. Although one has come to take concepts such as these for granted, they imply a good deal that has remained unexamined. Caught between the Scylla of holistic theories which make social patterns or configurations appear as something apart from individuals and the Charybdis of atomistic theories

---

[1] N. Elias, " Problems of Involvement and Detachment," *British Journal of Sociology*, VII, 3, pp. 226ff., 1956. An enlarged version is to appear in this series.

which make them appear as masses of individual atoms, one is often not able to see and to say clearly what these terms mean.

If one looks back at the whole study, can one say that it is of some help towards clarifying the issue ? Were the groupings of people which have been presented, the sum total of actions of initially independent " Egos " and " Alters " who encountered each other in a no-man's land, who then began to interact and to form communities or other patterns, situations, configurations as secondary phenomena additional to their pure non-social " individuality " ? Was what one saw in keeping with the basic assumption of action theories and of other similar atomistic theories, that sociological research has to begin with the study of individuals as such, or of even smaller elements, of individual " actions ", which being the atoms form the " ultimate reality " to which one has to trace back the properties of composite entities—as one tries or tried in physics and chemistry to trace back the properties of composite entities like molecules, according to a theory which even there has somewhat dated, to those of physical atoms as the " ultimate reality " ? Could one really find the explanations for the configurations to be observed in a community such as Winston Parva in pre-social individual actions, in individual atoms conceived as antecedents to the composite units they formed ? Or, alternatively, was what one found in Winston Parva a " social system " whose parts fitted nicely and harmoniously together, or a " social whole " which represented the " ultimate reality " behind all individual actions and which existed as an entity *sui generis* apart from " individuals " ?

To refer theoretical constructs such as these to an empirical study shows their artificiality in better perspective. It is easy to see that theoretical assumptions which imply the existence of individuals or individual acts without society are as fictitious as others which imply the existence of societies without individuals. The fact that we are caught in the trap of so unreal a conceptual polarity as this—that we are tempted again and again to speak and to think as if one could escape from postulating individuals without society only by postulating societies without individuals cannot be circumvented simply by the assertion that one knows the polarity is fictitious.[1] Many linguistic and semantic traditions drive our speaking and thinking again and again into the same groove. Even academic institutions such as the strict division between two disciplines, psychology and sociology, the one supposedly only concerned with " individuals ", the other supposedly only with " societies ", are based on, and resurrect again and again, the fictitious polarity.

What is baffling in all these cases is the persistence with which we go on speaking and thinking in terms of a dichotomy which taken at its best, is an awkward working hypothesis obviously incongruent with any evidence one can produce, but which for reasons hardly stated explicitly and certainly not yet explained seems difficult to replace.

And yet, as one saw, the reason is simple enough. In this case, too, the capacity to observe and to study is disturbed by the concern for preconceived sets of values. The question which always seems to be at the back of the minds of people in discussions on the relationship of " individual " and " society " is not a factual question but a question of values. They ask and try to answer such questions as " what came first ? ", " what is more important ? ", " individual or society ? ". Here, too, a value polarity masquerading as a factual polarity is at the root of the difficulties. Because different groups of people attach different values to whatever the two symbols

[1] I have discussed these problems with E. H. Carr, who was good enough to acknowledge privately, though as far as I know, not publicly, that I have been of some help in clarifying these problems for him. Of all that has been written his approach in " What is History ? " comes nearest to my own. But in the last analysis his presentation does not go much beyond the point where the absurdity of the conventional conceptual polarity of " individual " and " society " is clearly shown. To release our standard forms of thinking from the trap something more is needed. The release is probably not possible as long as a power struggle in society at large keeps the ideas of many people locked in this value polarity, as long as the struggle perpetuates the need to assert, in terms of the current slogans, either that the " individual " is more important than " society " or that " society " is more important than the " individual ". But a theoretical clarification may, nevertheless, prepare the way for a gradual thawing of the frozen polarities. Only experience can show how far, given the power polarity, ways of thinking which go behind and beyond the corresponding value polarities, can enter public thinking, but as another experiment *in vivo* the attempt seemed worth making.

N.E.

" individual " and " society " stand for, one is apt to manipulate them in speaking and thinking as if the two concepts referred to two separate things. The protracted controversy between those who claim priority for " the individual " and those who claim priority for " society " is quite simply, in the guise of a discussion about facts, a controversy about two systems of belief. A wrong kind of conceptualisation has been hardened into a seemingly eternal polarity by polarities in societies at large, such as the cold war polarity, in which the greater or lesser importance of " individual " and " society " plays a central part. It is one thing to make confession of one's political faith, another to make a sociological enquiry. Nothing in the observable evidence corresponds to a conceptualisation such as " individual " and " society " which implies that there are, in fact, individuals without society and societies without individuals which form in some way separate groups of objects and can be studied separately without reference to each other.

The factual basis of the controversy about values is simple enough. Individuals always come in configurations and configurations of individuals are irreducible. To start thinking from a single individual as if it were initially independent of all others or from single individuals here and there irrespective of their relationships to each other is a fictitious point of departure no less persistent than, say, the assumption that social life is based on a contract concluded by individuals who prior to it either lived alone in the wilderness or with each other in absolute disorder. To say that individuals come in configurations means that the starting point for every sociological enquiry is a plurality of individuals who in one or the other way are interdependent. To say that configurations are irreducible means they can neither be explained in terms which imply that they exist in some ways independently of individuals, nor in terms which imply that individuals exist in some way independently of them.

Perhaps one might think theoretical considerations are somewhat out of place at the end of an empirical enquiry. And yet perhaps that is one of the places where they belong. It is precisely because neither atomistic theories, as for instance

Parson's action theory, which, in spite of all limiting provisos, treats individual acts as if they were things that existed prior to all interdependencies, nor holistic theories which, like some forms of contemporary Marxism, appear to be concerned with configurations without individuals, are particularly useful as guides in the conduct of empirical studies, that theoretical considerations such as these are not inappropriate at the end of an empirical study. For in the last resort, the crucial test for the fruitfulness or sterility of a sociological theory is the fruitfulness or sterility of empirical enquiries stimulated by and based on it. In many ways the study of Winston Parva was one such test. It showed a configurational theory in action. Communities and neighbourhoods are a specific type of configuration. The enquiry showed both the scope and the limitations of choices which they gave to individuals who formed them. One can imagine an individual newcomer settling on the Estate or in the " village ". Whether he came alone or with his family, he certainly had a number of choices. He could, as many Estate people did, " keep himself to himself". He could go with the unruly minority. He could try to make his way slowly into " village " society. He could soon decide that neither " village " nor Estate suited him as a neighbourhood and move away. But if he stayed on, if he became a " neighbour " he could not avoid being drawn into the existing configurational problems. His neighbours would start to " place him ". Sooner or later he would be affected by the tensions between the " established " and the " outsiders ". And if he lived long enough at the place, the particular character of his community would affect his life ; the configuration of which he formed part would gain some power over him. And that would be even more strongly the case if he lived in Winston Parva as a child. The study indicated at least one of the many ways in which the structure of community and neighbourhood could influence the personality development of young people who grew up there. The development from an identification with their families to a more or less individual identity is a crucial phase in the growing-up process of every human being. The enquiry indicated how different the pattern of this phase can be in neighbourhoods with a different structure. It pointed to the interplay between the place of a family in the status order of a neighbourhood and the growth of the self-image of children of that family. This was one way of showing why every theory which accepts, which does not explicitly overcome, the customary manner of speaking of "individual" and "society" and explain the futility of assuming a kind of existential separation between the two "objects", must fall short of its task. The identity problems of adolescents are one small example of the interdependence between what one may be inclined to classify as a purely "individual" and a purely "social" problem. It indicated once more the process character of configurations which showed itself throughout the enquiry whether one focused attention on the development of individuals or, taking a wider angle, on the development of neighbourhood and community.

There is no doubt that in many ways configurations such as those studied in this enquiry exercise a degree of compulsion on the individuals which form them. Expressions like "mechanisms" or "trap" used with reference to specific situations were meant to indicate this compelling force. One of the strongest motive forces of people who insist on starting their theoretical reflections about societies from "individuals *per se*" or from "individual acts" seems to be the wish to assert that "basically" an individual is "free". There is a certain abhorrence against the idea that "societies" or to put it less equivocally the configurations which individuals form with each other exercise some power over the individuals which form them and limit their freedom. Yet whatever our wishes may be, looking simply at the available evidence, one cannot get away from the recognition that configurations limit the scope of the individual's decisions and in many ways have a compelling force even though this power does not reside as it is often made to appear outside individuals, but merely results from the interdependence between individuals. The fear that one may magically deprive men of their freedom merely by saying, by facing up to the fact that configurations of individuals can have a compelling power over the individuals which form them, is one of the main factors which prevents human beings from lessening this compelling force. For it is only if we understand its nature better that we can hope to gain some control over it. Perhaps by understanding better the compelling forces at work in a configuration such as that of the established and the outsiders one may in time be able to devise practical measures capable of controlling them.

APPENDIX 1

Sociological Aspects af Identification

Problems of identification have been studied from various angles. S. Freud and G. H. Mead were among the first who, in this century, stimulated interest in these problems—Freud's contribution can be found in " Totem and Taboo " and " Group Psychology and the Analysis of the Ego " as well as in his " New Introductory Lectures on Psycho-Analysis " and in some of his smaller papers ; Mead's contribution in " Mind, Self and Society ". Many others have followed the trail or gone beyond it and any selection is arbitrary. But it might be useful to mention a few contributions which explicitly or implicitly point to the sociological significance of identification mechanisms.

S. H. FOULKES, On Introjection. *International Journal of Psycho-Analysis*, 1937, 18, 269ff.

L. P. HOLT, Identification, A Crucial Concept for Sociology. *Bulletin of the Menninger Clinic, 1950*, 14, 164ff.

L. P. HOWE, Some Sociological Aspects of Identification. *Psycho-Analysis and the Social Sciences*, Vol. IV, 1955, 61.

E. H. ERIKSON, The Problem of Ego Identity. *Journal of the American Psycho-Analytic Association, 1956*, 4, 56.

E. H. ERIKSON, Young Man Luther. *A Study in Psycho-Analysis and History*, 1958, 106ff.

Louisa P. Howe's emphasis on the connection between identification and social inheritance came to my notice after our experience in Winston Parva had drawn my attention to the same connection there. In both cases the emphasis is directed against the uncritical attribution to biological mechanisms of inheritance of continuities between the generations which can be quite well explained in terms of sociological mechanisms of inheritance. L. P. Howe's comments on Freud's biologistic tendencies are not unjustified and are useful in this context, although it is much more understandable that a man like Freud who received much of his training in the

174

nineteenth century should show biologistic tendencies of this kind than that they are still widespread and well received in the mid-twentieth century when it has become somewhat easier to distinguish between biological and sociological forms of inheritance and to study their inter-play.

" It is surprising," she wrote in ' Some Sociological Aspects of Identification ', "that Freud clung so tenaciously to his idea of primal murder and to the postulation that unconscious memories of this and other ' historic ' events are passed on through biological inheritance, when he himself described so insightfully the kind of social inheritance that occurs by means of identification."

Some effects of sociological inheritance have already been discussed in the text in connection with the transmission of prejudice and discriminatory attitudes from one generation to the other and its deepening effect (pages 132–33).   The example of the operation of sociological inheritance of outsider resentment through identification with socially rejected and disordered outsider families which has been given in the text points in the same direction.   It is more comprehensive as it links the identification to the whole social situation of parents and children.   It takes account of the interplay between the image people have of themselves, and the images which others have of them.   This sociological extension of the problems of identification beyond the relations between an individual child and his individual parents to the position, and particularly to the status position, of an individual family in relation to others may at first seem to complicate matters unduly.   In fact, it simplifies the problem, though perhaps not the collection of evidence.   It comes nearer to what we actually observe.

Even without systematic study one can easily observe in everyday life that the image children form of themselves is affected not only by their experience of their parents, but also by their experience of what others say and think about their parents.   The status consciousness of children, though perhaps more fantasy bound, is, if anything, even stronger than that of adults.   The assurance which a person gains as a child from the belief in the high status of his family often enough colours his self-assurance in later life even if his own status is less well assured or has become lower. In the same way the experience of a low status attributed to a child's family will leave its traces in his self-image and self-assurance in later life. It is identification in this wider sense which is relevant to the problems raised in the text, among them to the problems of young delinquents.

Erik H. Erikson in " Young Man Luther " (and in some of his other writings) has discussed a number of problems with which adolescents are faced in their search for identity, particularly page 106ff. He, too, has pointed to the need for developing further the psycho-analytic concept of identification :

> " Psycho-analysis has emphasised and systematised the sexual search of childhood and youth, elaborating on the way sexual and aggressive drives and contents are repressed and disguised to re-appear subsequently in compulsive acts and in compulsive self-restraints. But psycho-analysis has not charted the extent to which these drives and contents owe their intensity and exclusivity to sudden depreciations of the ego and of material available as building stones for a future identity. The child does have his parents, however ; if they are half-way worth the name, their presence will define for him both the creative extent and the secure limitations of his life tasks ".

The comparison between the working-class communities of Winston Parva points to the need for a more detailed typology of the social configurations which go into the making of a person's identity. In this field too the conventional limitation of one's attention to relationships within a family which make it appear that families live in a social vacuum obstruct our understanding. It is unlikely that one will be able to come to grips with problems such as these without systematic enquiries into types of communities as well as types of families and into the status order within which children grow up.

N.E.

APPENDIX 2

A Note on the Concepts " Social Structure " and " Anomie "

One could point to many instances in which " anomie " is treated as a problem while its opposite, the state of " well integrated " people or whatever one may call it, is made to appear as relatively " unproblematical ", as " normal " and sometimes, by implication, as a phenomenon which need not be studied.

It may be enough to choose as an example some of the concluding remarks of Merton's well-known essay " Social Structure and Anomie " [1] :

> " In so far as one of the most general functions of social structure is to provide a basis for predictability and regularity of social behaviour, it becomes increasingly limited in effectiveness as these elements of the social structure become dissociated. At the extreme, predictability is minimised and what may be properly called anomie or cultural chaos supervenes."

At the end of his essay Merton presents " social structure " and " anomie " as antithetic phenomena ; they are made to appear as opposite poles of a continuum : where " anomie " prevails, there is no, or little, " social structure " ; its place is taken by cultural (or perhaps social) chaos ; " predictability and regularity of social behaviour " are at a discount.

This concept of anomie, as one can see, is different from that of Durkheim. If its use in Durkheim's study of suicide means anything, it means that " anomie " is a specific type of social structure, not its opposite pole in a continuum of social phenomena.

Durkheim argued that when the particular type of social structure prevails to which he referred as anomie suicide rates are likely to be high. Contrary to Merton's idea that " anomie " diminishes predictability of social behaviour, Durkheim's theory implied that a better understanding of " anomie " as a

[1] Merton, R. K., *Social Theory and Social Structure* (Glencoe, Ill.), 1963, p. 159.

type of social structure might make it possible both to explain high suicide rates and to predict that, given anomic conditions, suicide rates are likely to be high.

Merton's idea of a polarity between " social structure " and " anomie " is based on a misunderstanding which is fairly widespread. " Social structure " is identified with a type of social order of which the observer approves, with a " good order ". Hence " anomie " regarded as undesirable and incompatible with a " good order ", also appears as incompatible with " social structure ". A " good order " is seen as an order in which social behaviour is well regulated. The identification of social structure with a " good social order ", therefore, leads to the assumption that sociological regularities of social behaviour diminish when " social structure " in the sense of a " good " and " well regulated " order gives way to the " bad order " of anomie. The semantic difficulties which arise if one equates the sociological concept of " social order " with what one regards in everyday life as a " good social order " and the sociological concept of " regularities of social behaviour " with the evaluating concept of a " well regulated behaviour " show themselves in such considerations clearly enough. Here as elsewhere the intrusion into one's sociological diagnosis of evaluations extraneous to the problem under consideration—of heteronomous evaluations—is at the root of the difficulties. Evaluations such as " good " and " bad " invading a sociological analysis give the impression of sharp moral dichotomies where factual enquiries reveal in the first place simply differences in social structure. In this respect Durkheim's approach can serve as a corrective. He was able to show that social behaviour which is " not well regulated " has its distinct sociological regularities. It is easy to evaluate high suicide rates as " bad ". It is much more difficult to explain why certain societies have higher suicide rates than others. If that is regarded as the primary sociological task—if one tries to correlate, as Durkheim did, different suicide rates with different social structures one soon becomes aware that the issues are more complex than simple value polarities such as " good " and " bad " suggest. A steady rise in suicide rates, for example, which one may judge to be " bad " may be connected with changes in social structure, such as increasing industrialisation, which one would find more difficult to evaluate as equally " bad ". Thus the concept of " social structure " can be used, and has been used among others by Merton himself, in a sense which is less disturbed by alien evaluations than that in which it has been used by Merton in the sentences that have been quoted. It can be used with reference to more closely as well as to more loosely integrated groups. There is no harm in speaking of the former as " well integrated " (which suggests approval) and of the latter as " badly integrated " or " dissociated " (which suggests disapproval) as long as the differences of structure and the reasons for these differences firmly remain in the centre of one's attention.

Both, forms of close integration and forms of loose integration, raise problems that require investigation. The comparison between " village " and Estate in Winston Parva showed that clearly enough. All sections of Winston Parva, including the unruly minority of the Estate, were " structured " sections. As such they all showed a degree of regularity and predictability of social behaviour.

At the beginning of his essay Merton himself uses the term " social structure " in a more sociological sense. There he represents " social structure " as a condition for deviant and, at least by implication, for conforming behaviour [1] :

" Our primary aim, " he wrote, " is to discover how some social structures exert a definite pressure upon certain persons in the society to engage in non-conforming rather than conforming conduct."

And he adds in the light of this sentence very appropriately :

" Our perspective is sociological."

The perspective ceases to be sociological if the term " social structure " is approximated only to " nomic " conditions and behaviour and if " anomie " is identified with " structureless " chaos. Sociology can come into its own as a scientific discipline only if it is understood that there is no chaos in any absolute sense. No grouping of humans, however disorderly and chaotic

[1] Ibid., p. 132.

in the eyes of those who form it, or in the eyes of observers, is without structure. But perhaps this is not the place to enlarge on this point.

Merton uses the term "social structure" in two different and not wholly compatible ways—once as a possible condition of deviant behaviour and of anomie and once as one pole of a continuum whose opposite pole is "anomie". In terms of one's immediate evaluations as involved participants, structures which encourage a more "orderly" and others which encourage a more "disorderly" behaviour may be experienced as independent and incompatible opposites. In terms of a sociological enquiry both can be approached as structures on the same level ; in many cases one can show them as interdependent. Again, the study of Winston Parva illustrates the point. The primary task was simply to enquire how the community and its various sections functioned, why they functioned in this particular way and, among others, why tensions arose and persisted within the community. When that had been done it appeared no longer as easy as it may have seemed before, to pass judgement on the various sections of Winston Parva in terms of a black and white design—in the simple terms "good" and "bad". The Estate showed to a fairly high degree the condition to which one refers as "anomie". The "village" might serve as an example of a "well integrated" community. Compared with the vivid and complex picture which can emerge from an empirical enquiry, the tendency to argue in general terms as if close integration of a group were a purely positive quality and loose integration a purely negative quality appears as a dry oversimplification. Close integration, as the example of the "village" indicated, is often bound up with specific forms of coercion. It may be bound up with specific forms of oppression. There can be too much social cohesion as well as too little, and too much as well as too little pressure for conformity. More empirical investigations alone can help us to understand what actually happens in communities to which we apply terms such as "close integration", and what in such cases "too much" and "too little" actually mean. At present one is apt to believe that value judgements used in such cases are wholly independent of the advances in knowledge. One often argues as if people acquired the values for which they stand from nowhere. They appear to be *a priori*, namely prior to all experiences. Without suggesting that they can be simply derived from empirical enquiries, one can certainly say that they are not independent of them. Men's sense of values changes with the changing conditions of their lives, and, as part of these conditions, with the advances in human knowledge.

The point is not without relevance in this context. The axiomatic evaluation of close integration as unconditionally " good " could be rectified with the help of a factual enquiry. That is one of many examples one could give of the way in which evaluations which at one stage are widely accepted as self-evident can be affected by advances in knowledge. It will require many more comparative empirical investigations of communities with varying degrees of cohesion and of the effects on the people who live there before one can with reasonable certainty define and evaluate some of them as better than others. At present, human organisations are still so imperfectly designed and our ignorance about them is so great that forms of malfunctioning and the suffering which results from it are ubiquitous and are widely accepted as normal and unavoidable. Although general and abstract value judgements of which the present form of moral judgements are an example may satisfy one's conscience, they are of little help as guides to actions with a long-term perspective. One can only hope to act more adequately with the help of a much improved factual knowledge about society. Without such knowledge it is not only difficult to say which actions, in the long run, are likely to be " good " and which will turn out to be " bad," one may also in order to remedy what one evaluates as " bad " take steps which make it even worse.

N.E.

APPENDIX 3

On the Relationship of " Family " and " Community "

Some of the notable characteristics of the Winston Parva " village " are similar to those observed before in other communities. One of the pioneer studies in this field was " Family and Kinship in East London " by Michael Young and Peter Willmott, published first in 1957 and, in a revised edition as a Pelican book, in 1962. As far as one can see, they were the first to point out that the " wider family, far from having disappeared, was still very much alive in the middle of London " (1962, p. 12). In the face of a tradition, probably modelled on the middle-class image of a " normal " family, which stressed the role of a father as the central figure of a family, they put on record the fact that in the working-class families which they studied the mother appeared to be the central figure of a type of family which was usually larger and in structure somewhat different from what was often regarded as the " normal " type of European family.

As record of a series of highly imaginative observations Young and Willmott's study broke new ground. It represented one step in a long series of steps which may one day help to revise the conventional picture of the structure and function of a " normal " family of which the concept of a " nuclear family " as the core and essence of families all over the world is an example. It would have been far less easy to perceive " mother-centred " families in Winston Parva without the precedent set by Young and Willmott in their study of families of Bethnal Green.

But perceptiveness of observations is not quite matched in their study by perceptiveness of conceptualisation. The authors seem to take pride in the fact that they simply " observe " without having a theory. In fact, their observations like everybody else's were guided by specific theoretical ideas. They were probably taken over from the fund of general ideas in society at large. They were not explicitly worked out and

182

critically examined. The authors seem to treat their theoretical ideas as self-evident. They did not regard it as part of their task to examine in the light of their factual observations the general concepts they used in making these observations.

Take the following passage which appears as a summary of the plan according to which they proceeded [1] :

> " We have, in the part of the book which is here to be ended, moved successively outwards from the married couple to the extended family, from the extended family to the kinship network and from there to certain of the relations between the family and the outside world. We shall now turn from the economic to the social, and consider whether, outside the work place, people in this particular local community unrelated either by marriage or by blood are related in any other way."

There is no need to comment on expressions like " the economic " or " the social." They are indicative of the kind of classifications at the back of the authors' mind. The procedure as outlined in this quotation is significant. It suggests that one moves outward from the married couple or the family which appears as the centre of the social universe in a number of stages to what appears as the shell called " the outside world ". It is a family-centred theoretical framework, somewhat vaguely conceived, which bears some resemblance to early geocentric conceptions of the universe according to which the earth was the kernel and the heavens the outer shell.

A family-centred concept of society is not unusual in the present sociological literature on the family. Because one confines one's attention to the selection of data about " the family ", the structure of families stands out clearly while that of other aspects of societies are summarily conceived as the world " outside " the family and remain rather dim. Young and Willmott were only mildly inhibited in their observations by their family-centred image of society. They assumed as a matter of course that families have their own independent structure. But they were not particularly concerned with examining this general proposition. Nor did it prevent them from noticing that some kind of relationship existed between family structure and community structure. But as they did not

[1] M. Young, P. Willmott, op. cit., p. 104.

reflect on the nature of this relationship, they had some difficulties in expressing what they observed about it :

" Since family life is so embracing in Bethnal Green one might perhaps expect it would be all embracing. The attachment to relatives would then be at the expense of attachment to others. But in practice this is not what seems to happen. Far from the family excluding ties to outsiders, it acts as an important means of promoting them. . . .
The function of the kindred can be understood only when it is realised that long standing residence is the usual thing. Fifty-three per cent of the people in the general sample were born in Bethnal Green."

Thus in this case too, as in that of Winston Parva, a specific type of family structure, mother-centred two-or-three-generation kinship networks were associated with a specific type of community structure ; they developed within the framework of an old working-class community. Perhaps in Bethnal Green too women went to work.

But as far as one can see Young and Willmott were only marginally interested in the structure of the community. Their attention was focused on types of families.

The difficulties engendered by this approach can be seen more directly in " Family and Social Network " by Elizabeth Bott. Two passages may be enough to indicate the problem [1] :

" On the basis of the facts collected from the research families, it is impossible to analyse the pattern of forces affecting their networks. In order to consider these factors at all, it is necessary to go beyond the field data to draw on general knowledge of urban industrialised society. . . ."

" In the literature on family sociology, there are frequent references to ' the family in the community ', with the implication that the community is an organised group within which the family is contained. Our data suggest that this usage is misleading. Of course, every family must live in some sort of local area, but few urban local areas can be called communities in the sense that they form cohesive social groups The immediate social environment

[1] E. Bott, Family and Social Network, London 1957, pp. 97-99.

of urban families is best considered not as the local area in which they live, but rather as the network of actual social relationships they maintain, regardless of whether these are confined to the local area or run beyond its boundaries."

One can see in these passages the author's strong tendency not only to " observe " families, but also to reflect on the general problem raised by the relationship of family and community. But her reflections are essentially elaborations of axiomatic beliefs common to many sociological studies of the family, particularly of the belief that " the family " has a structure of its own which is basic and more or less independent of that of the surrounding world. It is a belief which, as one can see, persists in spite of all the evidence which shows that the structure of " the family " changes with changes in society at large, e.g. with increasing urbanisation and industrialisation.

The line of thought, represented in these passages, is not uncharacteristic of the circularity of thinking which often results if one accepts specific research techniques as given and as absolute and allows one's conception of whatever one sets out to discover to become dependent on the results of these techniques irrespective of their limitations. E. Bott states first that the techniques used in her study for the collection of data limited the evidence to specific families ; they did not make it possible to consider factors from outside the " research families " which had an influence on their structure. This is a very legitimate acknowledgement of the limitations of the methods used and of the sections of the social tissue brought into focus with the help of these methods. But from the acknowledgement of these limitations the author goes on to say that only what her research methods have brought into focus has a firm structure and that the wider groupings, the communities within which families live have no recognisable structure. It is an example of a type of error common in studies of society : aspects of society which can be opened up with the help of conventional techniques of a given period and whose structure can therefore be recognised to a higher or lesser extent are treated as basic aspects of society. Other aspects of society which the techniques of a given period cannot open up with any degree of certainty are, as a matter of course, presumed to lack any firm organisation or structure.

Often enough the first are experienced as effective determinants of the flow of social events while the others believed to be without firm structure appear as more or less passively determined by them. Because the data collected by E. Bott made it appear that only the family has a firm structure, but not the community, the author implicitly assumed that one can neglect the community as a factor in the structuring of families. The example of the " village " in Winston Parva showed that it is not as misleading as E. Bott suggests to regard a community as a unit with a specific structure, and that it is quite possible to enquire into the structure of families and community at the same time. If that is done the interdependence of their structure becomes soon apparent.

The connection between family structure and community structure may be less apparent in residential middle-class neighbourhoods than in old working-class neighbourhoods. But although in their case families have many relationships outside their residential area, their neighbourhood is by no means unstructured.

N.E.

SELECTED BIBLIOGRAPHY

AICHHORN, A. *Wayward Youth.* London 1936.

ALEXANDER, F., HEALY, W. *Roots of Crime.* New York 1935.

ANGELL, R. C. *The Family Encounters the Depression.* New York 1936.

BAKKE, E. W. *The Unemployed Man.* London 1933.

BELL, LADY. *At the Works : A Study of a Manufacturing Town.* London 1907.

BENDIX, R. Concepts and Generalisations in Comparative Sociological Studies. *American Sociological Review.* Vol. 28, No. 4, 1963.
— *Max Weber.* London 1960.

BERNARD, J. An Instrument for the Measurement of Neighbourhood with Experimental Applications. *South Western Social Science Quarterly.* September 1937.

BLOCH, H. A. *Disorganisation : Personal and Social.* New York 1952.

—, NIEDERHOFFER, A. *The Gang.* New York 1958.

BLOS, P. *The Adolescent Personality.* New York 1941.

BLUMENTHAL, A. *Small Town Stuff.* Chicago 1933.

BOOTH, C. *Life and Labour of the People in London.* London 1902.

BOSANQUET, H. *Rich and Poor.* London 1899.

BOTT, E. *Family and Social Network.* London 1957.

BOWLBY, J. *Maternal Care and Mental Health.* Geneva 1951.

BRENNAN, T., COONEY, E. W. AND POLLIM. *Social Change in South West Wales.* London 1959.

BRIGGS, A. *Victorian Cities.* London 1963.

BURT, C. *The Young Delinquent.* London 1955.

CARR-SAUNDERS, MANNHEIM, RHODES. *Young Offenders.* Cambridge 1942.

CHOMBART DE LAUWE, P. *La Vie Quotidienne des Familles Ouvrieres.* Centre de la recherche scientifique, Paris 1956.

CLEMENT, P., XYDIAS, N. *Vienne sur le Rhone : La Ville et les Habitants situations et attitudes.* Paris 1955.

COHEN, A. K. *Delinquent Boys.* Glencoe 1955.

COLE, G. D. H. *Studies in Class Structure.* London 1955.

COLEMAN, J. *The Adolescent Society.* Glencoe, Ill. 1961.

CRUTCHFIELD, R. S. Conformity and Character. *American Psychologist.* No. 10, 1955.

DAHRENDORF, R. Sozialwissenschaft und Werturteil. In *Gesellschaft und Freiheit.* Munich 1961.

DAVIE, M. R.   Pattern of Urban Growth.   In MURDOCH, G. R. (ED.).
The Science of Society.   New Haven 1937.
DAVIS, K.   Adolescence and the Social Structure.   *The Annals of the
American Academy of Political and Social Science.*   Vol. 236, November
1944.
— The Sociology of Parent-Youth Conflict.   *American Sociological
Review.*   August 1940.
DURANT, R.   *Watling : A Survey of Social Life on a New Housing
Estate.*   London 1939.
DURKHEIM, E.   *Suicide : A Study in Sociology.*   London 1952.

EISENSTADT, S. N.   *From Generation to Generation : Age Groups and Social
Structure.*   Glencoe, Ill. 1956.
ELIAS, N.   Problems of Involvement and Detachment.   *British Journal
of Sociology.*   Vol. VII, No. 3, 1956.
— *Über den Prozess der Zivilisation.*   Basle 1939.
— *Die öffentliche Meinung in England.*
— *Nationale Eigentümlichkeiten der englischen öffentlichen Meinung.*   In:
Vorträge, Hochschulwochen für staatswissenschaftliche Fortbil-
dung in Bad Wildungen.   Bad Homburg 1960 and 1961.
ERIKSEN, E. G.   *Urban Behaviour.* London 1954.
ERIKSON, E. H.   *Childhood and Society.*   New York 1950.
— The Problem of Ego Identity.   *Journal of the American Psycho-
Analytic Association.*   1956.
— *Young Man Luther, A Study in Psycho-Analysis and History.*   1958.

FELLIN, P. H., LITWAK, E.   Neighbourhood Cohesion and Mobility.
American Sociological Review.   Vol. 28, No. 3, 1963.
FIRTH, R. (ED.).   *Two Studies of Kinship in London.*   London School
of Economics.   Monographs on Social Anthropology, No. 15.
London 1956.
FLEMING, C. M.   *Adolescence.*   London 1948.
FOULKES, S. H.   On Introjection.   *International Journal of Psycho-
Analysis.*   1937.
FREUD, S.   *Group Psychology and the Analysis of the Ego.*   London 1936.
— *New Introductory Lectures on Psycho-Analysis.*   London 1937.
FRIEDLANDER, K.   *The Psycho-Analytic Approach to Juvenile Delinquency.*
London 1947.

GENNEP, A. VAN.   *Rites of Passage.*   London 1961.
GLASS, D. V. (ED.).   *Social Mobility in Britain.*   London 1954.
GLASS, R.   *The Social Background of a Plan.*   London 1948.
GLUECK, S. H., AND E.   *Delinquents in the Making.*   New York 1952.
— *Unravelling Juvenile Delinquency.*   New York 1950.

GOLDFARB, W. Effects of Psychological Deprivation in Infancy and Subsequent Stimulation. *American Journal of Psychiatry.* Vol. 102, No. 1, 1945.

GOLDFARB, W. Psychological Privation in Infancy and Subsequent Adjustment. *American Journal of Orthopsychiatry.* Vol. XV, No. 2, 1945.

GORER, G. *Exploring English Character.* London 1955.

HANDLIN, O. *The Uprooted.* Boston 1951.

HAVIGHURST, R. J., AND H. T. *Adolescent Character and Personality.* New York 1949.

HINKLE, R. C. Antecedents of the Action Orientation in American Sociology before 1935. *American Sociological Review.* Vol. 28, No. 5, 1963.

HODGES, M. W., SMITH, C. S. The Sheffield Estate. In BLACK, E. I., SIMEY, T. S. (ED.). *Neighbourhood and Community.* Liverpool 1954.

HOLLINGSHEAD, A. *Elmstown's Youth.* New York 1945.

HUNTER, F. *Community Power Structure.* University of North-Carolina 1953.

ISAACS, S. *Social Development in Young Children.* London 1945.

JEPHCOTT, A. P. *Some Young People.* London 1954.

JOUVENEL, BERTRAND DE. *On Power.* Boston 1948.

JUNOD, H. A. *The Life of a South African Tribe I, Social Life.* London 1927.

KARDINER, A. *Psychological Frontiers of Society.* New York 1945.

KERR, M. *The People of Ship Street.* London 1958.

KLINEBERG, O. How Far Can the Society and Culture of a People be Gauged through their Personality Characteristics. In HSU, F. L. K. (ED.). *Aspects of Culture and Personality.* New York 1954.

KRAMER, D., AND M. K. *Teen Age Gangs.* New York 1953.

KUPER, L., AND OTHERS. *Living in Towns.* Birmingham 1950.

LANDER, B. *Toward an Understanding of Juvenile Delinquency.* New York 1954.

LÉVI-STRAUSS, C. The Family. In SHAPIRO, H. L. (ED.). *Man, Culture and Society.* New York 1960.

LEWIS, O. *Life in a Mexican Village.* University of Illinois 1951.

LIEBERSON, S. *Ethnic Patterns in American Cities.* New York 1963.

— The Old-New Distinction and Immigrants in Australia. *American Sociological Review.* Vol. 28, No. 4, 1963.

LINTON, R. What we Know and What we Don't Know. In HSU, F. L. K. (ED.). *Aspects of Culture and Personality.* New York 1954.

SELECTED BIBLIOGRAPHY

LIPSET, S. M., BENDIX, R. *Social Mobility in Industrial Society.* London 1959.
LOCKWOOD, D. *The Black Coated Worker.* London 1958.
LYND, R. S., AND H. M. *Middle Town.* New York 1950.
— *Middle Town in Transition.* New York 1950.

MAINE, H. S. *Village Communities in the East and West.* London 1872.
MANNHEIM, H. *Social Aspects of Crime in England.* London 1950.
MAYHEW, H. *London Labour and the London Poor.* London 1851.
MEAD, G. H. *Mind, Self and Society.* Chicago 1934.
MEAD, M. *Growing up in New Guinea.* London 1954.
MERTON, R. K. Social Structure and Anomie. In *Social Theory and Social Structure*, IV and V. Glencoe, Ill. 1957.
— Patterns of Influence : A Study of Inter-Personal Influence and of Communication Behaviour in a Local Community. In LAZARSFELD, P. F., STANTON, F. N. (ED.). *Communications Research 1948–1949.* New York 1949.
MITCHELL, G. D., LUPTON, T. The Liverpool Estate. In BLACK, E. I., SIMEY, T. S. (ED.). *Neighbourhood and Community.* Liverpool 1954.
MOGEY, J. M. *Family and Neighbourhood.* Oxford 1956.
MORRIS, T. *The Criminal Area.* London 1957.
MORRISON, A. *The House of the Jago.* London 1939.

NEUMEYER, M. H. *Juvenile Delinquency in Modern Society.* New York 1949.
NZEKWU, O. *Blade Among the Boys.* London 1962.

PACKER, E. L. Aspects of Working-Class Marriage. *Pilot Papers.* No. II, 1947.
PANETH, M. *Branch Street.* London 1944.
PARSONS, T. Certain Primary Sources and Patterns of Aggression in the Social Structure of the Western World. In MULLAHY, P. (ED.). *A Study of Interpersonal Relations.* New York 1949.
PARSONS, T., BALES, R. F. *Family Socialisation and Interaction.* Glencoe, Ill. 1955.
PIAGET, J. *The Moral Judgement of the Child.* London 1950.

RADCLIFFE-BROWN, A. R. *Structure and Function In Primitive Society.* London 1952.
—, FORDE, D. (ED.). *African Systems of Kinship and Marriage.* London 1950.
READ, M. *Children of their Fathers.* London 1959.
REDFIELD, R. *The Little Community.* Chicago 1955.

SCOTT, J. F. The Changing Foundations of the Parsonian Actions Scheme. *American Sociological Review.* Vol. 28, No. 5, 1963.

SEELEY, J. R. *Crestwood Heights.* London 1956.

SELF, P. J. P. Voluntary Organisations in Bethnal Green. In BOURDILLON, A. F. C. (ED.). *Voluntary Social Services.*

SHERIF, M. *The Psychology of Social Norms.* New York 1936.

SINCLAIR, R. *East London.* London 1950.

SLATER, E., WOODSIDE, M. *Patterns of Marriage.* London 1951.

SPAULDING, C. H. B. Cliques, Gangs and Networks. *Sociology and Social Research.* XXXII, 1948.

SPROTT, W. J. H. *Human Groups.* London 1959.

THRASHER, F. M. *The Gang.* Chicago 1927.

TITMUSS, R. M. *Essays on the Welfare State.* London 1958.

— *Problems of Social Policy.* London 1950.

TOWNSEND, P. *The Family Life of Old People.* London 1957.

TUMIN, M. M. *Caste in a Peasant Society.* Princeton 1952.

U.N. *Report on the World Social Situation.* U.N., New York 1957 and 1961.

U.N.E.S.C.O. *The Social Implications of Industrialisation and Urbanisation.* Calcutta 1956.

VEBLEN, T. H. *The Theory of the Leisure Class.* New York 1934.

VIDICH, A., BENSMAN, J. *Small Town in Mass Society.* Princeton 1958.

WARNER, W. L., LUNT, P. S. *The Social Life of a Modern Community.* New Haven 1941.

— — *The Status System of a Modern Community.* New Haven 1947.

—, HAVIGHURST, R. J., LOEB, M. B. *Who Shall be Educated?* London 1946.

WEBER, M. *The City.* London 1960.

— *The Methodology of the Social Sciences.* (Trans. and ed. SHILS, E. A., FINCH, H. A.) Glencoe, Ill. 1949.

WHYTE, W. F. *Street Corner Society.* Chicago 1943.

WILLIAMS, W. M. *The Sociology of an English Village : Gosforth.* London 1956.

WILSON, B. R. " Teenagers " in *Twentieth Century.* August 1959.

YOUNG, A. F., WESTON, F. T. *British Social Work in the Nineteenth Century.* London 1956.

— WILLMOTT, P. *Family and Kinship in East London.* London 1962.

INDEX

Printed in the United Kingdom
by Lightning Source UK Ltd.
135956UK00001B/223-279/A